INVESTING
IN
SECURITIES

Richard A. Haft is a graduate of New York University with a B.S. Cum Laude in Accounting and Economics. He has written for *California Business*, lectured, teaches an extension course in securities at the University of California at Los Angeles (UCLA), and is treasurer of the Christmas Seal Association of Los Angeles. He has been in the financial business for 25 years as a speculator, investor, broker, investment banker, and partner of a New York Stock Exchange firm. At present he is a broker and officer of Drexel Burnham & Company, Inc. member of the New York Stock Exchange.

INVESTING
IN
SECURITIES

A Handbook
for
Today's Market

RICHARD A. HAFT

A SPECTRUM BOOK

PRENTICE-HALL, INC., ENGLEWOOD CLIFFS, N.J.

Library of Congress Cataloging in Publication Data

Haft, Richard A.
  Investing in securities.

  Includes index.
    1. Investments. 2. Stock-exchange. 3. Securities-exchange.
  United States. I. Titles
  HG 4521.H223   332.6'32'0973   75-16153
  ISBN 0-13-504647-5
  ISBN 0-13-502708-x pbk.

© 1975 by Prentice-Hall, Inc., Englewood Cliffs, New Jersey

10 9 8 7 6 5 4 3 2 1

Printed in the United States of America

Prentice-Hall International, Inc., *London*
Prentice-Hall of Australia Pty. Ltd., *Sydney*
Prentice-Hall of Canada, Ltd., *Toronto*
Prentice-Hall of India Private Limited, *New Delhi*
Prentice-Hall of Japan, Inc., *Tokyo*
Prentice-Hall of Southeast Asia (Pte.) Ltd., *Singapore*
Whitehall Books Limited, *Wellington, New Zealand*

CONTENTS

PREFACE   ix

1

THE STOCK EXCHANGE   1

2

UNDERSTANDING AND ANALYZING FINANCIAL STATEMENTS:
A BASIS FOR DETERMINING VALUE   15

3

GROWTH AND INCOME INVESTMENTS   38

4

HOW TO FIND UNDERVALUED SECURITIES   61

5

THE FEDERAL RESERVE SYSTEM:
ITS RELATIONSHIP TO STOCK MARKET PERFORMANCE   76

6

THE TECHNICAL APPROACH   87

7

READING AND INTERPRETING THE FINANCIAL NEWS   106

8

PUT AND CALL OPTIONS   129

9

MUTUAL FUNDS, CLOSED END FUNDS, NO LOAD FUNDS,
AND PENSION FUNDS   148

10

SOME WAYS TO AVOID MAJOR ERRORS   162
IN SPECULATING AND INVESTING

GLOSSARY   174

INDEX   187

PREFACE

Gambling, speculating, and investing are three methods of dealing with the future in pursuit of gain. The differences among them are differences in motive and in the element of risk involved. Gambling, in its purest sense, involves risking money, or any other form of wealth, on any event over which the gambler has absolutely no control or foreknowledge. Rolling dice or flipping coins is gambling.

Speculation, on the other hand, is a form of business activity. A businessman is really a speculator. Proprietors expect and receive, when successful, higher returns than lenders of money. Speculation could be considered gambling if an individual had little or no intelligent idea regarding values or future values.

In this book I attempt to help an individual take as much of the gamble out of investing and speculating as possible. The assumption of risk is a necessity for gain, but intelligent knowledge of what the risks and rewards are separate the gambler from the speculator and the investor.

When a person has acquired any wealth above his needs, he must make a choice between speculating and gambling—unless he puts the excess in his mattress. Two factors will influence his choice; his temperament and his environment. An investor will have in mind the small but certain interest his money can command. His savings enable banks to keep industry growing. The daring, but less patient, man will seek a higher return on his money. He searches for superior opportunities in the hope of greater gain. Almost all men oscillate between speculating and investing and the act of choosing is often an unconscious one.

There are few who are qualified to be both an investor and a speculator. Those so qualified liquidate their stocks at the height of the market and place their money at interest. When the expected break in stock prices has occurred they then convert their holdings back into stocks. This ability is rare because they are usually acting counter to general public opinion and therefore have to have tremendous confidence in themselves. This confidence comes from their greater knowledge of what makes stock prices rise and fall.

It is hoped that this book can begin to help the reader become a better speculator and investor.

1

THE STOCK EXCHANGE

Without a central meeting place where people could buy and sell securities, thus creating liquidity for their investments, this country could not have become the leading industrial nation in the world.

THE NEW YORK STOCK EXCHANGE

In 1789 Congress authorized the issuance of $80 million in government securities to help pay for the Revolutionary War. There were no stock exchanges at that time and as a result brokers met at their individual offices to conduct business. Since all securities were difficult to sell without a central market place, investors were hesitant to buy. The need for a central security market was evident and in 1792 twenty-four brokers, the original members of the exchange, met under a sycamore tree on Wall Street, New York City, to exchange issues. Shortly thereafter they moved into a local coffee house that in 1801 became too small for their expanding operations. A new building was erected not far from the Bank of England near Capel Court in the Wall Street area, where they remained for 64 years. Securities were limited to the buy and sell orders of government issues. Later, New York State bonds were issued to pay for the Erie Canal and were sold together with the securities of fire insurance companies, banks, and railroads. In 1865 the stock exchange moved to its current location and two years later the first constitution of the exchange was adopted, providing for a president who called out the names of the stocks at 11:30 a.m. each business day as the brokers made their bids and offers.

The floor of the New York Stock Exchange today resembles a large arena with eighteen horseshoe-shaped trading booths in each of which are handled approximately 85 to 100 security issues. The specialists are located in these booths. As trades take place they are reported immediately to the high-speed ticker, which prints the trade within minutes.

The ticker was first installed in 1867. It prints the transactions in round lots of 100 shares, 200 shares, etc., that trade on the floor. The moving tape is then flashed on a screen so that observers in brokerage offices & around the country can keep up to date on the transactions taking place on the floor.

The first ticker printed 285 characters per minute and during frenetic trading periods it often ran several hours late. In 1930 a faster ticker system was installed that printed 500 characters per minute and a still more efficient, faster tape printing 900 characters per minute was installed in 1964. This is the way transactions are printed.

DD	GM	S	M
160½	1000 46 ⅛	2S 68¼	3S 27½

They would be interpreted as follows:

1. DD is the symbol for Du Pont and 100 shares (round lot assumed) traded for 160½ per share.
2. GM is the symbol for General Motors and 1,000 shares were traded for 46 1/8 per share. All sales of 1,000 and over are listed by exact number of shares traded.
3. S is the symbol for Sears, Roebuck and 2S, or 200 shares, traded for 68¼.
4. M stands for Marcor and 3S, or 300 shares, traded for 27½ per share.

The Function of the Exchange

The exchange, or Big Board, is a two-way auction market where buyer and seller meet through their brokers to achieve the best possible price on a stock transaction. The exchange itself neither buys nor sells securities. It merely provides a trading place where exchange members act as agents for the buyers and sellers of stock of approximately 1,500 corporations.

Membership in the Exchange

Today the New York Stock Exchange has grown to approximately 1,300 members. Each member must buy a "seat," so called because 100 years ago brokers sat at their desks on the floor of the exchange. These seats have sold from a low of $38,000 to a high of $515,000 in the last twenty years. Prospective seat buyers must pass a thorough examination on securities and the laws governing the handling of securities given by the exchange, and then must be approved by the exchange's Board of Governors. When a firm states that it is a "Member of the New York Stock Exchange" you should immediately understand that it owns at least one seat. Seat owners must meet rigid capital requirements and file monthly financial reports in order to retain their seats.

Types of Exchange "Seat" Holders

1. Specialists
2. Floor partners
3. Odd-lot Dealers
4. $2 Brokers
5. Traders
6. Bond brokers

Specialists. To ensure that each stock listed on the New York Stock Exchange gets proper representation on the floor, the exchange assigns specialists who are responsible for maintaining a fair and orderly market for stocks to which they have been assigned. They trade for their own accounts, thus adding liquidity and continuity to the auction market, and also execute orders for other brokers, for whom they act as agents. Their trading is closely supervised and they must follow strict exchange rules. Approximately 25 per cent of exchange members are specialists.

Floor Partners. Floor partners are individuals who represent their own firm on the floor of the exchange and who buy and sell as agents for their firms' clients. Approximately 70 per cent of the members of the New York Stock Exchange are floor partners.

$2 Brokers. When trading is hectic, one, two, three, or even four floor partners cannot handle all the business of their firm. In this event there are other brokers on the floor who help execute orders. They are known as $2 brokers, because many years ago that was the fee they were paid to execute a 100-share order. The fee has since changed but the name has not.

Odd-Lot Dealers. Any trader on the floor of the exchange who needs to fill an order for a client of less than 100 shares must purchase this stock from an odd-lot dealer. The odd-lot dealer is a principal, which means he owns securities and must sell less than 100 shares to any member based on the next round-lot price after receipt of the order. He also buys and sells for his own account and sells stocks to other brokers, floor partners, and $2 brokers who are acting as agents for their customers.

Traders. Traders buy and sell for their own accounts and are subject to severe restrictions by the exchange and the Securities Exchange Commission. Traders can act as $2 brokers if they do not trade in the same stocks for their own accounts.

Bond Dealers.   Bond dealers are also seat holders who buy and sell corporate bonds on the Big Board.

AMERICAN STOCK EXCHANGE

The American Stock Exchange, formerly called the New York Curb Exchange, is the second largest exchange in America. Securities may be listed on the New York Stock Exchange or the American Stock Exchange but not on both. There is little difference in the way each major exchange operates. The ASE performs the valuable function of making a market for many corporations that are still growing but cannot meet the more stringent requirements for NYSE listing.

The origin of the old "Curb" is hazy but it dates back to the Civil War when brokers met on William and Broad Streets in New York City. Brokers actually operated on the curbstones of these streets and often moved into the street. Overlooking the curbstones below were clerks watching from the windows of the surrounding buildings. These clerks, sitting next to telephones, would relay orders to the brokers either by shouting or using hand signals. Brokers wore colorful costumes so their associates could easily see them in the crowd. When the broker received the order from his clerk above, he raced to the particular mailbox, fire-hydrant, or lamppost where the stock was being traded. As the Industrial Revolution expanded so did the exchange, since more and more capital was needed by businessmen who now looked to the exchanges to provide capital from the public. Businesses expanded by selling shares of their stock to the public through the exchanges, thus assigning part ownership of the company to the public in exchange for money to promote their growth.

In addition to dealing in securities not listed on the NYSE, the American Stock Exchange specializes in foreign securities under a unique system known as American Depository Receipts. ADR certificates are issued by a New York Bank against deposits of the original shares held by a European branch of the New York bank. As foreign shares are deposited abroad, the equivalent ADR's are issued in New York on cabled advice from its European agency. As transactions (buying and selling) take place, the depository receipts change hands but not the stock certificates, which eliminates shipping the actual certificates back and forth from Europe to the United States. Instead, the investor receives an ADR that represents the actual certificate.

In 1921 the exchange moved to its present quarters on Trinity Place. In June, 1971, the American Stock Exchange celebrated the fiftieth anniversary of its move indoors. A memorial curbstone was unveiled that reads:

For more than a century the outdoor brokers, predecessors of the American Stock Exchange, conducted a market place on the curbstones of the financial district serving investors and aiding the nation's industrial growth. They moved indoors on June 27, 1921, from this site.

OVER-THE-COUNTER MARKET

Whereas the auction markets of the New York Stock Exchange and the American Stock Exchange handle transactions of approximately 3,000 corporations, the Over-the-Counter Market negotiates trades for over 18,000 companies. The over-the-counter broker does not need a seat to buy and sell securities. He is a "dealer" and as such may buy and sell as a principal. He often sells part of his inventory and at other times will buy stock to add to his inventory. He is in effect a "merchant" of stocks. The OTC broker, depending on his capital, may make markets in a few or as many as 100 or more stocks. If he is a local broker, he probably will make markets only for companies in his area.

Almost all members of the New York Stock Exchange employ OTC traders and make markets for unlisted securities in addition to buying and selling on both major exchanges. It is estimated the exchange members complete 50 per cent of all OTC trades.

All securities must first trade over-the-counter in order to get what the exchanges call "seasoning." Therefore, when shares of a corporation, no matter how large, are sold to the public for the first time, they must debut in the OTC market. When Ford first went public in 1955, it too had to be seasoned before it was approved for listing on the NYSE.

Inasmuch as the OTC market is the home of many young companies the analyst combs the list constantly looking for insipient growth stocks.

Over-the-counter brokers are called every day for quotes on each stock in which they make a market, and their quotes are listed in the "pink sheets." These sheets are printed on 8" by 14" pink paper and distributed by the National Quotation Bureau, which also publishes a book each month and one every six months of all stocks that have been quoted, listing dates, prices, and brokers. The pink sheets are mailed to all subscribers each business day. Next to each stock is a list of brokers who make a market in that stock together with bid and ask prices. In addition to the pink sheets many active over-the-counter stocks are quoted on electronic equipment in brokerage offices.

THE THIRD MARKET

The third market has evolved as a result of large institutional and pension fund demand for securities. These large buyers or sellers of stock place their orders "off the exchange" with dealers who specialize in trading with other large buyers or sellers.

REGIONAL EXCHANGES

Philadelphia was our earliest financial capital; New York City took over financial leadership of the nation two decades later and has not relinquished control since.

Today Philadelphia, Baltimore, and Washington together form a regional exchange and with Boston, Detroit, Cincinnati, Pittsburgh, and the Midwest and Pacific Coast stock exchanges account for about 5 per cent of all U.S. stock exchange sales. Although small in relation to the two major New York exchanges, they do provide markets for local companies and in addition list many companies on both major exchanges.

Regional exchanges:

1. Trade in issues also trading on the New York and American Stock Exchanges (known as dual trading);
2. Essentially do not make primary markets but instead follow the lead of the major market in New York;
3. Through dual trading tie the regional market to the New York and American Stock Exchange ticker tapes.

SECURITIES AND EXCHANGE COMMISSION

Prior to the crash of 1929, there were no federal laws requiring American corporations to provide financial and accounting information to shareholders and the general public. The crash caused widespread distrust and confusion in the investing public and a congressional investigation led to the creation of a new federal agency, the Securities and Exchange Commission.

The SEC Acts of 1933 and 1934 often referred to as the "truth in securities laws," have the following basic objectives.

1. To provide investors with financial and other information concerning securities offered for public sale;
2. To prohibit misrepresentation, deceit, and other fraudulent acts and practices in the sale of securities;
3. To ensure that just and equitable principles of trade are observed by exchange members and others;
4. To regulate the use of credit to purchase securities; margin rates (percentage the shareholder may borrow on his securities) would be set by

the Board of Governors of the Federal Reserve System and enforced by the SEC;

5. To regulate trading in securities by insiders in listed securities.

The acts also provide that before a corporation's securities may be sold to the general public a lengthy registration statement must be filed with the SEC. The SEC requires disclosure of pertinent facts about the issuing corporation, portions of which are set forth in a prospectus.
In general the registration statement must contain:

1. Description of the new issue as well as all other classes of securities outstanding for that company;
2. Data for up to five years on assets, liabilities, profits, and losses;
3. List of names of officers and directors together with salaries, bonuses, and ownership interests;
4. A brief description of the organization's operations;
5. A statement outlining the organization's competitive position within its industry.

The SEC does not pass on the quality or the value of the securities offered, it only passes on the truth of the statements made in the prospectus. It is up to the investor to determine the value and make his own decision.

The SEC Act of 1934, as amended in 1964, was extended to cover over-the-counter companies having more than 750 shareholders in mid-1965, then in 1966 to companies with more than 500 shareholders and more than $1 million in assets. The result has been that many of the corporations trading over-the-counter to avoid the SEC Act of 1934 were now required to register under this act. It induced many companies to apply for listing on one of the major exchanges. The SEC Acts of 1934 and as amended in 1964 and 1966 greatly expanded the SEC's power over the securities industry and even gave them power to bring proceedings directly against specialists and traders if the New York or American Stock Exchange fails to do so. But basically the SEC relies heavily on supervised self-regulation by the securities exchanges.

Congress authorized another special study of the securities markets in 1966 that brought out certain deficiencies in trading practices by both specialists and traders on the two major New York exchanges. New Requirements

1. Set a minimum capital standard for each trader;
2. Required that at least 75 percent of trading be against the tide (counter to the direction of the price movement of an issue);
3. Prohibited traders from trading in their own accounts and handling floor orders in the same issue on the same day.

These provisions restricted the trader to such an extent that 90 per cent of the 300 traders associated with the NYSE chose not to continue to work under the new requirements.

BROKER-CLIENT RELATIONSHIP

The Registered Representative

The registered representative, who may also be called an account executive, stock salesman, or stockbroker, is the client's closest contact with the stock brokerage firm. He may be a person introduced by a relative or a friend, but however a client meets him he must appraise the man's ability, his business and educational background, and his investment philosophies. A registered representative who is primarily interested in long-term investments for clients may not be the man for a client who wishes to speculate. Before becoming a registered broker:

1. A person's past conduct is investigated by the New York Stock Exchange;
2. He must pass an examination given by the NYSE;
3. He must be registered by the exchange before he can deal with the public.

A stock salesman may be merely an order taker or, at the other extreme, may actually be an investment counselor. More often, however, the client and the representative coordinate their ideas on the market, world affairs, internal business conditions, and individual securities before the client makes the final decision.

Opening An Account

The representative is aware of the New York Stock Exchange Rule 405 that requires every broker to "use due diligence to learn essential facts relative to every customer, every order, every cash or margin account accepted."

To comply with the exchange's regulations, new customers are required to fill out a new account form containing:

1. Full name, home, and business addresses;
2. Social security number, age, occupation, citizenship;
3. Present employer, address;
4. Bank reference;
5. Personal references;
6. Signature.

The registered representative must recommend the new account and sign the new account form. The branch manager must also pass on the account before sending it to a partner or officer of the firm for final approval. In practice, however, the registered representative will accept your order if he and the branch manager approve the account.

How Your Order Is Handled

1. Your order is entered and wired to the floor of the New York Stock Exchange or American Stock Exchange.
2. The floor broker goes to the "post" where the stock you want to purchase is traded and executes the order.
3. Confirmation is wired back to the branch office. If the order is traded quickly, you may still be in the office and actually see the trade printed on the stock ticker.
4. A confirmation of purchase is mailed to you and payment is due five business days after the transaction.
5. A certificate of ownership bearing your name and the number of shares is registered in your name and delivered in two to four weeks.

When securities are sold the same procedures are involved, except that now you must deliver the properly endorsed stock certificate that has been sold. Five business days later, the proceeds of the sale will be paid to you.

When you buy or sell securities on an exchange or over-the-counter, you usually buy them from or sell them to another individual. The corporation whose shares have been exchanged receives no money from these trades. The corporation, to raise capital, sells securities to the public and retains an investment banker (underwriter) to represent them in the sale. After these shares have been sold to the public in an initial underwriting, they are then freely traded by the original buyers. Some member firms also act as investment bankers (underwriters) and help corporations file the registration of their securities with the Securities and Exchange Commission in accordance with the SEC Act of 1933.

Types of Orders

Basically there are three types of orders:

1. Buy
2. Sell
3. Short Sale

These orders may be "at the market" or "at a specified price".

If a representative receives an order to buy 100 shares of General

Motors at the market, he writes out an order that is transmitted to the floor of the NYSE. The floor partner of the firm immediately goes to the "post" where General Motors is traded and buys the stock. A sell order at the market is handled in the same manner.

Short Sale

If an individual believes the price of a stock will fall, he sells stock "he does not own" fully intending to buy it back later at a lower price. In order to sell short, the following factors must be present.

1. The broker with whom you place a short-sale order can borrow the stock that you wish to sell.
2. A short sale cannot be exercised, according to the rules of both exchanges, unless the stock's last price is an up-tick. To illustrate: An order is entered to sell 100 shares of Ford short at 45 3/8. The preceding sale was at 45 3/8 down from 45½. The order cannot be executed since 45 3/8 is a down-tick from 45½. If the stock falls to 45¼ and then rallies to 45 3/8, your order can be executed. If the number of shares sold short in a particular stock exceeds 20,000 shares or if there has been a change of 10,000 or more shares during the month, the short position is reported in the *Wall Street Journal* around the third week of each month.

Limit Orders

If a client enters an order to buy 100 shares of General Motors at 47, the order is a "limit order." When this order is transmitted to the floor of the exchange, the floor partner can pay 47 or less for the stock but not more. A limit order to sell at 47 would mean that the client will not take less than 47 per share for his 100 shares of General Motors.

Stop Orders

A "stop order" is a limited order of a special type. Stop orders may be either a buy or a sell order, and it becomes a market order to buy or sell when the stock trades at the limit price the client specifies. To illustrate: If you bought 100 shares of GM for 47, you may place a stop order to sell at 44. If GM trades at 44, your order now becomes a market order to sell. You may get 44 or less depending on the next trade. A good rule to follow in using this type of order would be to place your limit orders at fractions instead of round numbers. Thus, a stop limit sell at 44 1/8 would most often mean that your stock would sell at 44 and not less.

Stop Order Uses:

1. To limit loss (as in above example).
2. To limit loss on a short sale. A short sale is the opposite of a buy. Instead of owning the stock, the short seller has sold stock he does not own because he expects the market to fall. The broker actually has to borrow the stock to deliver to the buyer. To illustrate: Client sells 100 shares of Texas Instruments short at 95 a share and places a stop order to buy at 99¾, thereby limiting his loss. If the stock goes down, he can buy it back and make a profit. If it rallies, his order becomes a market order as soon as the stock trades at 99¾.
3. To protect a gain.
   a. If 100 shares of GM were bought at 47 per share and it rallied to 58 per share, the client may enter a stop order to sell at 54¼, thereby protecting most of his profit.
   b. If 100 shares of Texas Instruments were sold short at 95 per share and it dropped to 85, the client could place a stop order to buy, thereby protecting his profit.

Other Types of Orders

Good 'til Canceled. This is an order that stays open on the specialist's books on the floor of the exchange until either it is executed or canceled by the client.

Good for Week or Month or a Specific Date. This is similar to an open order except that it is canceled on the specialist's books on the date specified.

Fill or Kill. If a client enters an order to buy 100 shares of Ford "fill or kill" at 45 1/8 per share and the quote is 45 bid - 45¼ offered, the floor broker goes to the post where Ford is being traded and places the order. If he buys the stock immediately, he reports the order; otherwise he wires back "100 shares buy Ford at 45 1/8 killed."

Not Held Orders. These are orders that may be given to a broker when the client has a large block of stock (several thousand shares). It relieves the broker of all responsibility regarding the price and time of the execution of the order. In effect the client is saying, "You're on the floor, use your judgment, and if you make a mistake it's not your fault."

At the Close. If a client wants to buy 100 shares of Texas Instruments at 85 1/8 and if not executed at that price, it becomes a market order "at the market, at the close." Client is trying to execute the order at a limit price, and if he doesn't buy it he's willing to pay the market price at the close.

At the Opening. Client specifically wants to buy or sell only at the opening price. If his order reaches the floor too late for execution at the opening price, it is automatically canceled.

All or None.   A client may place an order to buy 200 or more shares at a price marked "all or none." If the floor trader cannot buy all the shares at that price or lower, he will not buy any.

There are other variations of the above orders but these cover the vast majority of executed orders.

Implicit in every order is the good faith between client and representative, since most orders are verbal. Billions of dollars of securities are bought and sold over the telephone.

GOING PUBLIC

The legal and accounting ramifications of selling securities to the public for the first time is an intricate process, and the step-by-step procedure is knowledge a speculator or investor does not need to master. However, the prospectus contains information that the SEC believes is necessary for an individual to make an intelligent investment decision. Inasmuch as the SEC has been in existence since 1933 and represents over 150 years of investing experience, we can learn a great deal about a corporation by examining its prospectus, or S-1 form, as it is called.

Following are some of the requirements of the SEC Act of 1933 that are important to an investor.

1. Who is the underwriter? The vast difference between an astute investment banker and a mediocre one can be critical to an investor. Investigate the background of the major underwriter to determine his reputation.

2. What is the company going to do with the money it receives from the sale of securities? An investor can learn from this section of the prospectus the future plans of the company.

3. The Capital Structure of the Corporation. This section informs an investor of the number of shares to be outstanding if all securities being registered are sold. In a subsequent chapter on "Understanding Financial Statements," the importance of capital structure will be outlined completely.

4. Summary of Earnings. Probably the first section read by most analysts and investors. It contains a five-year history of sales and earnings and in capsule form traces the financial growth of the corporation.

5. Description of the Corporation's Business. The prospectus contains a brief description of the business the corporation does and its future business plans and portrays the general development of the business during the past five years.

6. Pending Legal Proceedings. Any material pending litigation other than ordinary and routine is reported in this section. If the case involves a patent necessary to the sale of the corporation or a suit jeopardizing a substantial part of the corporation's net worth, the investor may decide not to buy stock in the company.

7. Directors and Executive Officers. The names of all directors and executive officers of the registrant and all persons chosen to become officers and directors are listed. Also listed is the principal occupation of each officer during the past five years.

8. Remuneration of Directors and Officers. Each director and each of the three highest paid officers of the registrant whose aggregate direct remuneration exceeds $30,000 are listed. An investor can determine for himself is he believes that the key officers are paying themselves too much. If possible, it is wise to compare these salaries with the salaries of other officers in a similar business of approximately the same size.

9. Options to Purchase Securities. The registrant must furnish all information concerning options to purchase securities from the registrant, or any of its subsidiaries, which are outstanding as of a specified date within thirty days prior to the filing. This section provides another indication of whether management is being fair to the shareholders. If options to the officers compare favorably with other corporations and if salaries being paid are fair, the investor can feel that management is honest.

10. Principal Holders of Securities. An investor is informed who owns more than 15 per cent of any class of security. The holder does not have to be an officer or director to hold more than 15 per cent; however, he may be an important force behind the officers and directors.

SUMMARY

The New York Stock Exchange, the largest and most important of all the exchanges, began operations in 1792 when twenty-four brokers organized themselves into a cohesive unit to provide liquidity to the securities market. Because securities could not, at that time, be bought and sold readily, most people completely avoided investments.

An exchange is a meeting place for buyers and sellers of stocks and bonds, and only members, or seat holders, may buy and sell on the floor of the exchanges. Some buy for their own account but the vast majority of floor partners act as agents for their clients.

Registered representatives are employees of brokerage firms and are usually the public's closest contact with the securities market. Their duties range from order takers to investment counselors, depending on the kind of relationship a client seeks.

The need for securities markets began when our country was still young and before the Industrial Revolution began here. Securities markets helped finance the Revolutionary War, the War of 1812, and the Civil War; the building of canals and railroads in the nineteenth century; and the automobile, steel, chemical, and electronics industries during the first three quarters of the twentieth century.

As a result of the crash of 1929 the government passed the Securities and Exchange Acts of 1933 and 1934 that have helped prevent fraud and manipulation in securities dealings and have required improved financial reporting. In effect our securities markets are like thermometers—they register the temperature of the entire Western World. They are voting booths where investors cast their daily ballots. A healthy securities market is an absolute necessity to a healthy society.

QUESTIONS

1. Why, and when, was the New York Stock Exchange begun? What is its main function?
2. What is a seat? To what does it entitle its owner?
3. Name and describe the different types of seat holders.
4. What is the Over-the-Counter market and how does it differ from the New York and American Stock exchanges?
5. What is the function of a regional exchange?
6. What are the basic objectives of the Securities and Exchange Act of 1933?
7. What were the original goals of the SEC Act of 1934? How and when were they amended?
8. Name and describe the three types of orders a client may place with a broker.
9. Explain a stop order. What are its uses?

2

UNDERSTANDING AND ANALYZING FINANCIAL STATEMENTS: A BASIS FOR DETERMINING VALUE

Securities can be either stocks or bonds, and a major problem for an investor is determining the value of these securities. Without knowledge of security analysis, an individual assumes that on any given day the price reported in the newspapers determines the value of the security. To a large extent this is correct since the public through its purchases and sales in the open market have placed a price on a stock or a bond at which they are willing to buy and to sell.

An individual could ask, "Who am I to say a security is worth more or less than the price listed for that day?" In most cases he cannot, but as he learns more and more about evaluating a security he will begin to make value judgments. In order to learn what some of the elements are that determine value, a person must understand the basic meaning of the financial statements issued by corporations, and prepared by certified public accountants.

Accounting is not a science but to the non-accountant it appears that because everything balances the accounting is, therefore, precise.

Accountants express an *opinion* but do not offer guarantees because the values of many assets and liabilities on the balance sheet cannot be accurately measured and many items of income and expense are estimates. Nevertheless, accountants' opinions are necessary and helpful in both understanding and analyzing financial statements. The principal accounting statements are the balance sheet and the statement of income, which are interrelated and must be examined together to get a complete picture of the status of a business enterprise.

The *balance sheet* is a statement of a company's financial position and lists the assets, liabilities, and stockholders' equity. The balance sheet derives its name from the fact that it *always* balances. The *statement of income* lists all revenues, expenses, and income or loss of a corporation for the period. The income or loss of a corporation at the end of the year is then transferred to the retained earnings account of the balance sheet, and is, therefore, complementary to it. Retained earnings is part of the stockholder's equity section and reflects the accumulation of profits or losses of the corporation. Dividends are paid out of retained earnings. The balance sheet may be viewed as a temporary listing of assets that will be used to produce future sales and income. How rapidly these assets are consumed to produce income can determine the quality of earnings.

At the turn of the century the balance sheet was the most important statement as far as investors were concerned. They reasoned that since earnings derived from the statement of income were included in the assets and net worth of the corporation, it was not necessary to give much consideration to earnings.

Since World War I this emphasis has gradually changed. More and more analysts and investors began reading and studying the income statement and ignoring the balance sheet. Consequently, especially during the 1960's, many corporations were resorting to a variety of auditing and accounting devices to keep earnings rising. Investors seldom, if ever, asked questions about the balance sheet, only about the earnings and price-earnings ratio of a stock. The price earnings ratio is determined by dividing a corporation's annual earnings into the current price of the stock. If earnings are $2 per share and the stock sells for $16 per share, the price earnings ratio is 8 times. Perhaps the marriage of the balance sheet and the statement of income is on again!

THE BALANCE SHEET

All business begins and ends with the balance sheet. To illustrate: *Five* individuals form a new company, the PDQ Corporation, and *each* invests $10,000 in $10 par value common stock in it. Following is the balance sheet of the corporation after the shares have been issued and paid for.

ASSETS
 Current Assets
  Cash $ 50,000
  Fixed Assets   -0-
             Total assets $ 50,000

Liabilities and Stockholders' Equity

Current Liabilities	-0-
Long-term Liabilities	-0-

Stockholders' Equity

Common Stock Par Value $10 10,000 Shares Authorized 5,000 Shares Outstanding	$ 50,000
Total Liabilities and Stockholders' Equity	$ 50,000

Current Assets. These are *cash,* and other assets that presumably will be converted into cash, generally within a year.

Fixed Assets. These are assets of a relatively permanent nature that are not intended for resale.

Current Liabilities. These are the liabilities that must be paid within one year.

Long-Term Liabilities. These are bonds, mortgages, and debts not maturing within one year.

Stockholders' Equity. (owners' equity). This is the proprietorship interest or net worth of the corporation.

Authorized Shares. These are the number of shares the corporation may sell.

Shares Outstanding. These are the actual number of shares the corporation has sold.

To illustrate further, the corporation buys a machine for $20,000 that makes WARFS. It pays $5,000 cash and finances the balance of $15,000 payable in five equal installments. At the same time the steel to make the WARFS has been delivered. The invoice price is $6,000. If a balance sheet were prepared following these transactions it would look like this:

Assets

Current Assets		
Cash	$ 45,000.00	
Inventory (steel)	6,000.00	
Total Current Assets	$ 51,000.00	
Fixed Assets		
Machinery & Equipment	$ 20,000.00	(Total amount is asset— see Liability)
TOTAL ASSETS	$ 71,000.00	

Liabilities

Current Liabilities
Accounts Payable $ 9,000.00 ($ 6,000 owed for steel;
                                                  $ 3,000 current portion
                                                  of machinery debt)

Total Current Liabilities $ 9,000.00
Long-term Liabilities
    (machinery)   12,000.00
Stockholders' Equity
    Preferred Stock   -0-
    Common Stock Par Value
    $10
    10,000 Shares Authorized
    5,000 Shares Issued and
    Outstanding $ 50,000.00

Total Liabilities and
    Stockholders' Equity $ 71,000.00

The assets of the corporation increased $21,000 and so did the liabilities. Inventory is a current asset and the amount of debt incurred to pay for it is a current liability, an exchange of a liability for an asset. In addition, the first payment on the machinery of $3,000 is a current liability, leaving the remaining balance of $12,000 as a long-term liability.

Some other current assets:

1. U.S. Government securities
2. Accounts receivable
3. Notes receivable
4. Inventory

Each of the above assets presumably will be turned into cash within a year.

In the stockholders' equity section, 5,000 shares of stock have been issued out of a total authorization of 10,000 shares. Par value of $10 per share is an arbitrary figure. It could be any amount management chooses to place on its stock or if it chooses it can place no par value on its shares. Once, however, par value is established the corporation may not sell its shares below the par value but may sell them above. If in the above example par value was $1.00 per share instead of $10 per share and the shares were sold for $10, the stockholders' equity section would appear like this:

Common Stock Par Value $1.00	
10,000 Shares Authorized	
5,000 Shares Issued	$ 5,000.00
Capital Paid in Excess of Par Value	45,000.00
	$ 50,000.00

The capital paid in excess of par is part of the equity of the corporation. Not too many years ago this account was known as capital surplus and it was extremely confusing to the reader of the balance sheet. How can you invest money in a corporation and immediately produce a surplus? You cannot!

Accountants have been making great strides in changing their terminology over the years, removing as many ambiguous terms as possible in order to help the non-accountant understand statements more readily.

THE ANNUAL REPORT

When you read the annual statement of a corporation you will probably overlook the single most significant part. It is the accountant's report, which must appear with every company's financial statement. The Certified Public Accountant will give one of the following evaluations:

1. An unqualified opinion
2. A qualified opinion
3. An adverse opinion
4. A disclaimer of opinion

An Unqualified Opinion. Only this opinion can be construed by the investor to mean that there are no problems or no changes have taken place during the year that is reflected in the financial statement. A word of caution—fraud and deception are always possibilities. A certified public accountant may issue an unqualified opinion only to learn subsequently that there was fraud on the part of an employee or management itself in preparing the statement. The CPA is not a detective, although he uses techniques such as financial ratios to analyze progress and to detect discrepancies.

A Qualified Opinion. This opinion is issued if accountants have not been able to apply all the generally accepted auditing standards and procedures. It is a signal for the investor to investigate the reasons for this qualification before he invests. The CPA will make his qualifications clear in his report.

An Adverse Opinion. This opinion occurs if the CPA objects to the ways in which the generally accepted accounting principles have been used or if these principles have not been applied consistently in the financial statement. In any event, the CPA must disclose his reasons in a middle paragraph. Therefore, an auditors' report with *three* paragraphs is a flashing red signal to halt and check thoroughly before going ahead.

A Disclaimer of Opinion.   This opinion is given by a CPA if the scope of his audit is limited by either circumstances or by management. The public company is rarely confronted with such a set of circumstances since as we learned from the SEC acts the corporation must report earnings quarterly and submit a fully audited report to stockholders once a year. Disclaimers of opinion are usually issued to smaller, privately held corporations that either do not wish or cannot afford a complete audit.

Therefore, only one opinion, the unqualified opinion, gives the green light to continue analysis. Fortunately, the vast majority of opinions issued are unqualified.

Example of Unqualified Accountant's Report

We have examined the consolidated balance sheets of XYZ Corporation as of December 31, 1974 and the related statements of income, retained earnings and charges in financial position for the year then ended. Our examination was made in accordance with generally accepted auditing standards, and accordingly included such tests of the accounting records and such other auditing procedures as we considered necessary in the circumstances.

In our opinion, the aforementioned financial statements present fairly the consolidated financial position at December 31, 1974 and the consolidated results of their operations, and changes in stockholders' equity and financial position for the year then ended, in conformity with generally accepted accounting principles applied on a consistent basis.

In these two simple paragraphs the certified public accountants have informed us that they have examined all records using generally accepted auditing standards and generally accepted accounting principles applied on a *consistent* basis. The letter, signed by the accountant and included in the company's annual report, is formally called an unqualified opinion or a "clean opinion."

NOTES TO FINANCIAL STATEMENTS

All financial statements that have been audited conclude with a "notes" section that contains some or all of the following:

1. Principles of consolidation
2. Inventory policies

3. Income taxes (how computed)
4. Pensions (explanation of plan—liability of corporation)
5. Retained earnings (any restrictions)
6. Long term debt (maturity—interest—amount of debt)
7. Contingent liabilities

Note 1 will always read "Summary of Significant Accounting Policies," and will include some of the following, which should be studied because they are a part of the total financial statement.

Example
1. PRINCIPLES OF CONSOLIDATION
   The financial statements include the accounts of the company and its subsidiaries. Significant intercompany accounts and transactions have been eliminated in consolidation. This practice is in accordance with generally accepted accounting principles and eliminates sales among subsidiaries of the same company.
2. INVENTORIES
   Inventories are stated at the lower cost (last-in-first-out) or market.

In reading a balance sheet, and especially a statement of income during an inflationary period, the treatment of inventory by the management of the corporation is most important in arriving at profits.

Three Important Inventory Terms

1. FIFO: First In—First Out
2. LIFO: Last In—First Out
3. Moving Average: Average of all inventory on hand

These methods (there are others) of applying costs of inventory are acceptable to the accounting profession and are in accordance with generally accepted accounting principles.

Examples
The following figures have been exaggerated for purposes of illustration.

Three units of inventory have been purchased:

1st unit cost	$ 10	First In-First Out cost
2nd unit cost	15	
3rd unit cost	20	Last In-First Out cost
	$ 45	Total cost 3 units
	$ 15	Moving Average—1 unit

FIFO: We sell 1 unit for	$ 25	
FIFO cost	10	
Gross profit		$ 15
MOVING AVERAGE: We sell 1 unit for	$ 25	
M.A. cost	15	
Gross profit		$ 10
LIFO: We sell 1 unit for	$ 25	
LIFO cost	20	
Gross profit		$ 5

FIFO inventory accounting records the highest gross profit and therefore the highest earnings per share. LIFO inventory accounting reports the lowest gross profit and therefore the lowest earnings per share. The company using FIFO, in this exaggerated example, shows three times the profit as the company using LIFO, but these are not *real* profits. They are, in reality, non-recurring inventory profits attributable to inflation.

Therefore, in an inflationary environment it is far more conservative to use LIFO accounting and report lower profits. By reporting lower profits the corporation pays lower taxes. By paying higher taxes under FIFO, in inflationary times, it is possible for a corporation to become insolvent because it might not have enough capital to replace its inventory. The stock market, which places a value on earnings, examines the quality of these earnings and will value FIFO earnings *less* than LIFO. Generally, companies using FIFO accounting in this type of environment should be carefully scrutinized. FIFO inventory evaluation can be effectively used even in an inflationary economy if the merchandise turns over rapidly (twelve times a year or more) such as in the food industry.

One word of caution: If *inflation* turns into *deflation*, LIFO inventory accounting can turn profits into losses quite suddenly. There is no rest for the analyst. Rapid changes are built into our society and the investor must adapt to these changes in order to reduce the inherent risks.

EIGHT KEY RATIOS IN ANALYSIS OF FINANCIAL STATEMENTS

In broad terms a "ratio" expresses the numerical relationship between two numbers. Understanding some of these relationships can aid in making important investment decisions.

1. Current Ratio, Also Called Working Capital Ratio

Current ratio is the ratio of current assets to current liabilities. Among industrial companies, a 2 to 1 ratio is considered standard.

XYZ CORPORATION
Statement of Income and Retained Earnings
as of December 31

	1974	1973	
Net Sales	$ 32,501,030	$29,451,045	(Total amount billed for year)
Costs and Expenses			
Cost of Sales	24,267,125	22,198,830	(Raw material, direct labor, overhead, fuel, supplies)
Selling and Administrative Expenses	5,497,522	5,377,303	(Salesmen's commissions, advertising, officers' salaries)
Interest Expense—Net	687,234	604,175	(Interest on debt, less interest earned)
Total Expenses	$ 30,451,881	$ 28,180,308	(Total expenses to be deducted from sales)
Income before Taxes	$ 2,049,149	$ 1,270,737	(Taxes computed from this figure)
Income Taxes (Note 5)	854,000	529,000	(Total taxes on income)
Net Income	$ 1,195,149	$ 741,737	(Total income to be transferred to "Retained Earnings" on balance sheet)
Retained Earnings at Start of Year	6,659,693	6,271,135	(Retained earnings on balance sheet at start of year)
	$ 7,854,842	$ 7,012,872	
Cash Dividends Paid ($ 0.20 per share)	353,178	353,179	(Dividends paid to stockholders)
Retained Earnings at End of Year	$ 7,501,664	$ 6,659,693	(Retained Earnings at end of year [see Balance Sheet])
Net Income per Share	$ 0.68	$ 0.42	(Earnings per share, used to compute price-earnings ratio)

XYZ CORPORATION
Balance Sheet
as of December 31

	1974	1973	
ASSETS			
Current Assets			
Cash	$ 475,885	$ 105,080	(Cash, or assets usually turned into cash within one year) (Self-explanatory)
Receivables (less allowance of $130,000 in 1973 and $75,000 in 1972)	5,259,260	5,095,507	(Amounts owed by customers, less estimated amounts uncollectable)
Inventories (Note 1)			
Finished Goods and Work in Process	3,766,216	3,596,691	(Products that are completed or in process)
Materials and Supplies	2,944,719	2,805,836	(Materials and supplies not yet in manufacture)
	$ 6,710,935	$ 6,402,527	
Prepaid Expenses	288,257	245,834	(Payments made in advance of utilization [insurance, rent, etc.])
Total Current Assets	$ 12,732,337	$ 11,848,948	
Other Assets			
Deferred Product Development Costs, Less Amortization (Note 1)	620,200	707,788	(Expenditures for research relating to net products)
Property, Plant, and Equipment (Notes 1 & 2)			
Land	215,020	211,354	(Cost of land—no depreciation; does not wear out)
Buildings and Improvements	5,395,999	5,493,545	(Buildings, equipment, furniture, fixtures subject to deductions for wear and tear)
Machinery and Equipment	9,291,253	8,644,272	
Furniture and Fixtures	263,296	257,478	
	$ 15,165,568	$ 14,606,649	
Less Allowance for Depreciation and Amortization	4,654,869	4,287,038	(Total accumulated deductions)
	$ 10,510,699	$ 10,319,611	
	$ 23,863,236	$ 22,876,347	

XYZ CORPORATION

Balance Sheet
as of December 31

	1974	1973	
LIABILITIES AND STOCKHOLDERS' EQUITY			
Current Liabilities			(All debts due and payable within one year)
Accounts Payable	$ 1,624,024	$ 1,121,703	(Amounts owed to suppliers)
Accrued Payrolls	584,554	500,549	(Amounts owed to employees not yet paid)
Income Taxes	458,881	87,871	(Amounts owed for taxes, 1974)
Other Liabilities	978,402	905,337	(Assortment of many liabilities)
Long-term Debt Due within One Year	1,425,314	1,403,934	(Amount of long-term debt that must be paid this year)
Total Current Liabilities	$ 5,071,178	$ 4,019,389	
Other Liabilities			
Long-term Debt (Note 2)	6,108,537	7,108,851	(For money borrowed, excluding current portion due)
Deferred Income Taxes (Note 5)	676,365	654,329	(Different accounting methods used for financial and tax purposes)
Deferred Pension Payments (Note 4)	250,692	179,285	(Amounts to be put into pension funds)
	$ 7,035,594	7,942,465	
Stockholders' Equity (Notes 2 & 3)			
Common Stock, $1 Par Value*	1,765,893	1,765,893	(Amounts originally invested in business by stockholders)
Capital in Excess of Par	2,488,907	2,488,907	(Additional amounts received in excess of par)
Retained Earnings	7,501,664	6,659,693	(Retained earnings reinvested in business—available for dividends)
Total Stockholders' Equity	$ 11,756,464	$ 10,914,493	
	$ 23,863,236	$ 22,876,347	

*Authorized: 3,000,000 shares; issued and outstanding: 1,765,893 shares.

However, an investor should compare his company's current ratio with other companies within the same industry. If we review our definition of a current asset, we find it is made up of items that are either cash or will be turned into cash within a year. (There are exceptions. In the case of the liquor or lumber industries, wherein it takes years to develop the product, the inventory is still considered "current.") Therefore, if the current ratio is 2 to 1, we have twice as many current assets to pay off the current liabilities. To a businessman it translates into the following advantages:

a. He may take advantage of all discounts offered by suppliers for paying on time.
b. He may buy in quantities and thus effect substantial savings.
c. It may prevent his going further into debt.

Example (*See* XYZ Balance Sheet"):

$$1973$$

$$\frac{\text{Current Assets}}{\text{Current Liabilities}} = \frac{\$\ 11,848,948}{4,019,389} = 2.9 \text{ times current liabilities}$$

$$1974$$

$$\frac{\text{Current Assets}}{\text{Current Liabilities}} = \frac{\$\ 12,732,337}{5,071,178} = 2.5 \text{ times current liabilities}$$

This company's current position declined slightly in 1974 but remains quite strong.

A high ratio for a company, say of 5 to 1, may not necessarily be a sign of business health. Many companies may report a high current ratio but a deficit in earnings. This is another reason for the investor to examine both the balance sheet and profit and loss statement.

2. Quick Ratio (Liquidity Ratio) (*See* XYZ Balance Sheet)

This ratio is often termed the "acid test." It is an estimate of the immediate ability of the corporation to satisfy current obligations. In this acid test, inventories are omitted.

$$\text{Formula: } \frac{\text{Cash} + \text{Temporary Investments} + \text{Receivables}}{\text{Current Liabilities}}$$

No temporary investments were made in 1973 and 1974 in XYZ Corporation. Temporary investments are those made by a corporation in U.S. Government treasury bills or other securities bought to be held for a short period of time, usually less than one year.

1973

Cash   Accts. Rec.

$$\frac{\$\ 105{,}080 + \$\ 5{,}095{,}501}{4{,}019{,}389} = \frac{\$\ 5{,}200{,}581}{4{,}019{,}389} = 1.3 \text{ to } 1 \text{ Quick Ratio}$$

1974

$$\frac{\$\ 475{,}885 + \$\ 5{,}257{,}260}{5{,}071{,}178} = \frac{\$\ 5{,}733{,}145}{5{,}071{,}171} = 1.1 \text{ to } 1 \text{ Quick Ratio}$$

This ratio is applied in conjunction with the current ratio and it reflects a corporation's ability to meet current liabilities without the necessity of selling inventory. A ratio of 1.0 to 1 or more represents an extremely liquid company and one with the ability to raise its dividend.

During periods of expansion, liquidity ratios suffer because of the increase in accounts payable and cost of capital equipment. If quick ratio continues to decline, the company may have to raise additional capital or even lower its dividend.

3. Capitalization Ratio

a. Long-term Debt
b. Common Stock and Surplus

This ratio or series of ratios is extremely important and should be used in conjunction with the current and quick ratios. As a company's debt increases relative to the funds stockholders have invested, the creditors may be financing the growth of the business. In times of stress, companies with heavy debt are susceptible to undue strain and may even face bankruptcy.

Example (*See* XYZ Balance Sheet)

a. Formula: $$\frac{\text{Long-term Debt}}{\text{Stockholders' Equity} + \text{Long-term Debt}}$$

		1973	1974
$$\frac{\$\ 7.1 \text{ in millions}}{\$\ 7.1 + 10.9 \text{ in millions}} = \frac{\$\ 7.1}{18} =$$		40%	
$$\frac{\$\ 6.1 \text{ in millions}}{\$\ 11.7 + 6.1 \text{ in millions}} = \frac{\$\ 6.1}{17.8} =$$			34%

b. Formula: Common Stock and Surplus
—————————————
Total Capitalization

$$\frac{\$ 10.9 \text{ in millions}}{\$18 \text{ in millions}} = 60\%$$

$$\frac{\$ 11.7 \text{ in millions}}{\$17.8 \text{ in millions}} = \frac{66\%}{100\%}$$

In 1973 the debt of XYZ Corporation was 40 per cent of the total capitalization. It was reduced considerably to 34 per cent in one year. The corporation is gaining in financial strength and if the need arises should be able to borrow from commercial banks at advantageous interest rates.

The interdependence of the current ratio and the capitalization ratio can be illustrated further.

Example

ABC CORPORATION

	1973	1974
Current Assets	$ 70 million	$ 110 million
Current Liabilities	50 million	55 million

If an investor computed the current ratio for 1973 and 1974, he would see that it improved considerably:

Current Ratio $= \dfrac{\$ 70 \text{ mil}}{50 \text{ mil}} = 1.4 \text{ to } 1 \text{ in } 1973$

Current Ratio $= \dfrac{\$ 110 \text{ mil}}{55 \text{ mil}} = 2.0 \text{ to } 1 \text{ in } 1974$

If the analysis is continued, the investor might learn that the corporation issued $50,000,000 in bonds during 1974 and his debt to equity (net worth) ratio rose. Creditors (all bondholders are creditors) are financing the business growth of the company. Since long-term bonds are not current liabilities, the current ratio improved at the expense of possible strain on the corporation in the event of recession.

These first three ratios are all keyed to the balance sheet without reference to the statement of income.

4. Net Income to Sales Ratio (*See* XYZ Statement of Income)

Formula: Net Income after Taxes
—————————————
Total Sales

$$1973 - \qquad \frac{\$ \ 741,737}{\$ \ 29,451,045} = 2.5\%$$

$$1974 - \qquad \frac{\$ \ 1,195,149}{32,501,030} = 3.6\%$$

Sales for 1974 increased approximately 10 percent over 1973 whereas earnings increased 60 percent. The 3.6 percent return on sales is still not satisfactory but shows a significant improvement. If growth continues into 1975, the company may have sales of $35 million and earnings of $1,750,000.

5. Sales to Fixed Assets Ratio

This ratio is computed by dividing the annual sales by the value before depreciation of property, plant, and equipment at the end of the year.

Formula: $\dfrac{\text{Annual Sales (see Statement of Income)}}{\text{Total Fixed Assets before Depreciation (see Balance Sheet)}}$

$1973 - \dfrac{\$ \ 29,451,045 \ \text{Annual Sales}}{14,060,649 \ \text{Property, Plant and Equipment before Depreciation}} = 2 \text{ to } 1$

$1974 - \dfrac{\$ \ 32,501,030 \ \text{Annual Sales}}{15,175,568 \ \text{Property, Plant and Equipment before Depreciation}} = 2.1 \text{ to } 1$

This ratio is significant because it illustrates whether or not management is spending money wisely on new plant and equipment. Any sizable increase in facilities should lead to larger sales volume. If it does not, then the additional capital invested is either not being utilized properly nor fully.

In our analysis of the XYZ Corporation, its annual sales increased from $2 in sales for each invested dollar of property, plant, and equipment, or from a 2 to 1 ratio in 1973 to a 2.1 to 1 ratio in 1974. This signifies that management improved its use of fixed assets.

Companies in heavy industries such as steel or paper usually have sales to fixed asset ratios of 1.2 or 1.3 to 1, whereas in the lighter industries such as services or drugs the sales volume would be larger in relation to fixed assets.

6. Net Income to Net Worth Ratio

This ratio is a percentage and is derived by dividing the net income by the total shareholders' equity. It is unquestionably one of the most important ratios.

$$1973 \quad \frac{\text{Net Income}}{\text{Shareholders' equity}} \quad = \frac{\$ 741,737}{\$ 10,914,493} \quad = 6.8\%$$

$$1974 \quad \frac{\text{Net Income}}{\text{Shareholders' equity}} \quad = \frac{\$ 1,195,149}{\$ 11,756,464} \quad = 10.2\%$$

If money is deposited in a savings bank a person would want to know how much interest will be earned on the money. This is essentially the same question. Stockholders have invested $10,614,493 in 1973 and have earned $741,737 or 6.8% on all assets.

In 1974 the Company earned 10.2% on shareholders' equity in the business which is a substantial improvement. This improvement could be caused by many factors the investor should analyze:

1. General prosperity within the country.
2. General prosperity within the industry.
3. Country and industry emerging from recession.
4. Management improvements.
5. New products.

Surveys of all manufacturing corporations in the United States report that a return of approximately 10% is slightly above average. Would you, if you were sitting on a board of directors, approve an investment in a company that returned only 4% or 5% on its invested capital? I don't think so. The steel industry in the United States could not attract capital for almost twenty years because of its poor return on capital.

These ratios or comparisons are not static but have meaning and help translate cold figures into major business decisions.

7. Sales to Inventory Ratio

This ratio is derived by dividing merchandise cost of sales by the year-end inventories. It is called "inventory turnover" and indicates the number of times the merchandise stock is replaced during the year. A turnover of four times per year might also be stated as three months. This comparison gives the investor a valuable clue about how efficiently management controls inventory.

a. A relatively slow turnover, *in relation to other companies in the same industry,* means an overinvestment in merchandise and stale inventory. It shows management inefficiency.

b. A relatively rapid turnover, *in relation to other companies in the same industry,* contributes to an efficient use of working capital and, therefore, higher profits for shareholders.

For each type of business there is a normal period during which inventory should be sold, turned into receivables, and then into cash. If merchandise is carried beyond this point, it means extra expenses for the company such as interest costs, warehousing charges, and other variable charges.

Example

Formula: Merchandise Cost of Sales (NOT SALES) (see Profit and Loss Statement)

Inventories   (see Balance Sheet)

$$1973 \quad \frac{\$\ 22{,}199 \text{ in millions}}{6{,}402 \text{ in millions}} = 3.4 \text{ times}$$

$$1974 \quad \frac{\$\ 24{,}267 \text{ in millions}}{6{,}711 \text{ in millions}} = 3.6 \text{ times}$$

Inventory turnover improved in 1974 from 3.4 times to 3.6 times, and shareholders' profits also improved from 42¢ per share to 68¢ per share.

8. Number of Days Sales in Receivables Ratio

This ratio analysis provides a rough estimate of the average length of time accounts receivable are outstanding. Comparing this answer with the credit terms of the company supplies another test of management's ability.

Example

If the terms of credit are 2 per cent, 10 days, end of month, it means that if the customer pays by the 10th of the following month, he may take a 2 per cent discount.

Overinvestment in receivables may result from any of the following:

a. Too liberal a credit policy
b. Failure to write off bad accounts
c. Laxity in collections

Example

Formula: Accounts Receivable x 365 days   (see Balance Sheet)

$$\frac{\text{Net Sales}}{} \quad \text{(see Statement of Income)}$$

1973 $\dfrac{\$5,095 \text{ (in millions)} \times 365}{\$29,451 \text{ (in millions)}} = 63$ days turnover of receivables

1974 $\dfrac{\$5,257 \text{ (in millions)} \times 365}{\$32,501 \text{ (in millions)}} = 59$ days turnover of receivables

The company improved its receivable turnover considerably from sixty-three to fifty-nine days. Management has undoubtedly improved its credit and collection policies, while at the same time increasing its sales.

Other Critical Statistics

In addition to the ratios we have already explained, the following are also important to the investor in his analysis of a corporation:

1. Earnings per share—common stock
2. Dividends per share and dividend payout
3. Book value per share
4. Price-earnings multiple
5. Sales per share of stock
6. Interest coverage (bonds)

Earnings per Share—Common Stock

This is the most significant single statistic issued by a corporation. After the dividends are paid on the preferred stock, the remaining income balance is divided by the number of common shares outstanding. If additional common shares were sold during the year, the average number of shares outstanding would be used.

Formula: $\dfrac{\text{Net Income}}{\text{Number of Common Shares Outstanding}}$ (see Statement of Income)

(see Stockholders' Equity section of Balance Sheet)

Net Income 1973 $\dfrac{\$741,737}{1,765,893} = 42\cent$ per share

Net Income 1974 $\dfrac{\$1,195,149}{1,765,893} = 68\cent$ per share

Earnings for 1974 increased 61 per cent over 1973, whereas sales increased only 10 per cent, from $29,451,045 to $32,501,030. Evidently these were unusual circumstances causing this large increase in earnings. The corporation's progress should be closely studied to see if management has made permanent changes or whether the 1974 earnings were non-recurring. Perhaps a new product was introduced with a high profit margin. Earnings per share have become so important to investors that in 1973 our financial newspapers began to list the price-earnings ratio every day next to each stock price.

Dividends per Share and Dividends Payout

Dividend policy is set by the board of directors. Common stockholders have no promise of a dividend. The board of directors bases its decisions on the earnings per share plus the corporations need for more capital. Usually, industries follow certain dividend payout percentages. Always compare the company you are analyzing with its industry leaders. There are always good reasons for leaders' being where they are.

Dividend Payout of XYZ Corporation (see Statement of Income)

	1973	Dividends per Share	20¢
	1974	Dividends per Share	20¢

In 1973 the XYZ Corporation earned 42¢ per share. What is the dividend payout? Here is a simple formula to derive it:

$$1973 \quad \frac{\text{Dividends Paid} \quad = 20\cancel{c}}{\text{Earnings per share} \quad = 42\cancel{c}} = 47\%$$

$$1974 \quad \frac{\text{Dividends Paid} \quad = 20\cancel{c}}{\text{Earnings per share} \quad = 68\cancel{c}} = 30\%$$

The *smaller* the *percentage* of dividend payout, the more secure the dividend. In 1973 the dividend was almost one-half of earnings. In 1974 the dividend payout dropped to 30 per cent of earnings.

If it is the board of directors policy to pay approximately 50 per cent of earnings in dividends, then the investor can expect a dividend increase. Stated another way, earnings in 1973 were a little more than double the dividend, and in 1974 were more than triple.

Dividend payouts vary according to many factors such as:

1. Stability of earnings. (Do earnings move up and down rapidly?)
2. The need for new capital. (Company may be in the middle of expansion and needs capital for new plant and equipment.)

3. What is the economic outlook? (Does management expect the company to continue growing in the face of a slowdown in the economy?)

On average, over the last number of years dividends on common stocks have averaged around 50 per cent of earnings. In the gas and electric utility industry, dividends average between 70 per cent to 75 per cent. In other industries such as office equipment, the leader of which is International Business Machines, the dividend payout is much lower than 50 per cent.

Book Value Per Share

This value will tell each shareholder how much is invested in the business. It is found by adding the par value of the company's common stock to the capital in excess of par plus the retained earnings and dividing by the number of shares outstanding.

Formula: (see Stockholders' Equity Section of Balance Sheet)		
	1974	*1973*
Common Stock, 1,765,893 Shares Outstanding $1 par	$ 1,765,893	$ 1,765,893
Capital in Excess of Par	2,488,907	2,488,907
Retained Earnings	7,501,664	6,659,693
	$ 11,756,464	$ 10,914,493
Number of Shares Outstanding	1,765,893	1,765,893
Book Value Per Share	$ 6.66	$ 6.17

Book value at the turn of this century was one of the most powerful influences on stock prices. However, analysts now feel that it is what the assets earn that determines a stock price, especially in industrial companies. In other industries, such as investment companies, banks, or insurance companies, book value is more important; many of the assets of these companies are in investments that can be turned into cash. Some investment companies sell at premium over book value whereas others sell at discounts. During periods of stress in the stock market, sound investment companies can be bought at substantial discounts from book value.

Utilities are regulated by government and are entitled to earn a fair return on their investment. Usually, the higher the book value, the higher the earnings. Because the utility industry is regulated, there is a tendency within that industry not to write expenses off on the statement of income but to capitalize them—that is, enter them in the balance sheet as a fixed asset. This increases the book value, which is the basis of rate increases.

Constant reinvestment of earnings usually adds to the financial strength of a company and increases its book value. It follows, then, that this constant increase ordinarily will result in higher earnings.

In the XYZ Corporation, book value increased 8 per cent, or about 50¢ per share. Almost all the increase, or approximately $647,000 of it, went into additional machinery and equipment (see Balance Sheet). This additional investment should increase earnings in 1975 if the economy remains strong.

Price-Earnings Ratio

Together with earnings per share, this ratio is used more than any other on Wall Street. If the common stock of a company was selling at 5½ per share, we arrive at the price-earnings ratio by dividing the price by the earnings.

1973

Formula: $\dfrac{\text{Price of Stock}}{\text{Earnings per Share}} \quad \dfrac{\$\,5.50}{.42} = 13 \text{ x Earnings}$

If the company's stock were still selling at $ 5.50 in 1974 and earnings were 68¢, the price-earnings ratio would be:

1974

$\dfrac{\text{Price of Stock}}{\text{Earnings per Share}} \quad \dfrac{\$\,5.50}{.68} = 8 \text{ x Earnings}$

Projecting the price-earnings ratio is one of the most frustrating problems for an investor. If the price-earnings ratio of 13 times earnings in 1973 had remained in effect in 1974, the company's stock would be selling for around 8¾, or almost 60 per cent higher than the current market price. No one knows what the price-earnings ratio should be or will be. Analysts, in their projections, use the past as a guide but changes occur frequently.

On a larger scale, the Dow Jones Industrial Averages, made up of thirty giant corporations, have ranged in price-earnings from 7½ to over 20 times earnings. If a company with this wide a range earned $2.00 per share, it could sell anywhere from $15 to $40 per share.

The price-earnings multiple varies with economic conditions as well as with the confidence of investors. In addition, low and stable interest rates and bond prices add to the desirability of stocks.

Years ago the rule of thumb was 10 times earnings. An investor could then expect to receive about 50 per cent of the earnings as dividends.

If a company earned $2.00 a share and paid a dividend of $1.00, it would sell at 10 x $2.00 or $20 per share, and yield 5 per cent. Many companies sell at higher and lower multiples depending on growth of earnings and investor psychology.

Sales per Share of Stock

This ratio is derived by dividing the total sales by the number of common shares outstanding.

Formula: $\dfrac{\text{Total Sales}}{\text{Number of Common Shares Outstanding}}$ = Sales per per Share of Stock

1973 $= \dfrac{\$29.5 \text{ (in millions) (see Statement of Income)}}{1.7 \text{ (in millions) Outstanding (Stockholders' Equity section of Balance Sheet)}}$ = $17 in Sales per Share of Stock

1974 $= \dfrac{\$32.5 \text{ (in millions)}}{1.7 \text{ Million Shares Outstanding}}$ = $19 in Sales per Share of Stock

The investor, by using this simple formula, reduces sales from millions, or even billions of dollars, to sales for each individual share. The XYZ Company's sales increased from $17 per share in 1973 to $19 per share in 1974. A steady growth in sales per share of stock is a healthy sign. Management is using the assets of the corporation well. As the sales per share of stock increase, the earnings usually increase, as will the price of the shares.

Interest Coverage (Bonds)

This ratio is derived by adding the interest paid on all bonds outstanding to the income before taxes and dividing by the annual interest charges (see Chapter 3, Growth and Income Investing). In this case we are given a net interest expense figure of $604,125 in 1973 and $687,234 in 1974. What is the interest coverage?

	1973
Interest Expense (Statement of Income)	$ 604,125
Income before taxes " " "	1,270,737
Total Earnings Available for Interest Payments	$ 1,874,862
Net Interest Expense, 1973	$ 604,125

$\dfrac{\$ 1{,}874{,}862}{\$ \ \ 604{,}125} = 3.1 \text{ times}$

	1974
Interest Expense	$ 687,234
Income before Taxes	2,049,149
Total Earnings Available for Interest Payments	$\dfrac{2,736,383}{687,234}$ = Approximately 4 times

Interest in 1974 is covered approximately 4 times. We add back the interest charges because they are a deductible item for income tax purposes. Therefore, XYZ *income before taxes* included a deduction for interest that has to be added back to arrive at the total earnings available for interest. The larger the interest coverage, the safer the bond. The interest coverage increased from 3.1 times in 1973 to 4 times in 1974, together with the reduction of the loan from $7,108,851 to $6,108,530. Although the 4 times coverage is below the average 5 times interest coverage of manufacturers, the bond is improving in quality.

Ratios are extremely useful aids to an analyst or an investor, just as batting, fielding, and pitching averages are important to a baseball manager and a fan. They do, however, have shortcomings.

Limitations of Ratios

1. Ratios are not ends in themselves, only indications.
2. Many companies are made up of several corporations in different industries and data through ratio analysis are, in effect, only averages.

QUESTIONS

1. Define the terms "balance sheet" and "statement of income". How are they related?
2. What is the "accountant's report"? Why is it important to an analyst and investor?
3. Define the terms "current ratio" and "quick ratio". What is the difference?
4. What are the "notes to financial statements"? Are they necessary to an understanding of financial statements?
5. Describe the inventory terms LIFO, FIFO, and moving average.
6. In an inflationary economy which method of inventory shows the highest earnings? Which the lowest? Why?
7. What is the "capitalization ratio"? What is its relationship to the current ratio?
8. What is the significance of "earnings per share" and what is the "price-earnings ratio"?
9. What is book value? What relationship does book value have to the price of a stock?
10. What are the advantages of applying ratios to financial statements? What are some of their limitations?

3

GROWTH AND INCOME
INVESTING

What is a growth company? Can an investor identify a growth company with reasonable accuracy? To what extent does the present price of a stock reflect its future growth?

The average growth of America's 1,000 largest corporations was approximately 7 per cent in the 1960s. This average may and probably will change and so, too, will our concept of growth. It is not static.

How can an investor find these exceptional companies?

Wall Street research departments and individual investors are constantly researching the market and uncovering many good growth stocks. There are also standard reference manuals, such as Standard & Poor's and Moody's, which analyze growth stocks. Several other investment advisory services specialize in growth stock investing. A publication that captured the idea of growth the earliest was John S. Herold's *America's Fastest Growing Companies*.

Investment manuals and research, then are excellent starting points for an investor interested in identifying growth stocks. As he pursues his investigations, what growth characteristics should he look for? There are three major ones:

1. A new product (preferably patentable) or unique service
2. A small capitalization
3. Successful management

In addition, these other elements are important:

1. Low labor costs per dollar of sales
2. Management's ability to increase prices as costs increase to enable the corporation to maintain profit margins
3. Earnings and sales growth for a period of at least three years.

Let us examine some of the outstanding growth companies of this century to see if they exhibit the above ingredients. General Motors was founded on the genius of William C. Durant who conceived and built the Chevrolet. The single product was the automobile. The company was small at the time and management proved to be excellent. Although the product was not patentable, the American public's demand for automobiles grew to be insatiable and General Motors thrived on the tremendous success of the Chevrolet. Could General Motors be a growth stock today? Not likely, because it would be almost impossible for this giant to consistently earn more than the average.

A new product or service is the chief propellant to growth, but a successful product does not necessarily mean growth. A product can be extremely successful but not have much effect on earnings. In the late 1950s George Romney, as president of American Motors, gambled that a compact car would sell in the American market. He diverted a large portion of his company's production capability into the Rambler. The car was a huge success and the company's stock soared in price. Ford, at the other extreme, introduced the most successful car in the history of the automobile, the Mustang. Nothing happened. The corporation was already so large that even Mustang's outstanding success had little effect on Ford stock. Ford is not, and cannot be, a growth stock candidate. Like General Motors, it is a well-managed giant.

American Motors grew rapidly because its capitalization was comparatively small. However, its growth did not continue because the other automakers quickly introduced their own compacts, which cut into A.M.C.'s profits and growth. A single product, the Rambler, enabled the per-share earnings to grow markedly.

Lorillard, a tobacco company, introduced a new cigarette, called Kent, in the late 1950s, at the time when the link between cigarette smoking and lung cancer was being reported in all the newspapers. Later, a national magazine wrote that tests proved that Kent cigarettes contained the lowest percentage of tar and nicotine than any of the other leading brands and were therefore less harmful. Lorillard's stock price multiplied six times, but poor management practices negated Kent's huge success and subsequently Lorillard merged with another company. Ephemeral successes such as the Rambler and Kent often can be translated into extraordinary stock market profits, but true growth companies maintain their earnings gains for five, ten, or even more years.

Du Pont built an empire on nylon; IBM, on the computer; Eastman Kodak, on the camera; Rohm & Haas on plexiglass; Texas Instruments, on the semi-conductor; Xerox, on photocopying machines; and MMM, on Scotch Tape. These huge successes all began with a single product.

The second criteria of a growth company is small capitalization. It is axiomatic that the fewer the shares outstanding, the higher the possible earnings per share. Therefore, most young growth companies are not listed on the national exchanges. They are usually dealt over-the-counter. The risks are higher to the investor, but the rewards are even greater. I have known several investors who bought shares in young growth companies, only to sell them too soon. When you have risked buying into a young company, *do not* settle for small profits. Keep analyzing your investment as though you did not own the stock. Would I buy it now? Are sales still rising at 15 per cent to 20 per cent per year? Are profit margins remaining firm? Use the tests of good management, the ratios we learned to analyze in Understanding Financial Statements.

Ford illustrates this point. It already had 94 million shares outstanding when it introduced the Mustang. Its growth was inhibited because of its size.

Good management is the third ingredient of a growth stock and by far the most difficult of all for the investor to judge. A poet reminds us that "Success is a garden with too much sun, be careful it doesn't dry your roots." Inadequate managements usually do one of the following:

1. They overexpand;
2. They have inadequate capital for expansion;
3. The expand into product areas in which they are not informed;
4. They cannot handle success.

The investor can use the ratios and tests of the financial statements to uncover some of the inadequacies of management. The current ratio can show us that there is not enough working capital to expand. The capitalization ratio may show that the company is too heavily laden with debt. The fixed asset to sales ratio may show that the company needs a large investment in plant and equipment to expand.

Notwithstanding, analysis has shortcomings, since the tests are made after the events have taken place and in many cases the stock has already suffered a decline. Like the Dow Theory, which is late in affirming a bear or a bull market, analysis will at least tell us why, but it, too, can sometimes be late.

Good management uses sound conservative accounting and uses it consistently, even if earnings per share do not grow at the hoped for rate. Inadequate management will try to force the earnings growth by changing accounting policies. An investor must not only read the annual reports, but also study each quarterly report for any indication of a change. All changes, however, are not necessarily negative. If a corporation announces that it is changing its inventory pricing from FIFO to LIFO, we understand that LIFO will show lower earnings per share but is more accurate and conservative. However, if a corporation announces that it is changing its depreciation policy to a less rapid write-off, then we should immediately understand that it is trying to increase its earnings per share. Again, if a corporation's policy has been to write-off as an expense its research and development and then changes to capitalizing it as an asset, thereby increasing earnings per share, do not wait—SELL!

All three of the chief ingredients (new product or unique service, small capitalization, good management) characterize growth companies, and the most important for the short run is the single new product, if the capitalization is small enough. However, over a longer period of time, three years or more, it is good management that will determine if the initial success was ephemeral or is to last. It is good management that will use the profits of the new product to develop other new products. It is out of research and development that growth companies remain growth companies.

HOW TO FIND GROWTH COMPANIES

I have mentioned using the research departments of brokerage firms, together with many financial service organizations, as excellent methods of finding good growth stock candidates. In addition to these analyses, add some of your own. Be alert to everything around you. If you are a woman, you are constantly being exposed to new products and may tend, after a while, to become somewhat insensitive to them, even if they are excellent. If the product is good, find out who makes it. If the manufacturer is publicly owned, write for an annual report. Find out if they produce other products and if you can test them. If not, solicit opinions from others. It's a beginning step in individual analysis and can be fun. Avon Products, for many years one of the prime growth stocks, could have been discovered in this manner. Avon offered the woman at home an excellent product and an exclusive service. Of the two, it was Avon's service that gave the company strong growth impetus. Similar products could be bought elsewhere, but not the service.

After the new product or service has given the corporation its initial impetus, management must decide what to do with the large influx of cash from sales. A healthy corporation begins to plan for expansion in three ways:

1. *Horizontally*—If the service or product is well received in one area or region, management may wish to extend the same service or product to other areas. Sears, Roebuck has expanded its stores horizontally to a point where it is now considered the finest retail organization in the world. Growth came primarily from expansion of units.

2. *Vertically*—Instead of spreading out over wide geographical areas, management may decide to try to control more of the components that go into the production of its product. General Motors not only ex-

panded horizontally (Chevrolet, Oldsmobile, Buick, Cadillac), but also began controlling and manufacturing many of the products that went into the corporation's cars themselves.

3. *Helter-Skelter*—In the two methods of growth we have just discussed, management tries to stay within the product line it knows best. In the helter-skelter approach, growth of sales and growth of profits are all important, regardless of the kinds of industries or products involved. In the 1960s this method gave birth to the word "conglomerate," which was then synonymous with growth. As the conglomerates grew, so did management problems. Many conglomerates were forced into bankruptcy. One such giant, Litton Industries, fell into such disfavor with investors that its stock dropped from over $100 a share to less than $5. This helter-skelter expansion is dangerous and usually does not make for healthy growth.

METHODS USED FOR GROWTH

1. Growth from Within—A corporation that uses its own resources to improve its product, expand its product line, or expand geographically without acquiring other companies is following this method of growth.

Earnings growth is a key element in a growth company and research and development is a key determinant in producing this earnings growth.

The National Science Foundation estimated that in 1974 R & D expenditures would exceed $32 billion dollars. Approximately 18% of industry's R & D is spent on applied research, which is research that has definite new product goals. Development of these new products or processes takes another 78% and only 4% goes into basic research.

Chemicals, drugs and electronics are R & D oriented industries and are, therefore, growth industries.

2. Growth by Acquisition—Management in this instance decides to expand by acquiring other corporations rather than by the slower process of internal growth. They buy companies either to expand horizontally or vertically hoping to acquire good management, geographical diversification or products that dovetail with their own. This method has inherent risks. No one can analyze all the problems of or be expert in another corporation's business. There are always surprises. One has to wonder if General Telephone would make the same decision again to buy Sylvania Electric? Two methods of growth by acquisition are:

a. Exchange of stock or bonds
b. Purchase by cash

Exchange of Stock or Bonds

The stocks of many companies in the bull market of the 1960s sold for high price-earnings ratios—twenty to fifty or more times earnings. Growth from within, the slower and surer method, was passed over because now the corporation could use its overvalued stock to buy other companies, either public or private.

To illustrate:

	Price-Earnings Ratio	Market Price	Shares Outstanding
Corp.A earns $2.00 per share	20	$40	1 million
Corp.B earns $2.00 per share	10	$20	1 million

Corporation A issues 500,000 shares to Corporation B's shareholders. Corporation A's stock at time of issuance to B was worth 500,000 times $40 a share, or $20,000,000, which is the same value of Corporation B's old stock of 1 million shares at $20 per share.

After issuance of stock and merging of Corporations A and B, the following is the new capitalization structure:

	Shares Outstanding	Earnings	Earnings Per Share
A & B Corporation	1,500,000	$4,000,000	$2.67

Because Corporation A is considered a glamour stock by investors, the price-earnings ratio of twenty times would probably hold, or paradoxically, might even rise. At the same price-earnings ratio, the stock of A & B corporation would sell for over $53 per share, or a 35 per cent increase over the pre-merger price of $40.

At this point you may be asking yourself, why would Corporation B sell out so cheaply? There are several reasons:

1. Corporation A has received extensive publicity in the financial publications and investors have bid up the price of the stock. Corporation B is impressed.
2. Corporation A is an excellently managed company and deserves its high price-earnings ratio.

3. Corporation B's management does not feel capable of expanding as rapidly as it wishes.
4. Corporation B's management wishes to sell out, and this is the best method for them to follow.

Purchase for Cash.   Some corporations are cash rich either because they have retained most of their earnings and paid little to shareholders as dividends or have developed a new product that is increasing earnings, or a combination of both. Instead of exchanging its stock to buy another corporation, it pays cash.

To illustrate:

	Shares Outstanding	Total Earnings	Earnings Per Share	Price-Earnings Ratio	Market Price of stock
Corp. X	6 million	$24,000,000	$4.00	15	$60

Corporation X now buys for cash a company earning $3 million after taxes. Corporation X will then appear as follows:

	Shares Outstanding	Total Earnings	Earnings Per Share	Price-Earnings Ratio	Market Price of stock
Corp. X	6 million	$27,000,000	$4.50	15	$67½

Many advantages accrue to an investor when his corporation expands in this manner, since there is no dilution in the number of shares outstanding. Each shareholder now has more earnings and, more important to him, can command a higher price for his stock. If Corporation X sold at a price earnings multiple of 15 times, the price of the stock before the acquisition would be $60 per share, (15 x $4.00 earnings). After the acquisition the earnings increased to $4.50 per share. The earnings multiple would not decline but quite to the contrary might even rise. At 15 times the $4.50 per share, the Corporation X would sell for $67.50 per share or over a 10% increase in the value of the investors stock.

WHAT ARE GROWTH STOCKS WORTH?

This question is not an easy one to answer because many analysts themselves have completely divergent viewpoints on the subject. However, let us attempt to place some real value on a company and not just assume that its price-earnings ratio is correct.

The earnings growth of 1,000 selected corporations in the 1960s was approximately 7 per cent. Therefore we will define as a growth company one whose earnings grow at the rate of 10 per cent or more per year. Another assumption will be to project these earnings only five years into the future. Many growth stocks perform for much longer periods, but many do not. Five years into the future is a long enough period to look ahead.

To illustrate:

Growth at Different Rates

Company	Growth Rate	Presumed Earnings at beginning per share	1st yr	2nd yr	3rd yr	4th yr	5th yr	Max. Price Earnings Ratio investor should pay for growth
A	10%	1.00	1.10	1.21	1.33	1.45	1.60	16X
B	15%	1.00	1.15	1.32	1.52	1.75	2.01	20X
C	20%	1.00	1.20	1.44	1.73	2.09	2.50	25X
D	25%	1.00	1.25	1.66	2.07	2.59	3.24	32X

The table points out that a company growing at the rate of 10 per cent a year will be earning $1.60 a share at the end of five years. What is the company worth now?

Minimum   *Maximum*

10 x 1.00 earnings = $10   16 x 1.00 earnings = $16

1. If we buy Company A for ten times the $1.00 per share earnings ($10 per share) and hold it for five years and the company is still selling for ten times earnings ($1.60 per share) the shares will have appreciated to $16 per share, or 60 per cent over a five-year period (12 per cent per year).

A price-earnings ratio of ten times in effect means that a corporation will in ten years earn, in total, the amount the stock is selling for at present. This has been, as stated before, a rule of thumb among Wall Street analysts. Therefore, if a stock is growing at 10 per cent per year, the ten times earnings figure can be considered a minimum price-earnings ratio.

2. What usually happens in the market is that as the earnings of Company A increase each year, more and more research analysts and investors become aware of the company and will pay a higher price-earnings ratio for the stock. The chart shows the maximum price-earnings

ratio of 16 for earnings growth of 10 per cent per year: 16 x $1.60 (earnings end of five-year period) per share = $25.6, the projected market price in five years).

Therefore, if an investor bought the stock at the undervalued price of $10 per share the price can increase to over $25 per share in five years, representing more than a 150 per cent gain (30 per cent per year).

3. An investor may not be able to buy at the minimum price-earnings ratio and must decide how much more he will pay. He should not pay in excess of sixteen times earnings, or $16 per share for this stock, but preferably the figure should be around ten to twelve times earnings.

4. We project a 25 per cent growth rate per year for Company D. Although this growth is rapid, it is not unusual. Polaroid, Xerox, Schering and many corporations attained this rate and even exceeded it. If an investor bought Company D at ten times earnings, or $10 per share, he could watch his investment grow to over $100 per share (32 x $3.24 earnings). Even if the investor paid twenty-five times earnings, or $25 per share, his investment could quadruple.

If this approach sounds logical, why doesn't everyone buy growth stocks? Are there any disadvantages?

Disadvantages

1. The price-earnings ratio of the stock may be too high.
2. Earnings growth invites competition if the product is not patentable.
3. Earnings may not grow as projected.
4. Earnings not only may stop growing, but may decline.
5. Management becomes obsessed with growth and tries to show growth in earnings at cost of sound business and accounting methods.
6. Stock price can plunge when analysts, investors, and institutions become disenchanted.

These disadvantages are severe. Growth stocks that were sacrosanct one day became the devil incarnate the next. Polaroid, with which Wall Street had a twenty-year love affair, fell from $149½ per share to below $20 in a year and a half. Conglomerates, fell precipitously—growth stocks one day, avoided and sold the next.

A retreating market is a good place to look for growth stocks, because their price-earnings ratios will be low and the investment risks lessened. In an advancing market, growth stocks are usually the leaders and therefore sell at higher price-earnings ratios, thus increasing risks. Growth stocks are the most exciting facet of the stock market and notwithstanding numerous declines in growth stocks will again be the source of many new stock market successes.

From the mid-1950s to the present, most analysts, investors, and institutions have devoted a substantial part of their energies to this area, so much so that in the early 1970s a new phrase caught on in financial circles, "a two-tier market". It meant that most stocks fell into the category of slow growth and were therefore ignored by the major stock buyers whereas the growth companies were bid up in price to very high price earnings ratios. Growth stock investing became a mania.

INVESTING FOR INCOME

Income to many investors is of immediate concern. Go into a savings and loan company or a bank on the first of any month and you will understand how important it is to many people.

In order to increase the return on their savings, many investors turn to income securities. These securities may be government bonds, corporate bonds or notes, or common stock. Interest is paid to creditors (bondholders) and dividends to stockholders. The yield on these investments is expressed as *a percentage of the price paid for the security.* This is an important point to remember, because in an inflationary environment prices of income securities drop, thereby increasing the yield to *new* investors. The *old* investor receives the same yield as when he purchased the security.

An Investor Seeking Income Has the Following Characteristics:

1. He is usually a long-term investor.
2. The market value of his securities are of secondary concern, if the interest and dividends are paid.
3. He searches for securities with long histories of dividend and interest payments.
4. He is a person who must have income immediately (widows, the retired).
5. He needs income for specific goals, such as education for children or vacations.

Types of Income Securities

Government and Municipal Securities. U.S. Treasury Bonds Series H pay interest every six months and are very safe. These bonds, however, are not transferable.

U.S. Treasury Bonds Series E pay all interest in one lump sum at the maturity of the bond. These bonds are often purchased by people wishing to defer their income until a later date.

The U.S. Treasury issues 90-day bills that can be bought each Monday morning. A certified check must be on deposit with the Reserve Bank before the auction of the bonds. Interest rates may vary from week to week but the preceding week's rates give a good indication of what an investor can expect. These bills are purchased by institutions or individuals ($10,000 minimum) who do not wish to tie up their money in long-term obligations but wish to receive a higher yield than the savings institutions pay out.

Municipal Bonds issued by states, cities or municipalities have one salient feature. Income from these bonds is free from federal income taxes and often also free from state taxes. Municipalities, then, can raise money for improvements by paying a lower interest rate than either government or corporate bonds. Investors in high-income tax brackets are attracted to municipal bonds because they increase their yield without increasing their risk.

Example

An investor in the 50 per cent tax bracket buys $50,000 of tax-free municipal bonds yielding 6 per cent. His tax-free return is $3,000 per year. He would have to earn 12 per cent on another, probably riskier, investment to equal this return.

Municipalities, like corporations, are of different quality and therefore have varying degrees of risk. The State of California's bonds have a triple A (AAA) rating, but ratings of cities within the state may vary considerably. The table on page 49 explains the ratings on corporate and municipal bonds. Most institutions and individuals use these tables as a source of reference when they purchase bonds. *Moody's* provides a similar service and is used in conjunction with the *Standard & Poor's* ratings.

Corporate income securities can be broken down as follows:

1. Corporate Bonds (secured by collateral)
2. Debentures (unsecured bonds)
3. Preferred stock
4. Common stock

Corporate Bonds.   One of the key tests of the balance sheet was the debt to equity ratio, and, with the test for the interest coverage on these bonds, we can use to determine the quality of the bond. Corporate bonds can be of very high quality and will pay interest even in times of recession.

These bonds are secured by specific collateral, usually first mortgages on property. Railroads, in the past, issued "equipment trust" certificates (secured bonds) on their engines and equipment (rolling stock). Many of these roads later went through bankruptcy yet still paid interest

STANDARD & POOR'S BOND RATINGS

To provide more detailed indications of credit quality, our traditional bond letter ratings may be modified by the addition of a plus or a minus sign, when appropriate to show relative standing within the major rating categories. the only exceptions being in the AAA – Prime Grade category and the lesser categories below BB

CORPORATE BONDS

BANK QUALITY BONDS – Under present commercial bank regulations bonds rated in the top four categories (AAA, AA, A, BBB or their equivalent) generally are regarded as eligible for bank investment.

AAA Bonds rated AAA are highest grade obligations. They possess the ultimate degree of protection as to principal and interest. Marketwise they move with interest rates, and hence provide the maximum safety on all counts.

AA Bonds rated AA also qualify as high grade obligations, and in the majority of instances differ from AAA issues only in small degree. Here, too, prices move with the long term money market.

A Bonds rated A are regarded as upper medium grade. They have considerable investment strength but are not entirely free from adverse effects of changes in economic and trade conditions. Interest and principal are regarded as safe. They predominantly reflect money rates in their market behavior, but to some extent, also economic conditions.

BBB The BBB, or medium grade category is borderline between definitely sound obligations and those where the speculative element begins to predominate. These bonds have adequate asset coverage and normally are protected by satisfactory earnings. Their susceptibility to changing conditions, particularly to depressions, necessitates constant watching. Marketwise, the bonds are more responsive to business and trade conditions than to interest rates. This group is the lowest which qualifies for commercial bank investment.

BB Bonds given a BB rating are regarded as lower medium grade. They have only minor investment characteristics. In the case of utilities, interest is earned consistently but by narrow margins. In the case of other types of obligors, charges are earned on average by a fair margin, but in poor periods deficit operations are possible.

B Bonds rated as low as B are speculative. Payment of interest cannot be assured under difficult economic conditions.

CCC-CC Bonds rated CCC and CC are outright speculations, with the lower rating denoting the more speculative. Interest is paid, but continuation is questionable in periods of poor trade conditions. In the case of CC ratings the bonds may be on an income basis and the payment may be small.

C The rating of C is reserved for income bonds on which no interest is being paid.

DDD-D All bonds rated DDD, DD and D are in default, with the rating indicating the relative salvage value.

NR – Not Rated.

Canadian corporate bonds are rated on the same basis as American corporate issues. The ratings measure the intrinsic value of the bonds, but they do not take into account exchange and other uncertainties.

MUNICIPAL BONDS

Standard & Poor's Municipal Bond Ratings cover obligations of states and political subdivisions. Ratings are assigned to general obligation and revenue bonds. General obligation bonds are usually secured by all resources available to the municipality and the factors outlined in the rating definitions below are weighed in determining the rating. Because revenue bonds in general are payable from specifically pledged revenues, the essential element in the security for a revenue bond is the quantity and quality of the pledged revenues available to pay debt service. Although an appraisal of most of the same factors that bear on the quality of general obligation bond credit is usually appropriate in the rating analysis of a revenue bond, other factors are important, including particularly the competitive position of the municipal enterprise under review and the basic security convenants.

"Although a rating reflects our judgment as to the issuer's capacity for the timely payment of debt service, in certain instances it may also reflect a mechanism or procedure for an assured and prompt cure of a default should one occur, i.e., an insurance program. Federal or state guaranty or the automatic withholding and use of state aid to pay the defaulted debt service."

AAA-Prime – These are obligations of the highest quality. They have the strongest capacity for timely payment of debt service.

General Obligation Bonds – In a period of economic stress, the issuers will suffer the smallest declines in income and will be least susceptible to autonomous decline. Debt burden is moderate. A strong revenue structure appears more than adequate to meet future expenditure requirements. Quality of management appears superior.

Revenue Bonds – Debt service coverage has been and is expected to remain substantial. Stability of the pledged revenues is also exceptionally strong, due to the competitive position of the municipal enterprise or to the nature of the revenues. Basic security provisions (including rate covenant, earnings test for issuance of additional bonds, debt service reserve requirements) are rigorous. There is evidence of superior management.

AA-High Grade – The investment characteristics of general obligation and revenue bonds in this group are only slightly less marked than those of the prime quality issues. Bonds rate "AA" have the second strongest capacity for payment of debt service.

A-Good Grade – Principal and interest payments on bonds in this category are regarded as safe. This rating describes the third strongest capacity for payment of debt service. It differs from the two higher ratings because:

General Obligation Bonds – There is some weakness, either in the local economic base, in debt burden, in the balance between revenues and expenditures, or in quality of management. Under certain adverse circumstances, *any one such weakness* might impair the ability of the issuer to meet debt obligations at some future date.

Revenue Bonds – Debt service coverage is good, but not exceptional. Stability of the pledged revenues could show some variations because of increased competition or economic influences on revenues. Basic security provisions, while satisfactory, are less stringent. Management performance appears adequate.

BBB-Medium Grade – This is the lowest investment grade security rating.

General Obligation Bonds – Under certain adverse conditions, several of the above factors could contribute to a lesser capacity for payment of debt service. The difference between "A" and "BBB" ratings is that the latter shows *more than one fundamental weakness*, or *one very substantial fundamental weakness*, whereas the former shows only one deficiency among the factors considered.

Revenue Bonds – Debt coverage is only fair. Stability of the pledged revenues could show substantial variations, with the revenue flow possibly being subject to erosion over time. Basic security provisions are no more than adequate. Management performance could be stronger.

BB-Lower Medium Grade – Bonds in this group have some investment characteristics, but they no longer predominate. For the most part this rating indicates a speculative, non-investment grade obligation.

B-Low Grade – Investment characteristics are virtually nonexistent and default could be imminent.

D-Defaults – Payment of interest and/or principal is in arrears.

NCR – No contract rating. No ratings are applied to new offerings unless a contract rating is applied for.

Provisional Ratings – The letter "p" following a rating indicates the rating is provisional, where payment of debt service requirements will be largely or entirely dependent upon the timely completion of the project.

Reprinted with the permission of Standard & Poor's Bond Guide, © (1974).

on these certificates. Of all corporate income instruments issued, secured bonds offer the strongest guarantee of payment.

Debentures (unsecured bonds) are usually riskier investments and as such sell to yield a higher rate of interest. In order to make the debenture more saleable, a corporation may issue convertible debentures offering investors the opportunity to convert their bonds into common stock. During bull markets this is a favorite type of security for the corporation to issue for the following reasons:

    a. It attracts income investors.

    b. It attracts common stock investors.

    c. The corporation pays a lower interest rate on convertible debentures than on a straight debenture.

d. Corporations' costs are lower when they sell bonds instead of common stocks.
e. Corporations deduct interest on bonds before they pay taxes.
f. It is a method of selling stock above the market price. Conversion rate into common stock, may vary from 10 per cent to 25 per cent above stock price.
g. The corporation has a call privilege and may force the convertible debenture holder into becoming a stockholder when it wishes.

To illustrate: MNO Corporation issued 7% debentures for $1,000, convertible into forty shares of stock. The stock was then selling at $25 per share ($1,000 ÷ $25 = 40). If MNO rises to $35 per share, the convertible debenture will sell for $1,400 (40 shares x $35, common stock price, = $1,400). As the reader can see, the debenture is in reality no longer selling as a bond but as common stock.

The corporation now calls the debentures, according to the terms set in the prospectus, for $1,040 per bond. Since the bond is selling for $1,400 in the open market, the debenture holders have two choices. One, they can sell their bonds and take their profits in the open market, or, two, they can convert each bond they hold into forty common shares. There is, of course, a third choice, which is to accept the corporation's offer of $1,040. This is, in reality, no choice, but a command to make one of the two other decisions.

If the investor sells his bonds, he pays taxes on the profits. If he converts into common stock, he does not pay taxes until he sells the stock.

In this example, if the common stock falls to $15 per share, what will happen to the convertible debenture? It is still convertible into forty shares times $15 per share (market price of common stock). Will the bond sell for $600? Once the common stock dips far below the conversion price, the debenture will sell as though it were a straight bond and lose its relationship to the stock. It now is bought on the basis of income and will sell in line with other investments of the same quality. If other bonds of similar quality (See Standard & Poor's and/or Moody's bond ratings) were selling to yield 10 per cent, then the MNO bond would not drop to $600 but to $700.

$$\frac{\$70 \text{ interest}}{\$700 \text{ Market Price of bond}} = 10\% \text{ yield.}$$

If MNO's common stock continued its drop to $10 per share, the bonds would still hold around $700 if all other investment criteria remained the same.

Convertible debentures are, in reality, a hybrid investment. They can attract both investor and speculator and can be an excellent vehicle for both income and capital gains.

Preferred stocks are called preferred because holders receive dividends before the common stock investors. These dividends are generally higher than the bond yield or common stock dividends of the same corporation. A good preferred stock has a long history of unbroken dividend payments that are adequately covered by the corporation's earnings. Like debentures, preferred stock can be made more attractive by the following methods:

  a. It can be made *cumulative,* which pays all dividends in arrears before any payment is made to common stockholders.

  b. It can be made *participating,* which means that the dividend rate is fixed at a minimum, but if profits rise participating preferred stockholders may get higher dividends.

  c. It can be made *convertible,* similar to convertible debentures. This stock may be converted into common stock, thereby holding out greater possibilities for capital gains. It can be an excellent vehicle for the income investor who will receive a higher yield than he would from the common for a few years and then will switch into common when its yield becomes higher than the preferred.

Common Stock—For the income seeker, this stock is an inherently risky investment. All other securities holders receive either interest or dividend payments before the common stockholders. Notwithstanding the risk, the following advantages are quite impressive. Common stocks offer the potential for capital gains in addition to income. Although growth stocks have outperformed income stocks over the past twenty-five years, it has not escaped investors that many income stocks have turned into growth stocks, affording the investor a sizable return on his capital.

Disadvantages of Investing for Income Only

  1. Inflation can make income investing not only difficult, but also a risky investment.

  a. Bondholders lose purchasing power.

  b. Preferred stockholders lose purchasing power.

  c. Bonds and preferred stocks drop in price as inflation grows. If the investor is forced to sell at less than the price paid, he can lose more than the sum of his interest and dividends. The following example illustrates the loss that bondholders can suffer because of inflation.

265 Long-Time Dividend Payers— Records Unbroken for More Than 40 Years

A roster of 265 common stocks that have paid dividends for 43 to 190 years is presented below. This list comprised of issues traded on the principal exchanges or with active Over-the-Counter markets, and in which there is considerable investor interest. Dividend information has been obtained in most cases from official sources. This is a factual survey only, and is not intended as a blanket approval to purchase the stocks listed. However, these are companies which have weathered such problems as the Great Depression, various later recessions, and wartime dislocations, and have built up dividend traditions that will not be readily broken. Among the issues covered there is wide enough variety to satisfy the interest of most common stock investors.

	Dividends			Dividends	
	Paid Since	Current		Paid Since	Current
Abbott Laboratories	1926	$ 1.20	Castle & Cooke	1896	0.60+
Adams-Millis	1928	0.20	Caterpillar Tractor	1925	1.60
Airco Inc.	1917	0.80	Ceco Corp.	1921	1.00
Allied Chemical	1921	1.32	Central Hudson G. & E.	1904	1.72
Amerada Hess	1922	0.30+	Central Illinois Lt.	1921	1.60
American Brands	1904	2.38	Champion Int'l.	1915	0.92
American Can	1922	2.20	Champion Spark Plug	1919	0.52
Am. District Teleg.	1901	0.48	Charter New York	1908	2.00
American Elec. Power	1910	1.90	Chase Manhattan Corp.	1848	2.20
American Express	1870	0.52	Chemical New York Corp.	1827	2.88
American Home Products	1926	0.65	Chesebrough-Pond's	1883	1.12
American Natural Gas	1904	2.40	Chrysler Corp.	1904	1.40
American Sterilizer	1914	0.28	Cincinnati Bell	1879	1.46
American Tel. & Tel.	1881	3.08	Cincinnati Gas & Elec.	1853	1.64
AMF Inc.	1927	1.24	Cincinnati Milacron	1923	1.40
Anchor Hocking Corp.	1914	1.08	C.I.T. Financial	1924	2.20
Archer-Daniels-Midland	1927	0.25	Cleveland Elec. Illum.	1902	2.32
Arizona Public Service	1920	1.36	Coca-Cola	1920	1.90
Arvin Industries	1925	0.52	Colgate-Palmolive	1895	0.54
Atlantic City Electric	1919	1.50	Columbus & So. Ohio	1926	1.96

Atlantic Richfield	1927	2.00
Avon Products	1919	1.40
Baker Oil Tools	1929	0.37
Baltimore Gas & Elec.	1910	1.96
Bank of New York Co.	1784	2.00
Bankers Trust New York	1904	3.00
Becton Dickinson	1926	0.35
Bell & Howell	1915	0.84
Beneficial Corp.	1929	1.25
Blue Bell, Inc.	1923	0.72
Book-of-the-Month Club	1927	1.44
Borden, Inc.	1899	1.20
Berg-Warner	1928	1.35
Boston Edison	1890	2.44
Briggs & Stratton	1929	1.60
Bristol-Myers	1900	1.32
Brown Group	1923	1.60
Burroughs Corp.	1905	1.00
Campbell Soup	1902	1.18
Cannon Mills	1895	0.86
Carborundum Co.	1922	1.60
Carpenter Technology	1907	1.30
Carter-Wallace	1883	0.45
Combustion Engineering	1912	1.51
Commonwealth Edison	1890	2.30
Cone Mills	1914	1.20
Consolidated Edison	1885	1.80
Consumers Power	1913	2.00
Continental Can	1923	1.60
Continental Corp.	1854	2.40
Conwood Corp.	1903	2.00
Corning Glass Works	1875	1.40
CPC Int'l.	1920	1.86
Dayton Power & Lt.	1919	1.66
Delmarva Pwr. & Lt.	1921	1.20
Dentsply Int'l.	1900	0.76
Detroit Edison	1909	1.45
Diamond International	1881	2.00
Dr. Pepper	1930	0.26
Donnelley (R.R.)	1911	0.48
Dow Chemical	1910	1.00
Duke Power	1926	1.40
DuPont	1904	5.75
Duquesne Light	1913	1.72
Eastman Kodak	1901	1.78
Eaton Corp.	1923	1.80

	Paid Since	Current		Paid Since	Current
Emhart Corp.	1902	1.32½	Int'l Business Machines	1916	4.48
Equimark Corp.	1872	0.80	Int'l Harvester	1918	1.60
ESB Inc.	1901	1.40	Iowa Power & Lt.	1916	1.74
Exxon Corp.	1889	4.55	Jefferson-Pilot	1913	0.52
Fairmont Foods	1904	0.62½	Jewel Cos.	1928	1.66
Fibreboard Corp.	1923	0.80	Johnson & Johnson	1905	0.55
Fidelity Union Bancorp	1893	2.20+	Johnson Service	1901	0.80
Firestone Tire & Rubber	1924	1.00	Kansas City Pwr. & Lt.	1921	2.20
First Nat'l Boston	1784	1.62	Kansas Gas & Electric	1922	1.56
First Nat'l City Corp.	1813	0.72	Kansas Power & Light	1915	1.48
First Nat'l St. Bancorp	1812	2.00	Keebler Co.	1928	0.70
First Penna. Corp.	1828	1.32	Kellog Co.	1923	0.54
Gamble-Skogmo	1929	1.40	Kraftco Co.	1924	1.77
Garlock, Inc.	1905	0.84	Kresge (S.S.)	1913	0.20
General Am. Transport	1919	1.80	Kroger Co.	1902	1.30
General Bancshares	1913	0.76	Liggett & Myers	1912	2.50
General Cigar	1909	1.20	Lilly (Eli)	1885	0.94
General Electric	1900	1.60	Lone Star Gas	1926	1.46
General Foods	1922	1.40	Louisville Gas & Elec.	1913	1.84
General Mills	1898	1.08	Ludlow Corp.	1872	1.08

Company	Year	Value	Company	Year	Value
General Motors	1917	3.40	Macy (R.H.) & Co.	1927	1.10
Georgia-Pacific	1927	0.80+	Mallinckrodt Chemical	1923	0.24
Gillette Co.	1906	1.50	Mfrs. Hanover Corp.	1909	1.56
Girard Co.	1837	3.24	Marine Midland	1929	1.80
Grant (W.T.)	1907	1.50	May Dept. Stores	1911	1.60
Great Northern Nekoosa	1910	1.60	Melville Shoe	1916	0.46
Hackensack Water	1887	2.48	Miles Laboratories	1894	1.28
Harcourt Jovanovich	1922	1.00	Minnesota Min. & Mfg.	1916	1.10
Hartford Steam Boiler	1871	1.68	Mirro Aluminum	1902	0.96
Hawaiian Electric	1901	1.56	Mobil Oil	1902	2.80
Heinz (H.J.)	1911	1.08	Monarch Machine Tool	1913	0.60
Heller (W.E.) Int'l	1920	0.84	Monsanto Co.	1925	2.00
Helme Products	1912	0.60			
Hercules Inc.	1913	0.80	Morgan (J.P.) & Co.	1892	1.60
Honeywell, Inc.	1928	1.40	Morton-Norwich Products	1925	0.88
Hormel (Geo. A.)	1928	0.84	Mountain States T. & T.	1911	1.52
Household Finance	1894	0.90	Murphy (G.C.)	1913	1.20
Houston Ltg. & Power	1922	1.48			
Idaho Power	1918	1.86	Nabisco Inc.	1898	2.30
INA Corp.	1874	2.10	Nalco Chemical	1928	0.43
Industrial Nat'l	1791	1.20	National Fuel Gas	1903	1.90
Ingersoll-Rand	1910	2.16	National-Standard	1915	0.80
Interco Inc.	1913	1.36	National Steel	1907	2.50

	Paid Since	Current
New England T. & T.	1886	2.36
N.Y. State Elec. & Gas	1910	2.20
NL Industries	1906	1.00
NLT Corp.	1924	0.36
Norfolk & Western	1901	5.00
Northeast Utilities	1927	1.02
Northern States Power	1910	1.84
Norton Co.	1922	1.50
Ohio Edison	1930	1.60
Oklahoma Gas & Elec.	1908	1.36
Olin Corp.	1923	0.88
Orange & Rockland Utils.	1917	1.20
Otis Elevator	1903	2.20
Outlet Co.	1926	0.65
Owens-Illinois	1907	1.48
Pacific Gas & Elec.	1919	1.88
Pacific Lighting	1909	1.68
Pacific Tel. & Tel.	1925	1.20
Penney (J.C.)	1925	1.12
Pennwalt Corp.	1863	1.20
Pennzoil Co.	1925	1.00

	Paid Since	Current
So. California Edison	1909	1.56
So. Connecticut Gas	1909	3.00
So. New England Tel.	1891	2.84
Southwestern Life Corp.	1910	0.80
Springs Mills	1898	0.60
Squibb Corp.	1902	1.62
Standard Brands	1929	1.83
Standard Oil, Calif.	1912	1.70
Standard Oil (Indiana)	1894	3.20
Stanley Works	1877	0.96
Stauffer Chemical	1915	2.00
Sterling Drug	1902	0.60
Sun Chemical	1929	0.40
Sun Oil	1903	0.98+
Tampa Electric	1900	0.88
Texaco Inc.	1903	2.00
Texasgulf Inc.	1921	0.76
Texas Utilities	1917	1.04
TI Corp.	1894	1.40
Time Inc.	1930	1.90
Times Mirror	1892	0.32
Timken Co.	1921	2.00
Toledo Edison	1922	2.00

Pfizer Inc.	1901	0.73	Travelers Corp.	1866	1.00
Philadelphia Electric	1902	1.64	Tucson Gas & Electric	1918	0.84
Philadelphia National	1844	2.00	UGI Corp.	1885	1.32
			Union Carbide	1918	2.10
Philip Morris	1928	1.40			
Pillsbury Co.	1923	1.64	Union Electric	1907	1.28
PPG Industries	1899	1.70	Union Oil of California	1916	1.70
Procter & Gamble	1891	1.80	Union Pacific Corp.	1900	2.40
Providence Gas	1849	0.80	U.S. Gypsum	1919	1.60
Public Serv., Colorado	1907	1.20			
Public Sev. Elec. & Gas	1907	1.72	U.S. Tobacco	1912	0.76
Pullman, Inc.	1867	1.50	U.S. Trust Co. N.Y.	1854	1.56
Quaker Oats	1905	0.76	Universal Leaf Tobacco	1927	1.76
			Upjohn Co.	1909	0.88
Rexnord, Inc.	1894	1.08			
Reynolds (R.J.) Inds.	1901	2.68	Virginia Elec. & Power	1925	1.18
Richardson-Merrell	1925	0.58	VSI Corp.	1921	0.52
Rochester Telephone	1926	0.73	Warner-Lambert	1926	0.76
			Washington Gas Light	1852	1.88
Rohm & Haas	1927	1.12			
Safeway Stores	1927	1.60	Washington Water Pwr.	1899	1.44
St. Paul Cos.	1872	0.72	West Point-Pepperell	1852	2.20
San Diego Gas & Elec.	1909	1.20	Westvaco Corp.	1899	1.10
			Whirlpool Corp.	1929	0.80
Scott Paper	1915	0.56			
Scovill Mfg.	1856	0.80	Wickes Corp.	1895	1.00
Security-Pacific	1881	1.40	Woolworth (F.W.)	1912	1.20
Sherwin-Williams	1884	2.00	Wrigley (WM.) Jr.	1911	3.15
Singer Co.	1873	2.60	Xerox Corp.	1930	1.00
SmithKline Corp.	1923	2.00			

Reprinted with the permission of United Business Service Company, © *(1974).*

American Telephone and Telegraph bonds are AAA in quality and have been so during this entire century, yet a recent *Wall Street Journal* issue listed the following quotations on ATT $1,000 bonds:

Interest Rate	Maturity Date of Bond	Market Value	Paper Loss Owing to Inflation
2 ⅝%	1986	$570	$430
2 ¾	1982	665	335
2 ¾	1980	730	270
3 ¼	1984	620	380
3 ⅞	1990	570	430

Inflation, and not the rating or the quality of the bond, has caused severe losses in principal to investors. Each day one group of investment bankers outbids another by a fraction of a percentage point to win the right to sell bonds to the public. Yet in a matter of months or even weeks, inflation takes its toll on the price of the bonds.

2. Investors feel secure buying income stocks with good records and tend to ignore periodic analysis. However this feeling of security may be undermined by:

1. Changes within the industry or the corporation itself.
2. Changes in earnings trend which may affect the safety of interest or dividends.

3. Common stocks, even of the highest quality, tend to fluctuate many times their dividend rates during the period of one year.

Example:

	1972 High Low	1973 High Low
Marine Midland Banks	36¼ 29	32¾ 21 5/8
Dividend per Share	$1.75½	$1.80*
1972 Range: 36¼-29	= $7.25	4 Times
	$1.72	
1973 Range: 32¾-21 5/8	= $11.128	6 Times
	$1.80	

*Dividend subsequently cut to 80¢ per year. Stock dropped precipitously to approximately $10 per share.

Marine Midland's price fluctuated four times its dividend in 1972 and six times in 1973, leaving little doubt that buying the stock at the right price is more important than the dividend it pays. This example is by no means the exception. Take any quality income stock or bond and subject it to the same analysis and you will discover the same wide fluctuation in price.

SUMMARY

Growth companies grow faster than the average corporation's growth of approximately 7 per cent per year. Three major ingredients for growth are a new product (preferably patentable) or unique service, a small capitalization, and good management. Because these elements mainly characterize smaller companies, analysts and investors will find most of them traded in the Over-the-Counter market. Corporations grow in three ways, horizontally, vertically, and helter-skelter, and from within or by acquisition. If by acquisition, other companies may be acquired for stock or for cash. If purchased for cash, all earnings accrue to the benefit of the current stockholders (no dilution of stock) and can mean a substantial earnings increase. This usually translates into stock market gains.

Many so-called growth stocks do not fit our definition of the term, and moreover, sell at a low price-earnings ratio. It takes extreme patience on an investor's part to find growth stocks once he has made his decision to buy.

The best time to look for growth stocks at a discount, thereby lowering the inherent risks, is when the market is retreating. The companies' growth can then be measured, and the chart of price-earnings can be used to determine when they are good buys.

Income investing attracts a different type of investor. He usually thinks of the longer term and market fluctuations are of secondary concern to him if the interest or dividend on his investment is paid. He does not look for small expanding companies but for giant complexes with histories of long interest and dividend payments. Whereas the aggressive and young invest for growth, the widows and the retired look for income. These sources range from U.S. Government and municipal bonds to corporate securities. Although corporate bondholders and preferred stockholders receive interest and dividends prior to common stockholders, many investors look to common stocks because dividends may be increased and appreciation is possible.

Inflation can make income investing quite difficult, for even topquality securities can tumble in price. Large losses will be sustained if the investor is forced to sell.

Few investors are solely income- or growth stock-oriented. Most have portfolios that reflect elements of both.

QUESTIONS

1. Define in your own terms the meaning of a growth stock.
2. What are the chief elements of growth?
3. What are the three methods of corporate expansion? Describe each and give examples.
4. Is there any relationship between expenditures for research and development and the growth of a corporation?
5. Is it easy to determine the price-earnings ratio of a growth stock?
6. What are some of the advantages and disadvantages of buying growth stocks?
7. What are the characteristics of an income investor?
8. Name and describe the different types of income securities.
9. What is a debenture? What is a convertible debenture? Why do both corporations and investors like convertible debentures?

4

HOW TO FIND
UNDERVALUED SECURITIES

ELEMENTS OF THE IDEAL INVESTMENT

We have examined bonds, debentures, convertible debentures, all forms of preferred stocks, growth stocks, income stocks, and common stocks and have found advantages and disadvantages in each form of investment. What are the elements of an *ideal* investment?

1. Liquidity
2. Safety of principal
3. Stability of income
4. Appreciation potential
5. Tax-free income
6. Free from care
7. Realistic maturity date
8. Marketable denominations
9. Value as collateral

The *first three* elements listed receive the most attention from investors and analysts. All three, however, cannot exist in a high degree in the same investment.

If the investment were absolutely safe, it could not return a high rate of interest or dividend or rental and at the same time command an active and broad market allowing the investor to sell whenever he wishes. If there were such a security, the demand for it would be huge, thus forcing the price up and the yield down. All investment and investment analysis, then, involves juggling these three main principles.

The other six elements add to or detract from the ideal.

Liquidity

Liquidity refers to marketability of a security, the ease with which it can be bought or sold. It is possible for an investor to get a higher income if he will sacrifice some degree of liquidity. A corporation lists its securities, (bonds, preferred stock, and common stock) on the stock exchanges because liquidity is thereby enhanced.

The demand for "listed" (traded on a major exchange) bonds from institutions as well as private investors is perhaps overdone but liquidity is predominant in their minds and they will forego the additional income to secure it.

Savings institutions offer an individual who will buy one- or two-year certificates up to 50 per cent more interest than if they deposited their money in a regular savings account that allows deposits and withdrawals at will. The certificate is in the form of the normal savings bankbook but marked to indicate that the deposit is for one, two, or more years. They caution that if the certificate is cashed in prior to maturity that significant interest will be lost. The principle of liquidity applies. The investor, by giving up his right to withdraw (without penalty), may receive higher interest.

Safety of Principal

If it is possible to have principal returned on demand, or if it can be converted at will into some equivalent form of asset, not only equal in value but satisfactory to the investor, then the principal is secure. I know of no investment that fits this definition of safety of principal. If money is deposited in a savings account, it may be paid out on demand but it will not, in many instances, be equal in value to the amount deposited because of inflation. This is also true of government and corporate bonds, and no one has ever even hinted that an investment in common stocks is secure. Investments in such assets as mortgages, bonds, and bank deposits are safer than any speculative investments in stock, commodities, or real estate.

Stability of Income

The last of the three major investment ideals is a fixed income or rental on an investment. This income is usually paid in regular installments, which further lends itself to stability.

Ideally, the income should be as safe as the principal. If it is not, the principal is suspect. Our test for interest coverage on bonds is essential in order to determine if the interest is secure.

Appreciation Potential

To some investors and to most speculators this ideal is considered number one. The bondholder wants his interest payment on time and to be paid his principal at maturity. The speculator buys discount bonds as he would stocks because he feels that developments within the corporation or municipality warrant an increase in bond price. These bonds usually sell at substantial discounts from par ($1,000). He also may foresee a declining prime rate, which would increase the value of the bond.

The stockholder views *appreciation* as an inherent right and expects it to be on a par with liquidity and security of principal as one of the prime investment ideals.

Tax-free Income

The one major investment that is free from federal and state taxes is the municipal bond. However, states will tax the interest on a resident's bond if the bond is an out-of-state security. A resident of California, to earn interest free from both federal and state taxes, must buy a California municipal bond. If he buys a Florida bond, the interest is deductible only on his federal tax return.

Free From Care

"Clipping coupons" is the quintessence of security. Coupons are attached to bearer bonds, which are negotiable by anyone. Bearer bonds are just that; they are not registered to any particular person. The coupons attached to these bonds are clipped off on specific due dates and presented to the bank for cash.

A landlord who collects rents on his property does not have such an easy life. His can be a full-time job, as full of care as the coupon clipper's is free from care.

Bonds and stocks may be kept at home (not recommended), in a vault at the bank, or with a brokerage firm. If the stocks or bonds are registered in your name, the dividends and interest will be mailed to you. If they are being held by your broker in "street name"—that is, in the name of the brokerage house—then dividends and interest will be mailed to the broker and in turn remitted to you.

Realistic Maturity Date

Only bonds have maturity dates. Stocks and income-yielding property do not. In selecting bonds, an investor should be careful to buy only those with a maturity date that suits his purpose. Those investors who are interested only in short-term security may either deposit their funds in a bank or buy 90-day Treasury bills. For those dealing in trust funds, a ten- or twenty-year maturity may be wise. Brevity of life, however, tends to preserve the principal of the bond. The longer the maturity date, the greater the risk to the principal.

Marketable Denomination

For the vast majority of stocks listed on the major exchanges, 100 shares is the standard trading unit. Anything under 100 shares is considered an odd lot. Odd lots, as we have discussed, are handled by odd-lot dealers and a fee of 1/8 of a point per share is paid either to buy or sell. In bonds, the round-lot denomination is $1,000 and few corporations deal in smaller amounts. Treasury bills of the 90-day variety must be purchased in quantities of at least $10,000. Banks, on the other hand, accept bonds of any denomination. Investors accumulate funds in savings institutions to buy the round-lot bond ($1,000) or the $10,000 minimum Treasury bill.

Value as Collateral

An investor often finds himself in a position where he must raise capital. Listed and many over-the-counter bonds and stocks can be purchased on margin from New York Stock Exchange firms. Loans may also be advanced by banks against this collateral. Both bonds and stocks are considered strong collateral by lending institutions.

No single investment will exhibit all of these desirable characteristics, since many conflict with one another. The investor should determine what his essential needs are and proceed to find the investment that satisfies his needs. If an investor can find a security that affords liquidity, security of principal, stability of income, appreciation potential, tax-free income, freedom from care, and in marketable denominations with a realistic maturity date and value as collateral then he is a miracle worker. As mere mortals, we shall be content merely in realizing as many of these ideals as possible in seeking investments.

Being able to read a balance sheet and a statement of income and knowing what an ideal investment should be, will enable an investor to make sound financial decisions. He should understand, moreover, that there are two methods that will guarantee the financial success of his investments. These methods are:

1. Buy low! Sell high!
2. Dollar-cost averaging

The first of these methods is what most speculators, and even some investors, dream constantly of accomplishing. Every neophyte envisions making a killing in the market by selling out ten minutes before a price decline. Somehow, the dream never seems to come true.

The second method, dollar-cost averaging, is a sound principle that involves investing the same dollar amount in the same security at fixed periods of time.

Example

| | Dollar-Cost Averaging | |
| | Monthly Investment | |
Dollar Amount	Price of Shares	Number of Shares Purchased
$100	$100	1
100	50	2
100	25	4
100	10	10
100	25	4
100	50	2
100	100	1
$700		24

In this example, the total amount invested was $700, which grew to be worth $2,400, yet the price of the stock was the same for the first and last purchase. Dollar-cost averaging is based on taking advantage of buying large quantities of stocks when prices are low.

The long-term trend in the American economy since the Revolutionary War has been UP. The economy has passed through periodic recessions and even depressions but has always emerged from them to continue to grow.

The D.C.A. principle should only be applied when buying into strong companies such as Eastman Kodak, Dow Chemical, General Motors, Du Pont, Exxon, and American Telephone. If it is used for small or poorly managed companies, an investor might "average down" into bankruptcy. The company he selected to continue buying may not survive and petition for bankruptcy.

Major Weakness of Dollar-Cost Averaging

The greatest strength of D.C.A. is at the same time the source of its most serious drawback. In our example, as the stock dropped in price, the investor was able to purchase more and more shares for the same dollar amount; and then when the stock rallied he was able to recover his loss and show a profit. An investor can buy more shares when the market declines. But will he? I think not, for the following reasons:

1. When the stock first starts to fall, the investor will continue to buy; however, as the decline continues he begins to have doubts.
2. These doubts increase.
3. The market continues to slide. It is possible that the investor has now become discouraged and disillusioned. He stops buying.
4. When the D.C.A. principle is most advantageous to the investor, he is too fearful to invest.

BASIC APPROACHES TO UNDERVALUED SECURITIES

There are two basic approaches to finding undervalued securities:

1. Industry approach
2. Searching the "new lows" in the *Wall Street Journal.*

The Industry Approach

This approach, has probably contributed more to investment success than any other method. In any stage of the economy some industries are moving ahead while others are either static or slumping. It is up to an investor to isolate growth industries and concentrate his research on them. As a general rule, an individual should limit his choice to the six most undervalued industries. Six industries may include over 100 companies, which is an adequate number for any investor to analyze.

Prior to America's entry into World War II, coal, shipping, shipbuilding, and air transport stocks led the market in spite of the fact that the market fell. Consumer stocks were weak, among them gold mining, retailing, automobiles, and tire and rubber companies. In the same market an investor who held shipping stock gained over 200 per cent on his investment, and an investor who held gold mining shares lost 65 per cent of his capital.

Prior to the war's end, and in anticipation of victory, the favored groups were:

1. Printing and publishing (gained over 200%)
2. Radio—TV (gained over 140%)
3. Tires and rubber (gained over 140%)
4. Motion pictures
5. Fertilizer
6. Paper

During the war, industry was tooled up to make guns, tanks, planes, and other war materials. Consumer goods had largely been ignored. To further help quash consumer spending our government increased taxes and put on an extensive "Buy U.S. Bonds" campaign. At the end of the war the tremendous pent-up demand by the consumer was unleashed. The above mentioned industries appreciated the most.

In the 1950's tobacco, motion picture, food, metal fabricators, and printing and publishing stocks were strong whereas textiles, lead, zinc, copper, sugar and petroleum issues were weak. In the 1960s, when investment trusts and pension funds became a major investor force, the "two-tier market" developed. One tier was made up of stocks these institutions held and the other tier was made up of those they didn't own. Growth stocks, or stocks labeled growth stocks, were bid up to very high price-earnings ratios. Many of these institutional favorites have now plunged to more realistic prices.

A detailed year-by-year study would further reveal the wisdom of analyzing industries in order to maximize stock market profits.

Searching the "New Lows" in *The Wall Street Journal*

A wise nineteenth-century investor once observed, "I buy my straw hats in the Fall". This method of investing requires more patience than the industry approach. It assumes two points:

1. Industries move in and out of investment favor.
2. Companies making lows today *may* have had most of the price risk removed.

A Polaroid or an Avon can be in great demand for years and then fall precipitously. Analyze the reasons why. Use the tools of research at your disposal. Their sickness may not be terminal and resumption of growth is possible. The reason why more patience is needed in this approach is the fact that new investors are not quickly attracted to a fallen angel.

FACTORS TO STUDY

Book Value

Book value is derived, as we've learned, by taking the total of *all* the assets less all liabilities and the liquidating value of any preferred stock. During the past decade the average stock on the New York Stock Exchange sold for slightly more than twice its book value. This situation has occurred because institutions and investors have looked at earnings and have bought stocks based on price-earnings ratios.

Assets on corporations' balance sheets are listed at cost and cost less depreciation. Many corporate assets are carried at values far beneath their true market or replacement value. Since many of these assets are, in reality, understated, it stands to reason that, if anything, the book value of most corporations is understated.

If a stock's price is well below book value, the company may well be "worth more dead than alive." Very few companies liquidate their assets and remit the cash to their shareholders, but high book values attract other corporate buyers who attempt to take over. In addition, many corporations buy some of their own shares and thus further increase their book value. When these corporations buy their own stock, it is usually at a premium over the current market price. A shareholder, then, can profit, if other corporations buy his company's stock or, if the company buys its own stock.

Book value alone is not a sufficient reason to buy a stock, but for the reasons mentioned it is an excellent place to begin looking.

Net Working Capital Assets per Share

This figure is derived by taking the total current assets and subtracting *all* liabilities plus liquidating value of preferred stock and dividing the balance by the number of common shares outstanding.

To illustrate: Please refer to XYZ Corporation's balance sheet. In 1973 it listed its current assets as $11,848,948, its current liabilities as $4,019,389, and its long-term liabilities as $7,942,465. It does not have any preferred stock outstanding. Let's fill in the formula:

$$\frac{\text{Current Assets minus Current Liabilities minus Long-Term Debt}}{\text{Number of Common Shares Outstanding}}$$

$$\frac{\$11,848,948 - \$4,019,389 - \$7,942,465}{1,765,893} = \frac{(\$112,906)}{1,765,893} = 0$$

After making the necessary deductions, we arrive at a negative figure, which indicates that XYZ Corporation has a deficit net working capital on assets per share. Therefore, if we can find not only a company selling below book value but one below new working capital assets per share, we have a running start at finding an undervalued security.

If you will again refer to the XYZ balance sheet, you will see that its "Net Property, Plant, and Equipment" account totals $10,319,611 for 1973. In a company selling for less than net working capital assets per share, you would be buying the stock without paying anything for these assets. Are there securities that sell below this figure? Yes, but let's proceed further with the analysis.

Cash Flow

Cash flow is simply the earnings of a corporation plus depreciation and depletion. The expenditures for both depreciation and depletion do not require cash outlays but are listed as an expense on the statement of income. Therefore, the corporation generates cash from net income plus these two bookkeeping charges.

Corporations, in compliance with income tax laws, use several methods of computing depreciation. Some methods permit them to write off these assets more rapidly than others. By writing off their depreciation rapidly, they show lower earnings and therefore pay lower taxes. This is legal. To the shareholder the earnings per share are conservatively stated. On the balance sheet the assets are also carried at a lower figure, since they are reduced by the depreciation.

Refer again to XYZ balance sheet for 1973. It lists its total "Property, Plant and Equipment at $14,606,649 and its accumulated depreciation at $4,287,038. In other words, the corporation has written off approximately 30 per cent of its fixed assets against taxes. If a corporation depreciates its assets at a slower but acceptable rate, its earnings will be higher than those of a company with an accelerated depreciation policy. An analyst must reconstruct the earnings of both corporations as if their depreciation policies were the same. The faster a corporation writes off its assets, the higher the quality of its earnings.

To illustrate: A corporation pays $150,000 for a piece of machinery and following its depreciation policy (this information appears in the "Notes to the Financial Statement") writes off this piece of equipment over a five-year period at an accelerated rate. The first year at 5/15, second at 4/15, the third at 3/15, the fourth at 2/15, and the final year at 1/15. A 5/15 write-off means the corporation is deducting 5/15 of $150,000, or $50,000, the first year. Earnings will be lower but more conservative. If no more equipment is purchased, the depreciation will decline to $40,000 the second year, $30,000 the third year, and so on, until $150,000 is totally deducted. Cash flow will decline each year as the depreciation declines. We, therefore, want to find companies with large depreciation and a consistent cash flow.

Earnings per Share

Earnings and stock prices, over a period of time, have an exceptionally close relationship. The higher the earnings, the higher the price of the stock. However, sometimes in undervalued situations, corporations may show deficits and still represent an outstanding purchase. Deficits, in this case, may be the result of a non-recurring strike, a non-recurring write-off of inventory, or a write-off of an unsuccessful product.

Management

If the company passes all the above hurdles, this last test might still eliminate the stock from being considered an undervalued security. Management, no doubt, has kept its company in line statistically, but does it live up to its predictions? Does it exaggerate projections? Do the workers strike too often? If an investor feels that management is not of the highest quality although the stock is statistically cheap, he should still avoid buying.

The following examples are an attempt to find some securities that pass all of these tests:

	Company A				
	1st yr.	*2nd yr.*	*3rd yr.*	*4th yr.*	*5th yr.*
Cash Flow	$ 2.33	$ 2.32	$ 2.79	$ 3.08	$ 3.50
Earnings per Share	1.15	1.00	1.45	1.76	2.07
Book Value	11.79	12.73	14.29	14.21	15.20
Net Working Capital Assets per Share	4.20	4.30	6.60	8.30	10.80

At the time of analysis, this corporation's stock was selling for $9 per share, which is less than two-thirds of its book value and more than a 15 per cent discount from its net working capital assets per share. Its earnings of $2.07 were being capitalized in the market place for less than 5 times and its cash flow at less than 2.6 times.

During previous years this stock sold at an average multiple of twelve times earnings and a correspondingly lower price-earnings ratio cash flow. Its earnings are now at an all-time high, and the projection for next year is for earnings to increase over 15 per cent.

The company is a leading manufacturer of visual communication and information transfer products, which produce over 90 per cent of its profits. Its return on invested capital is 12.5 per cent and has increased the past four years. Approximately 75 per cent of profits comes from foreign sales, although these sales are only 53 per cent of total sales. Domestic sales and profits should pick up this year and earnings are projected at $2.25 per share. The company's sales totaled around $157 million in fiscal 1974 and are expected to increase to at least $175 million in fiscal 1975.

An investor should be alert to the projection of increased domestic sales and earnings. If projections are not met, perhaps the company's domestic marketing operation should be investigated.

This stock meets all the criteria of being undervalued and could be purchased along with several other companies in a similar situation. Diversifying commitments will increase the percentages that one of your stocks will have a substantial market rise as a result of a tender offer by the company or a buyout offer from another company or recognition by the market that the stock is indeed undervalued.

Financial analysis has limitations, and the two most serious are:

1. Reading financial statements of the past cannot predict the future.
2. Even if your projection of the future is correct, you still cannot predict how investors will react.

Financial analysis gives an investor a feeling of confidence that he is fully acquainted with the company's past. It can alert him to the possible problems that might develop within the company. It can uncover what appear to be undervalued situations, but it is, at best, only a forecasting tool.

| | Company B | | | | |
	1st yr.	2nd yr.	3rd yr.	4th yr.	5th yr.
Cash Flow	$ 3.11	$ 2.47	$ 3.45	$ 5.27	$ 6.20
Earnings per Share	.51	.05(d)	1.04	2.62	3.40
Book Value	30.62	29.69	29.62	32.09	34.45
Net Working Capital Assets per Share	15.69	13.72	14.07	14.18	15.04
(d) = deficit					

This company is one of the largest manufacturers of textiles in the world, and at the time of analysis its stock was selling at $13 per share, or over a $21 discount from book value and a full $2 discount from its net working capital assets per share.

Its earnings of $3.40 a share were being capitalized at slightly less than four times, with cash flow at just over two times. Over a ten-year period the investors paid an average of approximately eleven times earnings. In addition, earnings have recovered remarkably from the recession of 1970, but nonetheless the stock is selling at its lowest price-earnings ratio in its more than 25 years of public trading. Demand for the company's products are strong, with the backlog up over 5 per cent from last year. The return on invested capital is 10 per cent, which is the highest profit margin since 1966. The current ratio of almost 3 to 1 should be adequate to finance the company's expansion.

About 50 per cent of corporate sales is to apparel manufacturers, with over 31 per cent sold for household use and the balance for industrial applications. The emphasis on apparel has been relaxed in recent years, and household use products have risen from 25 per cent to 31 per cent of sales in the past five years.

If investors' appetite for this stock improves and it returns to its ten-year price-earnings ratio of 11, it could sell for over $37 per share, or almost three times its current price. In the interim, the company is a good candidate to buy back some of its own shares at prices above the current price, and while you're waiting the dividend return is 7.7 per cent.

This company, whose stock cannot be considered a growth stock, is nevertheless severely undervalued.

	Company C				
	1st yr.	2nd yr.	3rd yr.	4th yr.	5th yr.
Cash Flow	$ 5.56	$ 5.17	$ 4.90	$ 5.50	$ 6.20
Earnings per Share	1.02	1.04	1.40	2.38	3.15
Book Value	37.33	38.88	39.87	42.27	44.55
Net Working Capital Assets per Share	1.56	8.00	10.68	13.60	16.30

The stock was selling at 40 per cent of book value and approximately at its new working capital assets per share. Its earnings of $3.15 were capitalized in the market place for only 5.5 times and at less than 3 times its cash flow.

These earnings are conservatively stated, since the corporation writes-off its assets at as rapid a rate as is allowed by tax laws. Notice that in each year the cash flow is more than twice its earnings and in some years, as high as five times.

The average price-earnings ratio of this stock over a ten-year period was twelve times, which if applied today would result in a price exceeding $37 per share. The return on the stockholders' invested capital is a low 7 per cent, whereas for the five-year period from 1964 to 1968 it averaged 14 per cent. A return to anywhere near these profit margins would double earnings. This is not a prediction, only a possibility.

The corporation is the largest producer of commercial jet aircraft in the world, and its sales account for almost 60 per cent of the market total, in excess of $3 billion. It is difficult to predict future demand for aircraft but this company's equipment meets the current needs of most major airlines and should continue to hold on to its commanding position in the market.

Notice that whereas its book value increased only $7 in the five-year period, or less than 20 per cent, its net working capital assets per share increased over $14, or 900 per cent. The corporation reduced its debt during this period from $623 million to $149 million, which accounts for the remarkable increase in net working capital assets per share. This company's stock passes every test for an undervalued security.

More important to an investor than whether the market is bullish or bearish is the knowledge that with a little research stocks with values such as these can be found. Tests other than the state of the market may be applied, as we have learned, and together with an investor's own business acumen, can lead him to undervalued securities.

We have set an extremely difficult standard by which to measure undervalued securities, and the reader should realize that securities do not have to meet all of these criteria to be included in this exclusive group. There are times when growth stocks with low book value in relation to their market prices are undervalued. We use a table of price-earnings ratios to determine this condition.

Basic changes, if recognized by an investor, can lead to substantial gains. Now, in the mid-seventies, one such change appears to be taking place within the steel industry. For fifteen years steel suffered through low profit margins as a result of intense competition from Germany and Japan. President Kennedy's confrontation with the industry over prices only added to its problems. Steel prices are now free from government intervention. In 1974, despite general economic turndown, curtailed homebuilding, and cuts in automobile production, the industry increased its earnings substantially. How? The oil and gas drilling equipment industry increased its steel orders 45 per cent that year and railroad car manufacturing was up 27 per cent and shipbuilding up 39 per cent. The industry's dependence on the two giants, autos and homebuilding, was lessened. In addition, the impact of the energy shortage was felt by steel's major competitors abroad and curtailed their production without seriously affecting our own. Another favorable development was the agreement reached in 1973 between the steelworkers union and the leading United States producers. The union withdrew its threat of a strike in return for certain arbitration rights and a guaranteed wage increase. This agreement continues through 1977, which meant that the steelworkers did not have to build inventories in anticipation of a strike. This increased buying in the past had disrupted the industry's competitive position and prompted users to place their orders for steel overseas. Moreover, many of our domestic steel companies had sufficient iron ore reserves, which was another major plus as many smaller nations began to flex their nationalistic muscles and threaten to withhold ore supplies.

SPECIAL SITUATIONS

In the stock market a "special situation" is a stock that will advance rapidly because of internal factors such as:

1. Tender Offer
2. Spin-offs
3. Mergers
4. Payment of bond interest or preferred dividend arrearages
5. New management

Tender Offer

In the analysis of undervalued companies, we attempted to find stocks selling well below their asset value. By diversifying, and with patience, it is possible for an investor to assemble a portfolio that will include a company that will buy back its own shares at substantially higher prices. It is also possible that another corporation will become interested and make a "tender offer." Either way, tender by the company or by another corporation can result in rapid gains. Special situations during the market breaks of past years have been extremely lucrative. Tender offers have become a popular method of acquiring controlling interests in other corporations.

Spin-Offs

A "spin-off" is another type of special situation that occurs when a corporation distributes shares of a company it owns to its stockholders.

In 1967, the Grinnell Corporation spun off Holmes Electric Protective Company, Automatic Fire Alarm Company, and American District Telegraph because earlier the Supreme Court had ruled that Grinnell's ownership of these companies created a monopoly. Olin Corporation spun-off Squibb in the late fifties. The stockholder of the parent companies in the examples above, Grinnell Corporation and Olin Corporation, receive shares in the companies they are spinning off. Spin-offs aid the stockholder because the sum of the parts seems to be greater than the whole.

Mergers

Mergers are probably the best known special situation. They occur when one corporation buys out another corporation. The price the buyer pays is usually much higher than the current market price of the company that is being bought. From 1966 through 1969 more than 2,000 mergers a year took place. Cash, common stock, and convertible preferred were the instruments used to buy these companies. If cash is given for stock, an investor immediately realizes a capital gain. However, if common stock or its equivalent (convertible preferred) is given, the stockholder does not pay taxes until he sells the securities.

Payment of Bond Interest or Preferred Dividend Arrearages

Many bonds and preferred stocks on which interest payments are skipped have a cumulative feature. This feature stipulates that no dividends may be paid on the common stock or preferred stock until all back bond interest payments have been made. A company must have turned around and become profitable for a few years before management decides to distribute any back interest or dividends. This gives an analyst time to discover this special situation.

New Management

In the search for growth companies, we mentioned that good management is probably the most difficult facet of a business enterprise to analyze, but in the long run is the most important ingredient of all. Good management can turn a struggling company around and bad management can destroy the finest. Management changes should be studied with extreme care.

QUESTIONS

1. To an investor, what are the three main elements of an ideal investment? Would a speculator agree? If not, why not?
2. What is a municipal bond? Why is it tax free?
3. Define dollar cost averaging. What are its weaknesses?
4. What method of investment has probably contributed more to investment success than any other? Could you use this method today? If so, give three examples.
5. Define cash flow. Why is it significant to an investor?
6. Over a period of more than fifty years, is there a direct correlation between the earnings of a corporation and the price of its stock? During what periods of time might this correlation not exist?
7. What are the major drawbacks in depending on the analysis of financial statements?
8. Write a corporation for a copy of its latest annual report and analyze it step by step, using the ratios learned in Chapter IV.
9. What is a special situation?
10. Define, tender offer, spin-off, and merger.

5

THE FEDERAL RESERVE SYSTEM: ITS RELATIONSHIP TO STOCK MARKET PERFORMANCE

Why, how, and when do bull markets begin and why do they end? It is impossible to estimate the number of words written on this subject, and the answers range from reasons as diverse as sunspots, stars, economic cycles, and wars. Since World War I a major thesis could be advanced showing that the Federal Reserve System had more to do with booms and busts than all other elements combined. What are the system's powers? How did they originate? How are they exercised?

America was one of the last countries in the world to establish a central bank, although the need for one was totally evident long before the Federal Reserve System was set up. The crash of 1893 is considered by many authorities to have been the worst the country had ever experienced before 1929, and it was. Ten years later another devasting slump occurred, and still another in 1907. It was then that Congress appointed a U.S. Monetary Commission, headed by Senator Nelson Aldrich of Rhode Island, to study the need for a central bank.

Because of the victory of the Democratic party in the 1912 elections, the committee's recommendations were turned down, although many of them were incorporated in the Federal Reserve Act passed in 1913. In order to do away with periodic economic crashes, the Fed was formed.

The Federal Reserve consists of a seven man board of governors, all appointed by the president for fourteen-year terms. One of the seven is appointed chairman and is the chief executive officer. Instead of only one central bank, our system has twelve Federal Reserve banks geographically dispersed throughout the nation to handle affairs in their area.

The twelve banks are located in Boston, New York, Philadelphia, Cleveland, Richmond, Atlanta, Chicago, St. Louis, Minneapolis, Kansas City, Dallas, and San Francisco. Each has a reserve bank. The chain of command of the Federal Reserve System is shown below.

SEVEN MAN BOARD OF GOVERNORS

,

,

,

REGIONAL 12 RESERVE BANKS

,

,

,

MEMBER COMMERCIAL BANKS

,

,

;

,

AMERICAN PEOPLE

Although each of the twelve Federal Reserve banks is privately owned, that ownership does not control them. Power resides in the Board of Governors. Each member bank is required by law to subscribe to stock in its regional bank in an amount equal to 6 per cent of its own paid-in capital and surplus. To date they have not been required to put up the entire 6 per cent, because the regional banks have maintained adequate capital levels. Should the need for capital arise, however, the regional banks may require the member banks to subscribe to more stock up to the maximum of 6 per cent of their own paid-in capital and surplus. The regional (or reserve) banks are not government banks, but since they are fiscal agents of the government and are closely supervised by it, they are in effect quasi-governmental banks.

A few words on how the seven man board is chosen. There is a sentence in the Federal Reserve Act that states "In selecting the members of the board, not more than one of whom shall be selected from any one federal reserve district, the president shall have due regard to a fair representation of the financial, agricultural, industrial and commercial interests, and geographical divisions of the country".

Now we can examine in some detail exactly what powers the Federal Reserve has and how these powers affect us all.

Robert V. Roosa, former Undersecretary of the Treasury, once wrote in a book, *Federal Reserve Operations,* "When the Federal Reserve system was established at the outset of World War I, there was a wide belief in the United States that the monetary system was a primary cause of periodic depressions, which appeared invariably to be set off by financial stringency and crisis". Whether the system has succeeded in preventing these periodic depressions should be for each reader to decide.

The Federal Reserve's main function is to guide the "credit policy" of the country, which it does by adjusting the money and credit supply to the banks within the Federal Reserve System. Following are methods the Fed uses.

1. It can raise or lower the reserve requirements of member banks.
2. It can raise or lower the discount rate of member banks.
3. It can buy or sell government securities in the open market.

The Federal Reserve has direct authority to establish margin requirements on loans against securities.

The reserve requirement of member banks is set by the Fed. If, for example, the reserve requirement is 10 per cent, member banks must keep on hand or on deposit with the regional bank $1 for every $10 of customer deposits:

Banking Deposits	$5,000
Reserve Required	500
Total Reserves	1,000
Excess Reserves	500

With reserve requirements at 10 per cent, the bank may extend $10 in credit for each dollar of excess reserves. Thus the bank's credit-making capability is $5,000.

If the Fed raised the reserve requirement to 20 per cent:

Banking Deposits	$5,000	Same
Reserve Required	1,000	Doubled
Total Reserves	1,000	Same
Excess Reserves	0	Increase in Reserve Requirements Eliminated Excess Reserves

The Bank's credit-making capability is thus $0. With reserve requirements at 20 per cent, the same bank with the same deposits has no lending power.

Thus we can see from these examples that by raising or lowering the reserve requirements, the Federal Reserve can expand or contract the money supply. In practice, however, the Fed rarely uses this method. It has used the discount and open-market operations far more frequently.

In the original Federal Reserve Act the only instrument for credit control was the provision for discounting commercial paper promissory notes presented to the regional banks by member banks. The intention was that a bank needing additional reserves would sell some of its assets to its regional bank for the needed reserves. The original act was amended in 1916 to enable member banks to borrow from regional banks on their own promissory notes. And finally, the Banking Act of 1935 granted permanent authority to the Federal Reserve banks to make advances for periods up to four months on promissory notes secured by any assets acceptable to the regional bank. In other words, if a regional bank were so disposed, it could extend credit to a member bank on mortgages, security loans, and bonds, all assets excluded in the original law. The reason behind this change was to enable regional banks to create bank liquidity in times of emergency.

A regional bank is in effect a bankers' bank. It does not do business with the public. Its purpose is to carry out the instructions of the Board of Governors in transacting business with the member banks in its geographical area. The Bank of America is a member bank and it does business with the regional bank in San Francisco, Chase Manhattan, also a member bank, discounts its promissory notes with the regional bank in New York City.

The regional bank charges interest for this service, and the transaction is called "discounting member banks' paper." The discount rate charged to the member banks is established by the regional banks' boards of directors and reviewed and finally authorized by the Board of Governors of the Fed.

Prior to World War II the discount rate was considered the most powerful tool of the Federal Reserve and Wall Street viewed several discount raises as extremely negative. Today when the Federal Reserve raises the discount rate they are in effect saying to the member banks, "you're borrowing too much. Slow down. The economy is expanding too rapidly. Don't use the discount window unless you must".

When the Fed raises the discount rate again, they are saying the same thing only this time more emphatically and at the same time alerting the Regional banks they may have to turn down a member bank's paper. On the third discount increase the Fed has lost patience as the economy is now probably fully expanded, unemployment low, and inflation beginning to get out of hand. The discount rate increase or decrease is in reality a signal from the Federal Reserve to its member banks that they either want the credit contracted or expanded. Whereas it takes three, four, or sometimes more discount increases to curb a boom, the first reduction is a good indication of an ailing stock market.

The original Federal Reserve Act gave the regional banks the additional power to buy and sell specific securities in the open market. Regional banks were to make their expenses discounting member bank's notes. At times this business slowed down but expenses did not. Therefore, regional banks sold securities to meet these expenses not covered by discounting. It was ten years after the passage of the Federal Reserve Act that the Federal Reserve discovered, and quite by accident, what is today the most powerful tool of credit control.

When the Fed buys securities in the open market it increases the reserves in the seller's (member) bank and the bank may now extend more credit. Here is how the procedure works.

Reserve Requirement 10 Per Cent

Bank's Deposits	$5,000
Reserve Required (10%)	500
Total Reserves (Money on hand or at regional bank)	700
Excess Reserves	200
Bank's Credit-Making Ability (10x excess reserve)	2,000

Reserve Requirement 10 Per Cent

Federal Deposit as Result of Buying Securities		$1,000
Bank's Deposits (includes federal deposit of $1,000)		6,000
Reserve Required (10%)		600
Reserves (money at hand or at regional bank plus federal deposit	$ 700 1,000	
Total Reserves		1,700
Excess Reserves = $1,700 less $600 required reserve		1,100
Bank's Credit-Making Ability		11,000

The Fed's purchase of a security for $1,000 increased the bank's lending capability $9,000. The reader only needs to extrapolate to realize the leverage in such a credit tool. You can now understand why our Federal Reserve is known as the "fractional reserve system."

There are two enemies of Federal Reserve policy that are under constant scrutiny. One is inflation; the other recession or increased unemployment. We have just examined the Fed's powers. How could you use these powers to stop a recession and to increase employment, thereby increasing demand for goods and services?

One, we could lower reserve requirements of member banks, thus creating excess reserves and thereby increasing the banking system's credit-making ability.

Two, we could lower discount rates, signaling member banks to borrow money from the regional banks.

Three, we could buy government securities in the open market, thus increasing deposits in the member banks, which increases reserves and thereby increases the bank's lending capacity.

If our economy was heading for inflation how could you decrease demand, thereby attempting to halt inflation?

One, we could raise reserve requirements.

Two, we could raise discount rates.

Three, we could sell securities in the open market.

What has trying to understand money and the Federal Reserve's powers got to do with the stock market and investing in securities? It has been my observation that more money can be made in the stock market by knowing which policies the Federal Reserve will pursue than through all the inside information ever received.

The Board of Governors meets every three weeks to discuss policy but does not release this information for ninety days. It is during this period of time that the investing public is confused about in which direction the Fed is moving. They may have reversed their policy from contraction to expansion of credit, but we can only try to learn this by studying other market conditions more closely.

During the ninety-day blackout period the following information can give some indication of the direction of Federal Reserve policy, especially if that policy has been changed from expansion of credit to contraction, or vice versa.

On July 15, 1974, the Dow Jones News Service printed the following release. It reported on the Federal Open Market Committee's meeting, which had taken place ninety days prior, in mid-April.

FED OPEN MARKET COMMITTEE TWICE IN MAY AGREED ON FURTHER CREDIT TIGHTENING

WASHN -DJ- THE FEDERAL RESERVE BOARDS' OPEN MARKET COMMITTEE VOTED IN MID-APRIL TO CONTINUE ITS TIGHT REIN ON THE NATION'S MONEY SUPPLY AND THEN IN THE NEXT MONTH AGREED TWICE TO PERMIT FURTHER RESTRICTIONS OF CREDIT CONDITIONS.
ACCORDING TO MINUTES OF THE APRIL 15-16 MEETINGS OF THE POLICY MAKING PANEL THE GROUP DECIDED TO ACHIEVE LESS RAPID GROWTH IN MONEY SUPPLY IN COMING MONTHS BECAUSE OF THE RAPID EXPANSION IN MONETARY AGGREGATES OCCURING THEN.
THE PANEL VOTED TO ALLOW THE MONEY SUPPLY TO GROW AT AN ANNUAL RATE OF

3 PC TO 7 PC FOR THE APRIL-MAY PERIOD
AND TO ALLOW THE WEEKLY AVERAGE FEDERAL
FUNDS RATE-FOR LOANS BETWEEN BANKS-TO
RANGE BETWEEN 9 3-4 PC and 10 3-4 PC.
    AT TWO SUBSEQUENT DISCUSSIONS ON
APRIL 24 AND MAY 17 MEMBERS OF THE
PANEL CONCURRED WITH RECOMMENDATIONS
BY FED CHAIRMAN BURNS THAT THE FUND
RATE CEILING SHOULD BE ALLOWED TO RISE
FIRST TO 11 PC AND THEN TO 11 1-4 PC
FROM 10 3-4 PC BECAUSE OF THE SURGE IN
DEMAND FOR CREDIT.
    REPORTS OF THE COMMITTEE'S PROCEEDINGS
GENERALLY ARE RELEASED ABOUT 90 DAYS
AFTER EACH MEETING.
-0- 3 25 PM EDT JULY 15-74

Members of the panel also agreed that the fund rate ceiling should be allowed to rise to 11 per cent and then to 11¼ per cent. Federal fund rates are the interest member banks charge one another when they borrow money to increase their reserves. On July 15, 1974, the day this report was released, the federal fund rate was at 14 3/8 per cent. The Fed, although agreeing to a ceiling of 11 per cent to 11¼ per cent for the federal fund rate, did not foresee the almost panicky demand banks would have for more reserves. It was during this period that the Franklin National Bank in Long Island, New York was forced to call on the Federal Reserve for almost $1¼ billion dollars. Other banks had similar problems, and the demand for money was seemingly insatiable. As a result, the federal funds rate soared beyond the Fed's highest anticipation. It is significant that the Fed allowed the fund rate to jump to 14 3/8%.

The Fed could have expanded the money supply by buying securities in the open market to alleviate the shortage of money, thereby relieving the upward pressure on interest rates. The fact that it did not signified a stronger determination on the Fed's part to fight inflation by trying to curtail the growth in the money supply.

OTHER MARKET CONDITIONS INDICATING CHANGES IN FED POLICY

1. Direction of Prime Rate

If the prime rate (the rate banks charge their best and strongest customers) rises during periods of blackout, it could signify a further tightening of credit. Several declines following a long rise could signal a strong technical rally in stock prices. Buy common stocks as the prime rate declines.

2. Direction of Bond Market

If investors are buying new bond issues at stable interest rates, the market is considered strong and advantageous for a buyer of common stocks. However, if bond yields are rising each week and bond prices are falling, the Fed is evidently restricting credit by selling bonds in the open market. It lowers the deposits and reserves of the member banks and this puts upward pressure on the prime rate. As the prime rate rises, bond prices fall. A falling bond market is not a healthy environment for common stocks.

3. Loan Demand Released Each Thursday by New York City Banks

If the loan demand is rising each week, there will be pressure to increase the prime rate. If you couple this condition with the federal fund rate, you can determine if the Fed is further restricting credit. If loan demand is heavy, the prime rate is rising, and the federal fund interest rate is high, you have a combination of factors suggesting that an investor should avoid common stocks.

4. A Change in Discount Rate During the Ninety-Day Period

One change in the discount rate does not of itself signal a reversal of Federal Reserve policy. However, a reduction in discount more often signals a change than an increase. If the Fed were to reduce the discount rate after three or four increases, the chances of a market rally are strong. Buy common stocks.

5. A Change in Federal Open Market Operations During Blackout

The only way to keep abreast of developments in this area is to read a good financial newspaper daily, preferably the *Wall Street Journal,* where you can follow the interest rates paid weekly on Treasury bills and commercial paper. The minimum that can be invested in a Treasury bill is $10,000 and may be exercised in $5,000 denominations. There is an auction every Monday morning that determines the rate of interest. If the Treasury bill rate continues to rise, it could signify a further tightening by the Fed. A Treasury bill rate 2 to 3 per cent higher than the current savings bank interest rate could lead to heavy withdrawals from these institutions. This condition prevailed in 1966 and aggravated a severe stock market decline. It again manifested itself in 1969-1970 and ended with the credit crunch that brought on the Penn-Central's bankruptcy and another serious market decline.

In July, 1974, the Treasury bill rate was approximately 7¾ per cent, and the savings and loan interest rate was 5¼ per cent. The Dow Jones Industrial Averages plunged almost 300 points. There is a euphemistic expression called "disintermediation" that describes periods when investors remove their funds from one institution to buy higher-yielding securities from other institutions. A more accurate description would be "chaos". Stocks during these periods should be avoided.

FEDERAL OPEN MARKET OPERATION

What is the Federal Open Market Committee (FOMC)? How does it work? I know of no other economic agency that has such power yet still remains such a mystery to the public.

The Federal Open Market Committee regulates the buying or selling of U.S. Government securities and foreign exchange. The FOMC consists of the seven-man Board of Governors and the presidents of five regional Reserve banks.

After each meeting, every three to four weeks, the Manager of the "open market operations" returns to New York to carry out the FOMC's instructions.

If, during the three-week interim between meetings, a problem develops, the manager consults with the Chairman of the Federal Reserve Board and the president of the Federal Reserve Bank of New York. If, in the manager's opinion, a crisis threatens, he can then call for a special telephone meeting of the Federal Open Market Committee.

The value of the transactions handled each day by the FOMC averages around $2.5 billion, or about four times the volume of the New York Stock Exchange. The trading takes place at the Federal Reserve Bank of New York. The overall policy of the Fed may be geared to expansion or contraction of credit, but the FOMC can and does change direction for short periods of time.

ELASTICITY OF CURRENCY

Before the Federal Reserve System was established banks had no central depository to call on for reserves during periods of heavy credit demand. During the holiday season from October through December of each year, the currency in circulation increases by over $1 billion. Consumers, retail merchants and business in general need more money to handle the increased business activity. If the Fed did not step in and help during these periods, the banks without excess reserves would have to call in short-term loans, or sell securities, or even use other drastic means, such as selling its real estate to raise cash. If many banks found themselves in this position at the same time, the stress could become great enough to cause a panic, as it did in 1907. Elasticity of currency, then, is what the Federal Open Market Committee provides to the banking system daily. It is an ingenious system designed to help prevent serious panics.

If the Federal Reserve has such powers why do we have recessions, unemployment, booms, and inflation? As in every system, there are many factors still outside the Fed's control and the most important of these is the federal budget. The president's staff prepares a budget that is submitted to Congress each year. This budget may call for spending more than the government receives, the term for which is "deficit financing." The fiscal policy of the government embraces taxation, borrowing and the management of the national, or public, debt and expenditures. If the Fed's policy (monetary policy) is toward restraint of credit and the government's fiscal policy inclines toward expansion, or vice versa, a conflict exists. The lack of coordination of fiscal and monetary policy has in the past exacerbated the financial problems of our country.

Since no government ever willingly chooses depression over inflation, the eventual choice of the Federal Reserve and the fiscal policies of the government are inevitable. Inflation is a problem that is not easily nor quickly solved, and as investors we must understand it in order to invest wisely in securities.

Investor optimism and expansion of credit by the Federal Reserve are not coincidental, and certainly the Fed's tight-money stance and past market declines usually have gone hand in hand. An understanding of the Fed's powers is just as necessary for a small investor as it is for a professional.

QUESTIONS

1. When and why did the Congress pass a law to form the Federal Reserve System?
2. Describe the chain of command of the Fed.
3. The Fed has three major powers it can use to expand and contract credit. What are they?
4. What does "margin requirement" mean? Who controls the use of margin?
5. What is a regional Reserve bank? What is its main function?
6. What is considered the most powerful tool of the Fed today? Why?

7. What is the "prime rate"? How does the prime rate affect the average investor?

8. Is there a relationship between bond prices and stock prices?

9. What is the blackout period and how long does it last? Can an investor learn what the Fed is doing before the blackout period ends?

10. Does the reader believe that there is a correlation between Federal Reserve policies and stock prices? If so, explain. If not, why not?

6

THE TECHNICAL APPROACH

The daily movement of individual stocks and of the market as a whole is of concern to all investors. Some of the factors causing these fluctuations are:

1. Federal Reserve policy
2. Government fiscal policy
3. Earnings of corporations
4. Psychology of investors
   a. Unemployment
   b. Consumer income
   c. Inflation
5. Foreign affairs

FEDERAL RESERVE POLICY

The policy of the Federal Reserve is, in this writer's opinion, the most important single short-run factor determining stock prices. We already have discussed this subject in some detail. If a bull market is to continue, the Federal Reserve must supply the necessary funds.

A bull market is an up or optimistic market, so called because of the actions of a bull who charges with his head low and attacks with a sweeping upward motion of his head. A bear, on the other hand, attacks by standing upright on his two back legs and engulfs his prey in a violent downward movement. Therefore, a bear market is one in which stocks are falling in price.

GOVERNMENT FISCAL POLICY

Government fiscal policy is set each year when the federal budget is presented to the Congress. The Treasury Department, together with the Budget Director, projects the income for the next fiscal year. The various departments of government submit their own estimated expenditures. After expanding some and eliminating others, the budget is submitted. If projected expenditures exceed projected income, the result is a deficit or vice versa. The federal government is the only agency allowed to operate at a deficit. Deficit financing results when projected income is less than projected expenditures. In its initial stage, deficit financing is bullish for the stock market because it supplies both money and jobs to the economy. However, once this type of financing gains momentum, inflation is the result. In order to curb inflation it is necessary to cut the federal budget while at the same time the Federal Reserve cuts back on the supply of money. The result is an increase in unemployment, a decrease in consumer income, a change in investor psychology and a decline in stock prices.

EARNINGS OF CORPORATIONS

In the long run, earnings of corporations are the primary cause of rising stock prices. Investors and speculators alike view the price-earnings ratio of a stock as the single more important statistic of corporate health.

PSYCHOLOGY OF INVESTORS

This condition is determined by many factors, such as war, the threat of war, interest rates, capital investment, inflation, and a myriad of government policies, all of which affect the psychology of the investor. High employment together with rising consumer income engender an ebullient investor mood. The Fed then supplies the necessary money to translate this optimism into real growth. A depressed mood causes the opposite reaction.

FOREIGN AFFAIRS

Foreign affairs can be a stimulant or a depressant to investors. Vietnam, the Arab oil embargo, the inflamed Middle East have all had a negative effect on the stock market, whereas progress toward the settlement of such problems has had a bullish effect.

The Dow Jones Industrial Average, and all other market averages, reflects, in essence, different movements. There are three major market trends an investor and a speculator should be aware of. The first trend is the most important, since it reflects the growth of the country over a long period of time. The second movement, or intermediate trend, charts temporary changes in this long-term movement. These secondary movements are usually caused by wars, recessions, and depressions. The third movement is caused by daily events that can affect individual citizens.

Examples
1. Changes in Federal Reserve policy
2. Unemployment
3. Wage and price controls
4. Consumer income
5. Strikes
6. Government confrontation with industry
7. Interpretation of daily events by media
8. Statements by government officials
9. Elections

THE DOW JONES INDUSTRIAL AVERAGE

When Charles H. Dow was editor of the *Wall Street Journal* prior to 1900 he was convinced, after much experimentation, that a small select group of stocks could indicate the direction of the market. The idea was very similar to the modern thinking behind the Gallup or Harris polls. Dow reasoned that these leading companies would most efficiently reflect the hopes and aspirations or the fear and pessimism of people and therefore predict the future trend of the stock market. He tried ten, then fifteen, then twenty stocks in his average before the present thirty stocks evolved as the correct sampling method. The thirty industrial stocks used in today's DJIA are:

Allied Chemical	Esmark Inc.	Minnesota Mining & Mfg.
Aluminum Co. of America	Exxon	Proctor & Gamble
American Brands	General Electric	Sears, Roebuck
American Can	General Foods	Standard Oil of California
American Tel and Tel	General Motors	Texaco
Bethlehem Steel	Goodyear	Union Carbide
Chrysler	Inco	United Technologies
Du Pont	International Harvester	U.S. Steel
Eastman Kodak	International Paper	Westinghouse Electric
	Johns-Manville	Woolworth
	Owens-Illinois	

These securities represent a cross section of American industry and each company listed is a giant in its field. Major movements in these stocks are interpreted by Dow Theorists as predicting the major trend of the stock market as a whole.

Because the railroads have lost ground to other methods of transportation, airlines and trucking issues have been added to the average. This list is now called the Dow Jones Transportation Average and consists of the following corporations.

American Air Lines	MoPack Corp.	Southern Pacific
Burlington North	Norfolk & Western	Southern Railway
Canadian Pacific	Northwest Air	Trans World Airlines
Chessie System	Pan Am World Air	Transway Inter-
Consolidated Freight	St. Louis-San Francisco	national-Corp.
Eastern Air Lines	Santa Fe Indust	UAL Inc.
McLean Trucking	Seaboard Coast	Union Pacific Corp.

The Dow Theory later was refined by William Hamilton and Robert Rhea. Hamilton was editor of the *Wall Street Journal* from 1907 until his death in 1929, and his work helped clarify many of Dow's theories on the market. Many people today feel that Hamilton was the real originator of the Dow Theory. After Hamilton's death and the crash of 1929, no one paid much attention to the Dow Theory until Robert Rhea wrote a book, *The Dow Theory.* It was Rhea who predicted the bull market of 1932 and the bear market of 1937. To further understand the complex Dow Theory, Rhea's book is recommended.

In its simplest terms, for the Dow theory to confirm a primary upward (bull) or downward (bear) trend in the stock market, *both* the DJIA and the DJTA would have to either hit new highs or lows. If one average made a new high without the other following suit, the Dow Theory would not confirm an upward trend.

While the DJIA may show short term aberations the *price earnings ratio* of all 30 stocks is an accurate barometer of optimism and pessimism.

Price-Earnings Ratio Steady
For Dow Jones Industrials

At the closing level of 988.36 Friday, the Dow Jones industrial average was 10.9 times the $90.68 per-share earnings of the 30 component stocks for the 12 months ended last June 30. A week earlier, at 989.11, it was 10.9 times the same earnings. A year earlier, at 809.29, it was 9.6 times the per-share earnings of $83.83 for the 12 months ended June 30, 1975.

The Dow Jones Averages

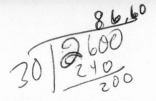

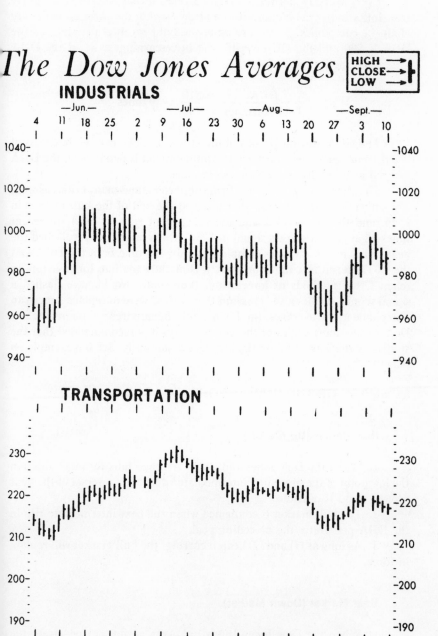

HIGH →
CLOSE →
LOW →

INDUSTRIALS

—Jun.— —Jul.— —Aug.— —Sept.—
4 11 18 25 2 9 16 23 30 6 13 20 27 3 10

TRANSPORTATION

Every Monday morning the *Wall Street Journal* reports on the thirty Dow Jones Industrial corporations and the total of the earnings per share of all the companies. If, for example, the total earnings per share of the DJIA is $90 and the DJIA is 810, the price-earnings ratio of the DJIA would be nine times earnings.

$$\frac{\text{DJIA} \quad = 810}{\text{Total Earnings} = \$90} = 9 \text{ times}$$

The DJIA, during periods of investor optimism, can sell in excess of twenty times earnings, and when the public mood is pessimistic, the DJIA can sell as much as below 8 times earnings.

The Dow Theory has many firm supporters, and many critics as well. The adherents firmly believe that it called the end of the bull market in 1929, and the low of 1932 and the subsequent rally in 1933. In recent times it gave a bull market signal in 1962, which lasted until it flashed the bear signal in 1966. Critics complain that by the time both the DJIA and the DJTA reach new highs or lows, it is already too late for investors to react. Other methods of forecasting, they claim, would have flashed a signal sooner. Critics also complain that if IBM were to replace American Telephone in the averages, the DJIA would be hundreds of points higher. Despite the many critics of the Dow Theory, it is recommended that the student of the market follow the averages assiduously. See the example on page 91.

SUMMARY OF THE DOW THEORY

Bull Market (Up Market)

1. When the Dow Jones Industrial Average fails to break through the low point of the preceding intermediate* decline, a reversal of the bear (down) trend is possible.

2. The bull market is confirmed when the next intermediate rise in the DJIA penetrates the preceding peak.

3. As long as (1) and (2) keep recurring, the bull market will remain in force.

Bear Market (Down Market)

1. When the Dow Jones Industrial Average fails to penetrate the peak of the preceding intermediate advance.

*If the average fails to break through the preceding high or low point, the trend is intermediate.

2. The bear market is confirmed when the next intermediate dip penetrates the low point of the preceding decline.

3. As long as (1) and (2) keep recurring, the bear market will remain in force.

In addition, Dow Theorists look for broad movements and increasing volume before they signal a primary trend (bull or bear market).

STANDARD & POOR'S INDEX

Standard & Poor's Index contains 500 stocks, including 425 industrials, 25 railroads, and 50 utilities of varying quality. It is more comprehensive than the DJIA and also more volatile.

1. The SPIA usually reaches its peaks and troughs at the same time as the DJIA and helps confirm the direction of the market.

2. SPIA is more volatile because it reflects what the public is doing more accurately than the DJIA, which is a reflection of activity in only the highest-quality stocks. If Standard & Poor's is rising relatively faster than the Dow Jones, it is a positive, or bullish, sign, and if it is falling faster than the DJIA, it is a negative, or bearish, sign. The SPIA can furnish a reliable forecast of the DJIA over a short period.

3. Standard & Poor's Index, when around 90, compares with the Dow Jones Industrial Average of 800. The ratio is approximately 1 to 9. If SPIA rises 50c for the day, the DJIA should rise approximately $4.50.

LOW-PRICED CONFIDENCE INDEX

Small investors suffer from the mathematical illusion that it is more likely for a $3 stock to rise to $5 or $6 than a $30 stock to rise to $50 or $60. As a result, an index of lower-priced stocks has been developed. Barron's, a weekly newspaper, prints a low-priced confidence index that measures public optimism or pessimism. While this index is advancing, a bear market is unlikely. It is another helpful index to aid the investor.

GM—A ONE STOCK INDEX

The late Charles Wilson, former president of General Motors and Secretary of Defense, once told reporters that "as General Motors goes, so goes the country," and the stock market often reflects his words. General Motors is followed by many Wall Streeters who reason that if General

Motors rallies strongly and breaks into new high ground, a strong market is indicated. General Motors is a one-stock index.

THE TECHNICAL APPROACH TO TRADING SECURITIES

The technical approach was developed after the Dow Theory and in the 1920s was used extensively by a new group of theorists. This approach consists of the use of charts by either an investor or a speculator to improve his timing in buying or selling securities. The wild and frenzied speculative atmosphere prior to the 1929 crash was, in part, blamed on these new "technicians." After 1929, charting and technical analysis fell into disfavor but emerged again in the 1960s.

Many fundamentalists, those who analyze a company in detail, completely disregard the technical approach to the market and view chart reading as a little better than astrology or fortune telling. Many technicians completely ignore the fundamentals of a company before they invest and regard the fundamentalist approach as antediluvian. Most investors and speculators use both techniques.

There are two basic methods a technician uses in charting:

1. VERTICAL BAR CHART

This chart is compiled with each bar representing the trading range of a stock within a specified period of time, usually a day, a week, or a month. The volume of trading for the period is shown directly beneath the bar it represents.

1. Bar charts can be maintained daily if the stock trades.
2. If the stock trades at a high of 30, a low of 29, and closes at 29¾, the bar chart will show a vertical line from 29 to 30 and a horizontal line crossing at the close of 29¾.
3. When the chartist draws this line, at the same time he draws another line upward from the bottom representing volume.
4. Each day the chartist should plot the price movement and the volume using vertical columns directly to the right.
5. This chart over a period of time will form patterns providing the basis on which the technician forms his opinion.

Many technicians who use the bar chart claim that volume is as important as price movement. One of the axioms followed by these chartists is that "volume goes with the trend."

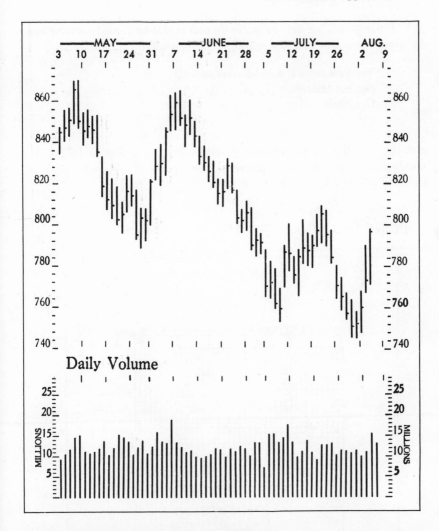

BASIC TECHNICAL RULES OF VOLUME

1. In a bullish (up) trend, the volume should increase on rallies and contract on declines.
2. In a bearish (down) trend, the volume should increase on declines and contract on rallies.
3. Drying up of volume signifies a bull market top or a bear market bottom.
4. Substantial volume sometimes signifies a market bottom since stocks are theoretically being transferred from weak (sellers) to strong (buyers) hands.

These charts are easy to maintain and would be a good exercise and discipline for a new investor to follow. He could plot the following:

1. The Dow Jones Industrial averages
2. General Motors
3. U.S. Steel
4. IBM

and possibly five or six additional stocks he would like to follow. If, however, time is a factor in plotting these charts, they are available at brokers' offices and can be studied there.

2. POINT AND FIGURE CHART

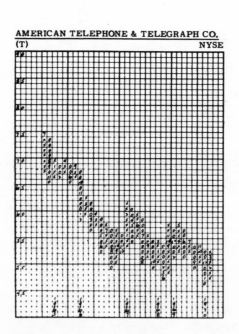

POINT & FIGURE

AMERICAN TELEPHONE & TELEGRAPH CO.
(T)   NYSE

(Chartcraft, Inc., Larchmont, N.Y.)   One dimensional. Both vertical and horizontal spaces record price alone. In this P&F service's method, years are shown at bottom and months in the price boxes with the month substituted for an X or O. One point = $1. X = rise, O = descending price.

Reprinted with the permission of Chartcraft, © *(1974).*

These charts indicate price changes in an individual stock, a group of stocks, or the market as a whole. Price changes are plotted only when the movement up or down is sizable enough to accomodate the point scale the technician is using. Small or minor changes are ignored. Most point and figure chartists claim that price changes are the most important element in investing and do not chart the time element or the volume.

1. The chartist determines the scale each point should represent. If the stock is low priced, under $20, he may decide to use a ½ point movement for each mark. Therefore, if a stock moved ⅛ or ¼ point in one day, the point and figure chartist would not plot this movement. If the stock is high priced, over $100, he may decide to make one point in the chart represent a two or three point movement in the stock.

2. If the chartist is plotting a stock selling at $40 and is using a mark for each point movement and it rises one point, he marks 41 with an X or with the number itself. If the stock falls, he marks descending prices with an O or the number itself. X's indicate ascending patterns and O's descending patterns.

3. Should the stock rise to 45, the chartist would plot five X's in a vertical line. Should the stock then decline to $38, he would slot seven O's in another column directly to the right in a descending vertical column.

4. Any change in the direction of the stock is represented by a new column.

SIMILARITIES BETWEEN BAR AND POINT AND FIGURE CHARTS

1. The chartist usually uses graph paper to plot changes in price.
2. Most of the basic terms and chart formations apply to both methods.
3. The main purpose of both methods is to help the investor or speculator improve the timing of his purchases and sales.
4. The technicians' conclusions are usually the same.

DIFFERENCES BETWEEN BAR AND POINT AND FIGURE CHARTS

1. Point and Figure chartists do not record volume, as they do not consider it important. The Bar chartist considers volume an important tool in forecasting price movements.
2. Price changes are recorded daily whereas in the Point and Figure method only changes in price that equal or exceed the number of points on which the chart is based are plotted. It is possible to make no entry on a Point and Figure chart for days or even weeks.

3. No dates are shown on Point and Figure charts whereas the date is clearly marked on the Bar Chart.

4. The charts are interpreted by different methods. In the Point and Figure method, the distance of the horizontal line will equal the distance the price may go up or down once the stock starts to move. In Bar charts "trendlines" are used. These lines are drawn to connect previous bottoms or tops in order to forecast price directions. Resistance or support levels to advances or declines can then be predicted.

Some chartists use both methods, although both generally indicate the same trend. An exception would be in a Bar Chart in which the price may indicate one trend and the volume another.

PROS AND CONS OF CHARTING

1. Even using the same charts, chartists may arrive at different conclusions based on the same data.

2. Charts can give false signals and the experienced chartist expects them. Successful technicians, however, claim to be right 60 per cent to 70 per cent of the time.

3. Charting by investors and speculators has been increasing over the years, as since many claim it helps them select the right stocks at the right time. No serious study confirms this fact.

EIGHT BASIC CHART FORMATIONS AND WHAT THEY MEAN

Bullish Patterns

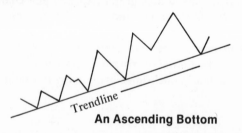

An Ascending Bottom

This is a bullish chart pattern, for each new bottom is higher than the preceeding one. Therefore, the stock remains in a strong technical position.

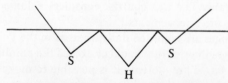

Inverted Head and Shoulders Bottom

This type of chart formation indicates to the technician that there will be a decisive upside breakout. The second or the right shoulder did not penetrate the head, thereby establishing an upward trend.

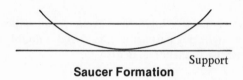

Double and Triple Bottoms

This pattern emerges when a stock sells off, rallies, and then sells off again, but does not dip below the first sell-off point. This double bottom is then considered a support level by the chartist.

Saucer Formation

This type of pattern usually signals a major uptrend. The technician watches the volume closely and hopes to find very light volume at the base of the saucer, which picks up strongly as it rises.

Bearish Patterns

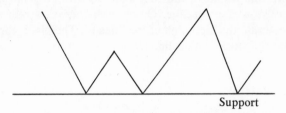

Descending Top

This is a bearish pattern, for each new high is lower than the preceeding one, thus establishing a downward trend in price. The rallies do not penetrate the preceding highs and confirm the decline.

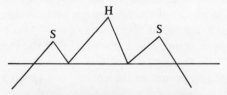

Head and Shoulders Formation

This pattern is the reverse of the bullish head and shoulder pattern. A technician reads this chart as follows: The first move he regards as the first shoulder followed by a slight decline. The second move takes the stock beyond the height of the first shoulder (forming the head), after which it suffers a sharp decline. On the third move, it rallies again but does not penetrate the high high of the "head". Therefore, the technician reasons that the stock will decline sharply.

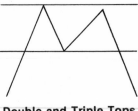

Double and Triple Tops

When a stock makes a high, then declines and rallies again but does not reach a new high, this pattern is considered a double top and is construed as bearish by the technician.

The Reverse Saucer, or the Umbrella Pattern

In this pattern new highs are usually made on light volume, whereas declines are heavier in volume. A sharp reaction could follow.

Gaps

When a stock moves either way more than ¼ of a point between trades, this is considered a gap. A trading gap may appear on the upside or the downside, and the first gap usually occurs at the beginning of an upswing or a downswing. If these gaps are accompanied by high volume, the advance or the decline can be substantial. Gaps that occur at the beginning of a move out of a saucer or any other classic bullish chart pattern on the upside are called "breakaway gaps." Many chartists carefully plot these jumps in price because they feel that the stock later will either fall or rise to "fill" the gap.

If a second gap occurs on the upside, it is called a "measuring gap" by the chartist because he feels that these gaps usually occur after approximately 50 per cent of the upward surge has been exhausted. Therefore, he "measures" the point at which he will sell. Sometimes there is a third gap in the same move, which is called the "exhaustion gap." A technician usually sells if a stock gaps the third time.

Tape Reading

This ability refers to an art that exceptionally few traders have mastered. After a stock is traded on the floor of the exchange, the information is reported on the ticker tape. All that is shown on the tape as we illustrated earlier are the symbols of the stocks traded together with the number of shares and the prices of the trades. From this information the tape reader attempts to determine the direction of the market and determine the direction of the stocks he is following.

An expert tape reader does not follow more than six stocks plus the overall market. He is usually an experienced chartist who has developed an ability to assimilate data quickly. For example, the tape reader may watch the ticker tape for hours, days, or even weeks, waiting for certain movements to occur. If a stock he is following usually trades approximately 8,000 shares a day and rarely in lots of over 500 shares, in his mind, or perhaps in a chart book close by, he sees one of the four bullish patterns forming—either the ascending bottom, the inverted head and shoulders, a double bottom, or the saucer. After watching every trade in this stock for perhaps a week, a 10,000 share block trades on a "gap" of a half point up from the last sale. He immediately sets out to buy the stock before it breaks out too fast. He knows that chartists will plot the activity by the next day and will probably place buy orders of their own.

The tape reader is extremely careful not to jump at false breakouts. He understands that the 10,000 share lot may be one sophisticated seller selling to a group of small buyers, in which case the signal is a false one and the stock will probably settle back and fill the gap. The tape reader realizes that thousands of traders have seen that 10,000 share trade and must use all his experience and knowledge to determine if someone deliberately purchased a large block hoping to attract many small speculators. He makes these decisions as he studies the tape.

If he is following the same stock with an average daily volume of 8,000 shares and observes the volume increase slowly to 10,000 shares, then to 12,000 shares, and finally to 20,000 shares without any significantly large trades, he may spot a new important trend. The stock pattern may be coming off a double bottom on the day it sold 20,000 shares and closed up ¾ of a point. No large blocks traded may signify to the tape reader than strong buying has been going on for some time and that the buyers were placing their orders in small lots in order not to attract attention.

Although 20,000 shares will not appear in the top ten as high volume stock for the day, it is indelibly imprinted on the tape reader's mind. He is convinced that the stock is ready to make a significant upward move and begins to buy.

The tape reader believes that all the information he'll ever need is on that tape, discusses the market with as few people as possible, and is usually looked on by others as a recluse. He doubts everything he reads, and almost everything he hears. He trades alone. He fully realizes that his tape-reading ability is far superior in picking bottoms than tops so he does not object to switching from one stock that has already made a move into another than appears ready to begin one.

INTERNAL MARKET TRENDS THAT INFLUENCE CHARTISTS

1. Basic trend of the market as a whole
2. Leadership (quality of stocks leading advance or decline)
3. Advance-decline ratio
4. Short position
5. Low-priced stock activity
6. Odd-lot ratio
7. Support levels of market and individual stocks
8. Barron's Confidence Index
9. Percentage of cash held by investment companies

Basic Trend of the Market as a Whole

Most securities analysts and technicians follow the same basic investment procedure.

a. They try to determine current market trend.

b. After the trend is established, they select leading industrial groups.

c. From these groups they choose the most promising stocks to buy.

d. If the market trend is down, they follow the same procedures by looking for industries and stocks that will fall faster than the market in order to find short sales.

Leadership

The quality of the stocks leading the advance or the decline is important to the chartist. If after a long advance low-priced stocks are attracting the most volume, he realizes that the public is heavily involved. This could signify a top. If, however, the volume leaders are still the country's major corporations, then the advance has further to go.

Advance-Decline Ratio

When the daily advances consistently outnumber the declines, the market is in a bullish phase. It is a bearish sign when declines are more numerous than advances. If the Dow Jones Averages advances and the advance-decline ratio either does not advance or levels off, it indicates that the advance is false. If the advance-decline ratio is strong but the Dow Jones has leveled off, then the DJIA should begin to rise.

Short Position

A speculator takes a short position when he sells stock he does not own hoping to buy it back later at a lower price. The greater the number of shares sold short, the stronger the technical position. The technician understands that short sellers are mostly speculators who must buy back the securities they have sold. Therefore, a market or a stock with a large short position is in a technically strong position to rally rapidly if the market remains strong. The short sellers usually become nervous during a rally and cover their short positions.

Low-Priced Stock Activity

Both the New York Stock Exchange and the American Stock Exchange list the ten most active stocks each day. If there is a preponderance of low-priced stocks among the leaders, the technician believes the market is nearing the end of a rally. He also reasons that in the beginning of an upswing investors prefer the quality stocks, and after they have been bid up in price he now turns to the lower-quality issues. The analysis follows that if the DJIA is rising and the average price of the leaders is high, then the bull market should continue.

Odd-Lot Ratio (less than 100-Share Purchase or Sale or Short Sale)

Each day the Wall Street Journal reports the following:

Example

New York-Carlisle DeCoppet & Co. reported handling the following odd-lot transactions on the New York Stock Exchange (in shares)

Customer Purchases	Short Sales	Other Sales	Total Sales
199,716	4971	278,365	283,336

Large institutions and investors do not buy in odd lots. The small investor does. The technician views the public as always being wrong and therefore, when the public sells more than it buys, he considers this a bullish sign. When the public purchases more than it sells, the technician interprets this as a bearish sign.

Support Levels of Market and Individual Stocks

The average closing price for the DJIA is plotted for the preceding 200 days (200 day moving average).

1. The market is in a bullish trend if the DJIA stays above its 200-day average but bearish if it breaks this trend line and continues to remain below it.

2. The same analysis holds true for an individual stock. A breakthrough on the downside is a bearish signal and an upside penetration of the 200-day average is bullish.

3. False penetrations of both the 200-day moving average of the DJIA and the individual stock may occur. Technicians use other trends to reenforce their interpretation of this type of situation.

Barron's Confidence Index

This is a ratio of Barron's ten highest-rated corporate bond yield average to the Dow Jones forty composite bond yield average.

a. When lower-grade bond issues outperform high-grade bonds, the Confidence Index rises, which is an optimistic sign for stock prices. The technician reasons that investors are not worrying about safety and are willing to buy a lower-quality bond. Therefore, they are optimistic about the market in general.

b. The converse is also true. When high-grade bonds outperform lower-grade bonds, the Confidence Index falls, signifying a lower market. The technician now reasons that the investor is seeking the haven of a high-grade investment and therefore is not bullish on the market.

Percentage of Cash Held by Investment Companies

During periods of declining market prices, investment companies sometimes hold a cushion of cash to invest at a latter date. A fully invested position (less than 3 per cent cash) is a bearish signal to the chartist, whereas a strong cash position (over 10 per cent) is considered bullish. The technician reasons that if investment companies have strong cash positions, they can make substantial purchases and help the market rise.

QUESTIONS

1. What are the main factors causing market fluctuations?
2. What is government fiscal policy? What relationship, if any, does it have to Federal Reserve policy?
3. What is the principle behind the Dow Theory?
4. Describe a bull and a bear market.
5. What are the main criticisms of the Dow Theory?
6. How does the Standard & Poor's Index differ from the Dow Index? Is there any relationship between the two? Describe.
7. Describe briefly the technical approach to the stock market.
8. What two basic methods do technicians use in charting? Describe. Is volume important to both methods?
9. What are the similarities and the differences between the two basic methods of charting?
10. List some of the pros and cons of charting.
11. Draw the four basic bullish and bearish chart formations and briefly describe their meaning.
12. What is a gap? Explain its significance to a chartist.
13. Tape reading is an art. What is it? In your opinion why is it an art?
14. List the basic internal trends that influence the chartist.
15. Fundamentalists and technicians seldom agree but most follow the same investment procedure. What is this procedure?
16. Describe: a. Advance-decline ratio. b. Short position. c. Low-priced stock activity. d. Odd-lot ratio.
17. Which approach to the stock market do you believe to be superior, the fundamental (analytical) or the technical (charting)?

7

READING AND INTERPRETING
THE FINANCIAL NEWS

A businessman seldom has unlimited time to read a financial news-paper thoroughly, so he skims most of the articles and reads closely only a few. In the United States today there are many daily papers with excellent financial sections but there is only one, the *Wall Street Journal,* that devotes itself almost entirely to business news. Any person who hopes to be a student of finance should read this paper every day. What does it contain? Can it help the fundamentalist? Does it provide tools for the technician? Can it help the businessman or woman, regardless of whether he or she owns stocks or bonds? The answer to all these questions is, yes!

It wasn't too long ago that only few people read the financial sections of newspapers because they were presented in a specialized manner and in the vocabulary of the professional. Today the business editor is well aware that what happens in Saudi Arabia, Pakistan, Japan, or Detroit has a direct impact on everyday life. The oil embargo was felt immediately at the gas pump and the proliferation of Japanese electronic products imported into this country caused unemployment in electronics factories in California and Texas. The everyday reader cannot afford to neglect the financial section of the newspaper, because even if the affect of what he reads is not immediate, he may be able to prepare for the eventuality. Reading the financial news has become part of over 30 million stockholders' daily lives.

The *Wall Street Journal* contains about twenty-two to thirty-eight pages. The "What's News" section is broken up into two columns, one for the most important news in "Business and Finance" and the other for "World-Wide" news. The Business and Finance section contains synopses of about fifteen of the most important business topics of the day, with full stories on each covered in the main body of the paper should the reader be interested in more complete information. The only other column appearing regularly on the front page is a section devoted to five different topics, one each day as illustrated on page 107.

Monday

The Outlook
Review of Current Trends In Business and Finance

Tuesday

Labor Letter
A Special News Report on People And Their Jobs in Offices, Fields and Factories

Wednesday

Tax Report
A Special Summary and Forecast of Federal and State Tax Developents

Thursday

Washington Wire
A Special Weekly Report From The Wall Street Journal's Capital Bureau

Friday

Business Bulletin
A Special Background Report On Trends in Industry and Finance

READING AND UNDERSTANDING STOCK QUOTATIONS

To the new reader of a financial paper, the method of quoting stocks appears as a mysterious code. These quotations are now well standardized and if you learn to read a few you'll be able to read the whole page. See the example on page 108.

The upper left corner of the page on which the quotations begin shows the volume of shares traded the preceding day and also the volume from January 1st to the present day, and compares this activity to the two preceding years.

Directly beneath this information is a tool used by technicians—the ten most active stocks showing the open, high, low, and close prices together with the volume and the change in price for the preceding day. To further help the technician, it reports the "average closing price of most active stocks." Following this information is the listing of the activity of each stock traded on the exchange the preceding day.

The first two columns show the highest and lowest prices of the year

THE WALL STREET JOURNAL,
Wednesday, Aug. 7, 1974

Tuesday's Volume
15,770,000 Shares; 110,400 Warrants

Volume since Jan. 1:	1974	1973	1972
Total shares	2,027,174,599	2,307,640,940	2,564,049,731
Total warrants ..	16,835,500	26,883,100	33,723,000

ACTIVE STOCKS

	Open	High	Low	Close	Chg.	Volume
Polaroid	29⅞	29⅞	27	27	−1⅛	181,400
McDonald	44	44	42⅜	42½	+1⅞	169,500
Fst Chart	6	6⅝	6	6¼	+ ¼	137,200
Howrd John	6¾	7	6⅛	6¼	− ⅜	129,100
Xerox Cp	98	98	95¼	95¼	+1⅜	128,400
East Kodak	90½	91¼	88⅛	89⅛	+2¼	122,600
Det Edison	10⅛	10⅛	9⅞	10⅛	+ ⅛	119,100
Gen Motors	44½	45¾	44⅜	44¾	+ ⅞	107,600
Disney W	40	41⅛	38	38⅞	+ ½	105,800
Am Tel&Tel	44¼	44⅜	43¼	43½	+1	105,300

Average closing price of most active stocks: 40.36.

— A–A–A —

	——1974——				P.E.	Sales				Net
	High	Low	Stock	Div.	Ratio	100s	High	Low	Close	Chg.
	61¼	49¼	Abbt Lb	1.32	13	43	50¼	49	49	− ¼
	61¼	35⅝	ACF In	2.60	8	61	36¾	35¾	36	....
	14⅝	10⅝	AcmeClev	1	6	9	10⅞	10⅝	10⅝	....
	5⅝	2⅝	AdmDg	.04e	3	44	2¾	2¾	2¾	...
(4)	13¼	9	AdmE	1.20e		52	9⅞	9⅜	9⅜+	⅛
	5¼	4	Ad Millis	.20	13	1	4¼	4¼	4¼	
	11¾	4½	Addres	.30p	...	77	5⅞	5⅝	5¾	
	11⅞	8¼	AdvInv	.30e	...	107	9½	9	9⅛+	½
	31	18⅜	AetnaLf	1.08	5	508	20¾	19¼	19¼+	½
	61½	36¾	AetnaLf	pf 2	..	1	35	35	35 −	1¾
	9⅛	5¾	Aguirre	Co	6	1	5⅞	5⅞	5⅞+	⅛
	13⅞	6⅝	Ahmans	.20	3	67	7⅞	7½	7½+	¼
	4¾	2½	Aileen	Inc	5	73	2⅞	2⅝	2⅝	
	58	40	AirPrd	.20b	17	128	47	46	46 +	⅜
	14⅞	10⅝	AircoInc	.90	5	58	11½	11⅛	11½+	⅜
	2⅜	1¼	AJ Industris		...	2	1⅝	1½	1⅝	
	24	16¼	Akzona	1.20	4	3	17⅛	16¾	17⅛+	⅜
	15	9½	Ala Gas	1.18	11	6	9¾	9½	9½−	¼
	103¾	80	AlaP	pf8.28	...	z20	81	81	81	
	29⅛	8	Alaska Intrs		...	87	9¾	8¾	8¾−	¼
	24⅝	23⅛	AlbanyIn	.60	7	22	23¼	22½	22½−	¾
	11⅜	5	AlbertoC	.36	11	41	5¾	5¼	5¾+	¾
	17¾	12¼	Albertsn	.50	8	98	13	12¾	12⅞+	⅜
	41	26⅝	AlcanAl	1.20	7	376	31⅛	30⅛	30⅜+	⅝
	9⅜	7⅜	AlcoStd	.40	3	42	8⅝	8⅜	8⅜+	⅛
	32⅞	15¾	AlconLb	.20	21	67	20	18¾	19 +	¾
	7⅝	3	Alexdrs	.10e	16	39	3¼	3	3⅛	
	23½	10½	AlisnM	3.09e	3	113	10⅝	9½	10 −	⅝
	12⅛	8	AllegCp	.46e	10	6	8¾	8⅝	8¾+	⅛
	32¾	26⅝	AllgLud	1.40	4	130	28⅜	28⅛	28¼+	⅝
	41	35	AllgLud	pf 3	...	2	36½	36	36½+	½
	21¼	15¼	AllgPw	1.52	7	62	16	15¾	15¾+	¼
	9⅝	5⅞	AllenGrp	.40	4	3	6¼	6⅛	6¼	..
	54¼	33¼	AlldCh	1.50	8	126	38¾	37½	37¾+	¾
	22⅝	12¼	AlldMnt	.48	9	8	15⅜	15⅜	15⅜	
(1)	17½	12⅞	AlldPd	.80	4	11	15¾	15⅛	15½+	⅝
	25⅝	20	AlldStr	1.50	5	44	21½	20¾	21 −	¼
	4⅞	2¼	Alld Supmkt		25	89	3	2⅝	3 +	⅛
	10¾	7½	AllisChal	.26	4	48	8¾	8¼	8¼−	⅛
(2)	51¾	38¾	Alcoa	1.34	10	867	50	48	48¾+	½
	28½	21½	A Sug	1.60a	3	7	23¾	23¼	23¾+	¾
	52⅞	35⅝	Amax	1.65	7	x117	38⅛	37½	37¾+	¾
	12	7⅞	AMBAC	.50	4	14	8⅞	8⅝	8¾	..
(3)	5	3¾	Amcord	.22	3	21	3⅞	3¾	3¾−	⅛
	40	16	A Hess	.30b	2	328	18½	17⅜	17⅜−	⅞
	89¼	43	A Hes	pf3.50	...	35	47¼	45½	45½−	1⅝
	16¼	7½	AAirFilt	.44	6	36	8¼	7¾	8¼+	¼
(5)	13⅜	7¼	Am Airlin		...	496	8⅜	7¾	7¾	....
	7½	4⅜	A Baker	.20	...	5	5⅜	5¼	5¼−	⅜
	39¾	29½	A Brnds	2.56	6	91	33	32¼	32⅝+	1⅞
	[illegible]	[illegible]	[illegible]	.80	7	280	23⅛	22¼	22¼−	¼

for each stock listed. The third column lists the name of the stock and the fourth, the dividend paid in dollars on an annual basis. The fifth column indicates the price-earnings ratio, listed as P.E. Ratio. This ratio is based on the last twelve months' earnings and the closing price of the stock. The sixth column reports the sales for the day in 100 share lots. The seventh, eighth, and ninth columns show the high, low, and closing prices of each stock traded, and the last or tenth column reports the net change in the price of the stock for the day.

Number 1—Allied Stores shows a high for the year of 25 5/8 and a low of 20. It closed at 21, down ¼ point from the preceding day. It pays a dividend of $1.50 by the closing price of 21. The dividend return is 7.1 per cent. The price-earnings ratio is reported as 5. What are the earnings? The paper does not report earnings each day. They are easy to figure however. Divide the last price of the stock by the price-earnings ratio ($21 ÷ 5). Earnings are approximately $4.20 per share. The number 44 listed under "Sales" signifies 4,400 shares traded for the day. Only round lot sales (100 shares or more) are reported.

Number 2—American Sugar shows a high for the year of 28½ and a low of 21½. It closed at 23¾, up ¾ point for the day. The dividend listed is $1.60a. The "a" is explained under "Explanatory Notes" as "also extra or extras." American Sugar pays, in addition to its $1.60 per share, an extra dividend in cash. The yield is computed on the regular dividend of $1.60 since the board of directors may or may not continue to pay the extra dividend. The regular dividend, $1.60 divided by 23¾, the closing price, gives a yield of 6.7 per cent. The price-earnings ratio is 3, which you divide into the closing price of the stock, 23¾ to compute the earnings, approximately $7.92 per share.

Number 3—Amerada Hess carries a letter "b" next to the dividend of 30¢. Again refer to the "Explanatory Notes." The letter "b" refers to annual rate plus a stock dividend.

Number 4—Addressograph Multigraph carries the letter "p" next to the dividend of 30¢. The "Explanatory Note" informs us that "p" means paid this year, dividend omitted, or deferred or no action taken at last dividend meeting. The board of directors paid 30¢ per share so far this year but decided not to pay the dividend at the last meeting. The other difference in reading the quotation line of Addressograph is the price-earnings ratio. None is listed, which means that the company is operating at a deficit. Because of the deficit the board omitted the dividend. Therefore, do not compute the dividend return. Consider it as zero.

Number 5—American Airlines closed unchanged at 7¾ on a substantial volume of 49,600 shares, pays no dividend, and is currently operating at a deficit.

The technician would plot the high, low, and change on his bar chart then plot the volume directly beneath the bar. The point and figure technician would definitely not make any marks on his chart for Addressograph Multigraph and American Airlines since there was no change in these stocks for the day. He would undoubtedly mark an X, showing an ascending pattern, for American Sugar and an O for Amerada Hess, signifying a declining pattern. He may or may not plot the decline of ¼ point in Allied Stores, since the chartist may have predetermined that he will make a mark only when the stock rises or falls ½ point or more.

The American Stock Exchange

These quotations are listed exactly as are those on the New York Stock Exchange.

The Over-the-Counter Market

The National Association of Security Dealers is an organization of brokers selling stocks and bonds not listed on any exchange. The NASD supplies the quotations to the *Wall Street Journal* and other financial publications reporting the bid and asked prices for industrial stocks, insurance stocks, utility stocks, bank stocks, and foreign stocks. In addition, corporate bonds are quoted, as well as mutual funds.

Over-the-counter is not how securities are traded but in essence refers to the fact that brokers sell their product in the same manner as the retail merchant. He buys the product and then marks it up for resale, or in a declining market, marks it down and suffers a loss. As you will recall, members of the New York Stock Exchange have departments that trade in the Over-the-Counter Market. In many instances they do not act as retailers and sell securities out of their inventory but rather act as agents who buy and sell at the best possible price and charge a standard commission to the customer. The commission is the same as they would charge on the purchase or sale of a listed security.

The investor can always tell if he bought or sold through an agent or

THE WALL STREET JOURNAL, Wednesday, Aug. 7, 1974

Over-the-Counter Markets

3:30 p.m. Eastern Time Prices, Tuesday, August 6, 1974

All over the counter prices printed on this page are representative quotations supplied by the National Association of Securities Dealers through NASDAQ, its automated system for reporting quotes. Prices don't include retail markup, markdown or commission. Volume represents shares that changed ownership during the day. Figures include only those transactions effected by NASDAQ market makers but may include some duplication where NASDAQ market makers traded with each other.

Volume, All Issues, 4,532,200

SINCE JANUARY 1

	1974	1973	1972
Total sales	721,361,667	997,088,500	1,412,284,200

MARKET DIARY

	Tues	Mon	Fri	Thur	Wed
Issues traded	2,630	2,634	2,637	2,639	2,639
Advances	635	427	250	259	199
Declines	257	334	473	565	613
Unchanged	1,738	1,873	1,914	1,815	1,827

ACTIVE STOCKS

	Volume	3:30 Bid	Chg.
Rank Organisation ADR	139,300	3¾	......
Amer Express	103,900	29⅞	+ 1⅜
Anheuser Busch	94,700	33⅛	+ 1½
Natl Medical Care	93,700	4¾	......
Intel Corp	71,700	32	− 2½
BankAmerica Corp	59,200	30⅛	+ ½
Citizen Sthn Natl	50,100	9¼	+ ½
Chubb Corp	49,200	22⅞	+ ¾
Conn Gen'l Ins Co	45,300	35¾	+ ¼
Medtronics Inc	44,300	29	+ ½

--A A--

Stock & Div.	Sales 100s	Bid	Asked	Net Chg.
ACMAT Corp	3	2⅝	3⅛	..
Acushnet C .60	1	11¾	12¾	..
AddWesley .20	8	4⅞	5¼	+ ⅛
Advance Ross	24	1¾	2	...
Advan Mry Sy	19	2⅜	2¾	− ⅛
Advan MicroD	40	8½	9	+ ¼
Advent Corp	7	11½	13½	...
AES Technolg	1	3¾	4¼	...
Affil Bnksh .80	5	18	19½	...
AgMet Incorp	15	12½	13¼	+ ¼
Agnico Eagle	144	8⅜	8⅝	− ⅛
AITS Incorp	21	2⅜	2¾	
AlaBancp 1.32	11	19½	20½	+ ¼
AldrichCh .24d	x1	56	57	+ ⅛
AlexandrA .70	70	21¾	22½	+ ¼
AlexBaldw .80	34	14⅝	15⅛	− ⅛
AlicoIncp .10d	9	9¼	10	.
AllegBevrg 3i	20	1¼	1½	+ ⅛
Allergan Phar	13	9¼	10	+ ¼
AlliedBncs .60	27	21¾	22½	− ¼
Allied Leisure	46	3⅞	4⅜	+ ⅛
Allied Tel .33	29	9¼	9¾	...
Allyn Bacon	7	3¾	4¼	...
Alton Box .20d	3	16	17	...
Amarex Incor	46	6⅞	7¼	+ ¼
AmAppras .42	4	2⅝	3	...
AmBancsh .80	10	12	13	...
AmBkr Ins .20	18	5⅞	6¼	+ ⅛
AmBkTr Pa 1	z8	17¼	18	...
AmBkrAs .20g	21	7½	8½	+ ¼
Am Beef Pack	3	4½	5	+ ⅛
Am Biomedicl	11	1⅜	1¾	..
AmCmwl Fncl	1	3¾	4⅛	...
A ConHm .05b	1	3⅛	3⅝	.
Am Exprss .60	1039	29⅞	30⅜	+ 1⅜
AmFidlLf .08e	13	7½	8	...
AmFltrona .52	12	7½	8	...
AmFinancl .04	83	10¾	11⅛	..
AmerFncl pf 1	81	7 11-16	7⅞	+1-16
AmFletch 1.16	89	19½	20¼	+ ¼
A FoundLf .16	x13	7¼	8¼	− ⅜
AmFurnitr .28	2	4¼	4⅝	...
Am Greetg .25	158	20¾	21½	− ¼
Am Heritg .30	14	9⅝	10⅛	+ ⅛
AmIntlGrp .24	88	40¼	41¼	− ¾
AmIntlRes .14	37	29¼	30¾	+ ¼
Amer Marine	5	3½	5½	− ½

Stock & Div.	Sales 100s	Bid	Asked	Net Chg.
ChemedCp .52	59	13½	15½	..
Chesapek Inst	10	1¾	2⅛	− ⅛
ChicBridge .80	169	67	68½	+ 2
ChrisSec 2.80d	22	140	146	+ 2½
ChubbCrp 1.40	492	22⅞	23⅜	+ ¾
ChurFrCh .05d	191	12¼	12⅝	+ ½
Cinn FclCp .48	6	10	10¾	+ ⅛
CircleIncm 1d	z85	13½	14	...
CitzSthnCp .80	3	17½	18½	..
CitSoNBGa .52	501	9¼	9⅝	+ ½
CitzSoRlt 77wt	1	10¾	11½	...
CitzUtil B 1.76	44	21¾	22¾	..
CitzUtil A 4.2i	36	21¼	22	− ½
CityNatl Crp 1	6	17½	18½	+ ½
Clark J L .90	36	23¾	24¾	+ ½
Class Financl	1	2¾	3½	...
Clevepak .60	17	11½	12½	...
ClevTrRlt .76d	18	5	5¾	...
ClvTRl ut .76d	12	5	6	...
Clow Corp .68	15	6¾	7½	+ ¼
CoastalSCp .27	20	4⅛	4½	...
Cobe Labrator	6	10½	11½	.
CoburnOp .18d	94	13	13¾	+ 2¼
CocaCB La .68	54	10⅝	11	− ⅛
CCBtlMia .15d	z80	6½	7¼	.
CCBtlMidA .20	z25	5	5½	+ ⅛
Codex Corp	22	14½	15½	+ ½
Coherent Rad	32	9¾	10½	+ ½
Colemn Cable	10	7¼	7¾	− ⅛
ColonBnc 1.60	5	16½	18½	...
ColLifeAcc .24	1	9	10	...
ColoNtlBks .92	6	14½	15¼	..
Columbi Crp	15	3	3⅜	− ⅛
Combanks .40	5	18	19½	
CombndIns .52	348	7¼	7½	+ ½
Comb Propert	2	7½	9	...
ComrcBkshr 1	4	17	18	...
Com ClHo .15d	132	11½	12½	...
ComlShrg .60g	3	20½	22	...
ComTrNJ 1.20	1	18¼	19	...
CmwNR 1.16d	16	5½	6¼	...
CwthNtGs 1.62	2	15¼	16¼	− ¼
CmwTlPa 1.70	7	20¾	21¾	
Comunc In .28	7	10¾	11¼	+ ⅛
Commun Prop	8	1⅝	2	..
Computcorp	51	3⅛	3⅝	− ⅛
Compuscan In	2	5	5½	+ ⅛

Stock & Div.	Sales 100s	Bid	Asked	Net Chg.
FlaMgMtl .12d	11	9	9¾	+ ¼
Flying Diamd	33	3⅞	4¼	+ ⅛
FMIC Corp	26	5¼	5¾	− ⅛
Food Town .16	4	17¼	18¼	...
Foodways Nat	4	2¾	3½	+ ¼
Forest Oil Crp	91	6⅛	6½	...
Founders Finl	180	2⅜	2⅝	...
FrameHs .32a	12	11¾	12½	...
Frankln El .28	14	7½	8	− ⅛
FranklinLf .72	115	11⅞	12¼	+ ¼
FrasMtg 1.22d	1	8¾	9½	+ ¼
FredHerr .39d	49	3½	4	− ¼
Friedmln .30g	3	8	9	..
Frndly Ice .05	55	11½	12¼	+ ½
Friona Indust	15	3⅜	3⅞	.
Froz FdEx .30	7	5⅞	6¼	+ ⅛
Fuller H B .36	5	8½	9	− ¼
Funtime Inc	z55	6¼	7	..
Furrs Cafe .28	18	10	10½	+ ⅝
--G G--				
Gates Learjet	51	7⅜	7⅞	+ ⅛
GatewayTr .60	9	6¾	7¼	...
Gelco Cp .12d	29	6⅜	6⅞	..
Gelman Instr	97	3½	3⅞	+ ½
Genl Automat	130	27½	28½	+ 2
GenAutoPt .56	3	12¾	13¾	+ ¼
Genrl Binding	8	20½	22½	...
Gen Crude .30	119	46¼	47¼	+ ½
GenlEnrgy Cp	95	8⅝	9	...
GenFinSy .08d	37	5¼	5¾	..
Gen Hlth Serv	31	2¼	2⅝	+ ¼
Gen Reins .40	50	127	131	+ 5
GenrlShale .80	1	9⅝	10⅛	+ ⅛
GenTlCal5pf 1	1	9¾	10¾	− ¼
GenTlCal 56pf	3	8¾	9¾	− ¼
Generics Am	24	3⅜	3¾	+ ¼
Genova Incp	2	7⅜	7⅞	...
GeoWaCp .03d	2	1¾	2¼	...
Gilbert A .54	79	23½	24½	..
GilfordInst .13	9	3⅝	4⅛	+ ⅛
Girard Co 3.24	13	36	37½	..
GlobeLife .08g	39	6¾	7¼	+ ⅛
Godfrey Co .90	8	10	10¾	..
GouldsPump 1	2	28	30	+ ½
GovEmpln .80	113	22⅝	23⅛	+ ½
Gov Emp wts	24	6¾	7½	..
[illegible]	[illegible]	30¼	31¼	+ ½

a principal by looking at the confirmation slip he receives from the broker. If the transaction shows a "net amount" (no commission charged), it signifies that he bought or sold the stock from or to a principal. If the transaction shows the amount of the purchase and adds a commission, he knows the broker acted as his agent.

The same essential facts reported on the major exchanges are listed on the Over-the-Counter Market each day but there are a few differences in reading the quotations.

Instead of the ten column report given for all listed securities the over-the-counter quotations are condensed into six—stock, dividend, sales, bid, asked, and net change. See the sample on page 111.

Specifically, the bid refers to the amount the broker is willing to pay for the stock if an investor has placed an order to sell, and the asked is the price the investor would have to pay to buy the security. The difference in the price is the "markup," or retail profit for the broker. In many instances an investor can negotiate between the bid and the asked, just as he may on any listed exchange.

The net change column reflects the change in the bid side by the broker. As a general rule, the more brokers that trade in a specific over-the-counter security, the closer the spread between the bid and the asked price.

Bond Quotations

Reading a list of bond quotations is different from reading quotations. Bonds are traded in $1,000 denominations and all prices are quoted by omitting the last zero. A bond selling at par—that, is at its issuing price of $1,000—will be quoted in the bond tables as 100. See the sample of a bond table on the opposite page.

The American Telephone Bond (circled) is listed at 8.80s05. This informs an investor that the coupon, or interest rate, of this bond is 8.80 per cent and that its principal becomes due and payable in the year 2005. It closed at 95½, which means $955 for each bond, and at this price yields 9.2 per cent to the investor. Prices of corporate bonds are quoted in 1/8 points. Therefore, a bond selling for 92 1/8 is worth $921.25. Since most bonds pay interest twice a year, the buyer of the bonds not only pays the seller the price quoted but also the interest accrued to the date of purchase. For example, if a buyer purchases one bond at 92 1/8 exactly three months after the last interest payment and the coupon rate of the bond is 6 per cent, he will pay:

One bond at 92 1/8	$921.25
Interest 6% for 3 months	15.00
Total cost to investor	$936.25

The fact that it is selling below its offering price (usually at par, or $1,000) means that the bond is selling at a discount. Therefore, discount

THE WALL STREET JOURNAL, Wednesday, August 7, 1974

New York Exchange Bonds

Tuesday, August 6, 1974

CORPORATION BONDS
Volume, $15,440,000

Bonds	Cur Yld	Vol	High	Low	Close	Net Chg
AirRe 3⅞87	cv	1	53½	53½	53½	....
AlaP 9s2000	10.	3	89¾	89¾	89¾	− ⅛
AlaP 8⅞s03	10.	30	84	84	84	− ½
AlaP 8½s01	10.	15	84	84	84	−3
Alaska 6s96	cv	35	52½	52	52	....
AlldSt 4½s92	cv	5	56½	56½	56½	+1¼
AldSu 5¾87	cv	3	44	44	44	− ¼
Alcoa 9s95	9.3	4	96⅛	96	96	....
Alcoa 5¼s91	cv	181	99½	98	98	+ ¼
AMAX 8s86	9.5	23	85½	83½	83½−1½
Amerce 5s92	cv	3	60	60	60	− ⅛
AAirin 11s88	11.	13	95	94¾	95	+ ⅛
AAiri 4¼s92	cv	237	42	41¾	41¾	− ¼
ABrnd 8⅞s75	8.9	8	99	99	99	− ½
ABrnd 5⅞s92	7.8	15	74⅞	74⅞	74⅞	− ⅛
AHoist 5½s93	cv	8	61	60	60	+ ¼
AHoist 4¾s92	cv	25	70½	70	70	− ½
AInvt 9½s576	11.	2	85	85	85	....
AMF 4¼s81	cv	15	72½	72½	72½+ ⅛
AMed 9½s98	14.	15	64	64	64	−3
AmMot 6s88	cv	42	63½	62¾	62½+ ¾
ASup 5⅜s93	9.1	7	60	58	58	−2
ATT 8.80s05	9.2	457	95½	94¾	95½+1⅛
ATT 8¾s2000	9.1	360	95½	95	95¾+1⅝
ATT 8.7s02	9.1	52	95	93⅞	95	+ ¼
ATT 7.75s77	7.9	43	98½	98	98	− ⅛
ATT 7⅛s03	9.0	141	78⅞	78½	78⅞+ ⅜
ATT 7s01	8.9	107	79	78	78½+ ⅛
ATT 6½s79	7.2	15	89¾	89¾	89¾+ ⅜
ATT 4⅜s85	6.4	49	68⅛	68	68⅛+ ⅛
ATT 4⅜s85r	..	12	68¾	68¾	68¾	....
ATT 3⅞s90	6.7	4	57	57	57	+1
ATT 3¼s84	5.2	27	62¼	62	62	− ¼
ATT 2⅞s75	2.9	68	94	93¾	94	− ¼
ATT 2⅜s80	3.7	46	73¼	72½	73¼+ ⅜
ATT 2⅝s82	4.1	8	66½	66½	66½	....
ATT 2⅞s86	4.6	10	57	57	57	....
Amfac 5s94	cv	8	54¾	54¾	54¾− ⅜
Ampx 5½s94	cv	28	39	39	39	+1
Anhser 6s92	7.9	3	75¼	75¼	75¼+1
AppalP9s75	9.1	11	98	9-32	98	9-32 98	9-32
Aristr 9½s89	10.	5	89	89	89	− 2⅞
ArizP 8.5s75	8.5	6	99½	99	99½+ ⅛
AshlO 4¾93	cv	20	60	59	59	+1⅞
AsCp 9¼s90	10.	4	86	86	86	....
AsInv 5¼77	5.6	3	92½	92½	92½+2⅜
Atchsn 4s95	7.6	1	52	52	52	−6½
Atchn 4s95r	..	1	58	58	58	− ¼
AtlCst 4s80	5.1	2	78	78	78	−1
AtRf 8¾s2000	9.3	1	92	92	92	− ⅛
ARF 7.7s2000	9.7	10	79¼	79¼	79¼+2⅞
AtlRich 7s76	7.3	9	95⅞	95	95¾+3
AvcoF 11s90	11.	20	99¾	99¾	99¾+ ⅝
AvcoF 8.35s	11.	5	75	75	75	....
Avco 7½93	13.	3	56	56	56	....
Avco 5½93	cv	42	42	42	42	....

Total Volume, $15,600,000

SALES SINCE JANUARY 1

1974	1973	1972
$2,306,258,500	$2,698,535,700	$3,574,043,300

	Domestic		All Issues	
	Tues	Mon	Tues	Mon
Issues traded	622	560	630	570
Advances	256	170	258	171
Decline	183	214	186	215
Unchanged	183	176	186	184
New highs, 1974	5	1	5	1
New lows, 1974	52	69	53	70

Dow Jones Bond Averages

	−1972−		−1973−		−1974−			−1974−		−1973−		−1972−	
	High	Low	High	Low	High	Low							
75.07	73.41	75.34	71.33	73.50	65.99	40 Bonds	65.99	− .15	71.76	− .12	73.91	+ .03
54.60	52.67	55.27	52.37	54.58	48.20	10 Hi Rails	48.20	− .77	52.72	− .36	53.05	− .06
69.01	66.16	67.73	65.05	68.36	62.85	10 2nd Rails	62.85	− .10	66.00	..	67.36	+ .21
91.97	89.55	92.00	88.85	91.70	80.95	10 Utilities	81.03	+ .08	88.85	− .17	90.43	− .02
86.09	84.05	85.90	77.55	80.82	71.68	10 Industrial	71.88	+ .20	79.47	+ .04	84.82	+ .01
55.08	51.67	54.61	49.97	54.26	45.82	Inc Rails	45.82	.....	50.73	..	52.23	− .01

Bonds	Cur Yld	Vol	High	Low	Close	Net Chg
Dressr 4⅛77	4.9	5	84½	84	84	− ½
DukeP 9¾s04	10.	10	93½	93	93½+ ⅛
Duq 8¾s2000	9.5	1	91¼	91¼	91¼+1¾
DuqL 2¾77	3.2	5	85⅞	85⅞	85⅞+2⅞
EasAir 5s92	cv	20	39	38¾	39	− ⅛
EaAir 4¾93	cv	7	39	39	39	.....
ElPas 8½s95	cv	45	84½	83¾	84	− ¼
ElPaso 6s93	cv	5	65¼	65	65¼+ ¼
Englh 5¼97	cv	10	73½	73½	73½+1
Essex 9¼s75	9.3	6	98½	98½	98½+1½
Evan 6¼s94	cv	12	53	53	53	+ ½
Exxon 6½s98	8.5	32	77	76½	76¼−1
Exxon 6s97	8.3	23	72	71	72	+1
Fairch 4⅞97	cv	7	46½	46½	46½	.....
Farah 5s94	cv	5	50	50	50	+1¼
Feddr 8⅞s94	14.	119	61	59	61	+2
Feddrs 5s96	cv	15	39¾	39	39	−1
FedN 4⅜s96	cv	622	75	72	72	+ ½
FPac 5½s87	cv	7	110	110	110	−7
Fiber 6¾s98	cv	10	97	96	97	.....
FinstMg 8¼s77	13.	10	62	62	62	.....
FNBo 7.6s81	8.6	10	88⅛	88⅛	88⅛−1⅞
FtNSt 7.2s79	8.4	3	85¾	85¾	85¾−1¼
FlexiV 4¾97	cv	3	62½	62½	62½+1
FlaPw 8⅞82	9.0	35	98	97¾	98	+ ½
FlaPw 8⅛75	8.3	35	98	97½	97½− ¼
FMC 4¼92	cv	16	55½	55½	55½+ ½

Bonds	Cur Yld	Vol	High	Low	Close	Net Chg
Mc Do 4¼91	cv	93	54	53	53	.....
MGM 5s93	cv	1	45	45	45	.....
MGIC 8⅜s88	..	5	78	78	78	+2
MGIC 5s93	cv	50	46½	45¼	45¼+ ¼
MichB 7¼s11	9.4	33	82½	82	82	+ ¾
Mile L 5¼s94	cv	5	61	61	61	.....
MRvCp 8s94	cv	6	82½	82½	82½− ½
MKT 5½s33f	..	8	6	6	6	+1
MoPac 5s45f	..	11	40¾	39¾	40¾+ ¾
M Pac 4¼90	8.4	7	50¼	50¼	50¼+ ⅛
M Pac 4¼05	9.7	9	43¾	43¾	43¾−1½
Moh D 5¼s94	cv	57	24⅞	24⅞	24⅞	.....
Mong 10½s75	10.	21	99½	99	99	.....
Monsa 9¼s00	9.3	20	98	98	98	.....
Mont W 9¼s90	10.	9	92⅜	92⅜	92⅜	.....
Mont W 9s89	9.8	15	91⅜	91½	91⅜+ ⅝
Mnt W 6⅛s87	9.8	3	66	66	66	.....
Morgn 4¾s98	cv	195	79¼	78	79¼+2½
vJMrE 3½s00	..	10	14	14	14	.....
MtS TT 9s10	9.2	33	97¼	96¾	97¼+ ¼
MtS TI 7¾s13	9.6	10	80¼	80¼	80¼−3¾
MtS TI 7¾s11	9.4	2	78	78	78	.....
N City 5½s88	cv	19	46	46	46	−4
N Cash 6s95	cv	6	73¾	73⅝	73¾+ ¼
N Dist 4¼92	cv	40	61⅞	59	59	−3⅝
NHom 4¾s96	cv	35	26	26	26	.....
N Ind 5⅛s88	cv	10	47½	47½	47½+ ½
N EnT 8⅜s09	9.5	8	90½	90	90	− ½

---

bonds are bonds selling below $1,000. The company, however, still is obligated to pay an investor the full $1,000 at maturity.

When the corporation pays the interest at the end of the six-month period, the investor will receive a check for $30. This is quite different from the way in which a dividend on stocks is paid. A buyer of stock may hold a security for only one day and be entitled to the full dividend.

Prices of Recent Issues

An investor can learn quite quickly what corporate bonds are yielding by referring to "Prices of Recent Issues. (See page 114). Moody's Rating, together with the current yield, indicate what investors are willing to pay for new corporate bonds. These new quotations are reflected immediately in the prices of the old bonds.

The Ashland Oil coupon rate (also circled) is 4¾ per cent and is due in 1993. In the space reserved for current yield, the notation "cv" appears.

Prices of Recent Issues

Current quotations are indicated below for recent issues of corporate senior securities that aren't listed on a principal exchange.

Issue		Moody's Rating	Bid	Asked	Chg.	Yield %
UTILITIES						
DukePwr-n	13s '79	Baa	101¼	101½	....	12.60
HoustonLP	10¼s '04	Aaa	99⅝	100	+ ⅛	10.13
IllPwr-n	10½s '04	Aa	99⅞	100⅛	...	10.49
MtStates	9¾s '12	Aaa	97½	97⅞	+ ⅛	9.95
NorIndPS	10.4s '04	Aa	99⅝	100	− ⅛	10.40
NorthwBell	10s '14	Aaa	99⅝	100	+ ¼	10.00
OhioEd	10s '81	Aa	99½	99¾	+ ¾	10.04
INDUSTRIALS						
AmBrnds	9⅝s 79	Aa	100	100½	+ ⅝	9.57
RCA	10.2s '92	A	98⅛	98½	....	10.31
n-New listing.						

This indicates that these bonds are convertible into the company's stock. It does not, however, give the price of the conversion. A Standard & Poor's or a Moody's bond book, or the financial statement of the company itself, will give this information.

The American Stock Exchange bond list is interpreted in the same way and appears directly below the New York Stock Exchange bond quotations. In addition the over-the-counter bond market reports "Government, Agency and Miscellaneous Securities."

Government, Agency and Miscellaneous Securities

Tuesday, August 6, 1974

Over-the-Counter Quotations: Source on request.
Decimals in bid-and-asked and bid changes represent 32nds (101.1 means 101 1-32). a-Plus 1-64. b-Yield to call date. d-Minus 1-64.

U.S. TREASURY BONDS

Rate	Mat. date			Bid	Asked	Bid Chg.	Yld.
3⅞s,	1974	Nov	....	98.18	98.26	+ .2	8.31
4s,	1980	Feb	....	80.10	80.26	+ .4	8.42
3½s,	1980	Nov	....	76.24	77.24	+ .10	8.09
7s,	1981	Aug	....	94.0	95.0	+ .8	7.94
6⅜s,	1982	Feb	....	88.24	89.24	+ .6	8.23
3¼s,	1978-83	Jun	....:....	71.20	72.20	+ .24	7.65
6⅜s,	1984	Aug	....	88.24	89.24	+ .6	7.87
3¼s,	1985	May	....	70.30	71.30	+ .6	7.00
4¼s,	1975-85	May	....	73.18	74.18	+ .2	7.78
6⅛s,	1986	Nov	....	87.24	88.24	+ .2	7.55
3½s,	1990	Feb	....	70.26	71.26	.....	6.39
4¼s,	1987-92	Aug	....	71.20	72.20	+ .8	6.93
4s,	1988-93	Feb	....	71.22	72.22	.....	6.57
6¾s,	1993	Feb	....	84.16	85.16	+ .6	8.29
7½s,	1988-93	Aug	....	91.8	91.24	+ .8	8.37
4⅛s,	1989-94	May	....	70.30	71.30	+ .10	6.70
8½s,	1994-99	May	....	99.28	100.12	+ .10	8.47
3s,	1995	Feb	....	71.0	72.0	+ .16	5.25
7s,	1993-98	May	....	85.24	86.24	+ .8	8.28
3½s,	1998	Nov	....	70.28	71.28	+ .8	5.64

The investor can glance at the yields on these securities and use the information as a basis of comparison for all other bonds.

Dividend News

Addressograph Multigraph Corp. directors, who indefinitely suspended dividend payments in June, continued the suspension by omitting a declaration at their Thursday meeting, the business machines company said Friday in response to an inquiry. The dividend, which had been 15 cents a share quarterly for the past three years, will remain suspended until earnings, cash requirements and overall financial conditions warrant a resumption, the company said.

Allyn & Bacon Inc., a textbook publisher, raised its semiannual dividend to 17½ cents a share from 12½ cents, payable Oct. 31 to stock of record Sept. 30. The concern paid a five-cent extra in April.

Westrans Industries Inc. declared an initial quarterly of five cents a share and a 10-cent extra, both payable Oct. 25 to stock of record Sept. 30. Westrans is an oil-and gas-exploration concern.

Longview Fibre Co. declared its regular quarterly of $1.50 a share and a year-end extra of 80 cents, both payable Oct. 10 to stock of record Sept. 25. A year before a 40-cent extra was paid.

Peerless Manufacturing Co., a maker of control equipment for the natural gas industry, boosted its quarterly to 14 cents a share from 10 cents, payable Nov. 27 to stock of record Nov. 13.

Canadian International Power Co. increased its quarterly to 32 cents (U.S.) a share from 27 cents, payable Sept. 30 to stock of record Sept. 24.

Yellow Freight System Inc. said it received Interstate Commerce Commission clearance to issue additional common shares to effect the already announced 100% stock dividend. The distribution will be made Oct. 8 to holders of record Sept. 24.

* * *

Dividends Reported Sept. 13-14

Company	Period	Amt.	Payable date	Record date
Abbott Laboratories	Q	.33	11–15–74	10–18
Addressograph-Multi		Omitted common dividend		
Allyn & Bacon Inc	S	c.17½	10–31–74	9–30
Banks of Iowa Inc	Q	.24	12–15–74	11–22
Big Three Indus Inc	Q	.15	10–25–74	10– 8

Company	Period	Amt.	Payable date	Record date
Canadian Int'lPwrCoLtd	Q	c.32	9–30–74	9–24
ChesapeakeLfeInsurance	S	.12	12–18–74	11–15
City Nat'l Corp	Q	.25	10–10–74	9–27
Commerce Group Corp	Q	.03	11–15–74	10–31
De Soto Inc	Q	.15	10–18–74	10– 1
Doyle Dane Bernbach	Q	.24	10–15–74	9–30
Drexel Utility Shares	M	.10	10–15–74	9–27
Ehrenreich Photo-Opt	Q	.05	10–21–74	10– 1
1st Conn Small Bus Inv	Q	.25	10–25–74	9–27
Fulton Nat'l Corp	Q	.14	10– 1–74	9–20
Gen'l Electric Co	Q	.40	10–25–74	9–23
Golconda Corp $1pf	Q	.25	11– 6–74	10–15
Gr Lakes Chemical Corp	S	c.08	10–25–74	10– 1
Hines Edward Lumber Co	Q	.50	10–10–74	9–25
Lin Nat'l Drct Pl Fd		.14½	11–14–74	10– 2
Longview Fiber Co	Q	1.50	10–10–74	9–25
Longview Fiber Co	E	.80	10–10–74	9–25
Manhattan Indus Inc	Q	.10	10– 1–74	9–23
Mark Twain Banchshrs	Q	.16	11– 7–74	10–11
Medalist Ind Inc	Q	.10	10–15–74	9–30
Mesa Petroleum Co	S	.02½	11–15–74	11– 1
Mesa Pet $2.20sr pf	Q	.55	10– 1–74	9–23
Montgoy St Income Securs	M	c.15	10–15–74	10– 2
Nat'l Securities Funds:				
Balanced Fund		.12	10–15–74	9–30
Bond Fund		.10	10–15–74	9–30
Dividend Fund		.05½	10–15–74	9–30
Northgage Exp Ltd		.25	10–15–74	9–30
Nucor Corp	Q	.06	11–11–74	9–30
Ohio Art Co	Q	.06	11– 8–74	10–18
Pay'N Pak Stores	Q	c.09	10–30–74	10–10
Peerless Mfg Co	Q	c.14	11–27–74	11–13
Pueblo Int'l Inc	Q	.07½	11–29–74	10–25
Putnam Funds:				
George Putnam Fd		.12	9–20–74	9–11
Putnam Voyager Fd		.25½	9–20–74	9–11
Rapid-American Cp	Q	.25	10–31–74	10–15
Rapid-American $2.25pf	Q	.56¼	10–31–74	10–15
Rapid-American $3pf B	Q	.75	10–31–74	10–15
Southern Indus Corp	Q	.25	10–11–74	9–27
Toro Co	Q	c.12½	10–14–74	9–27
Surveyor Fund Inc	E	h.01	10–21–74	9–19
Westrans Ind Inc	In	k.15	10–25–74	9–30

k-The amount consists of an initial dividend of 5 cents and a special dividend of 10 cents.

* * *

Stocks Ex-Dividend Sept. 17

Company	Amount	Company	Amount
Adams Express	.10	Manhattan Indus Inc	.10
Allied Thermal	.30	Mesa Petroleum $2.20pf	.55
Amerace Corp	.30	Motorola Inc	.17½
Can Hyrocrbns Ltd	.12½	Nat Air Inc	.12½
Central T&Util	.28	Nat Spinning	.05
Genl Elec Co	.40	Quaker Oats	.20
Hubbard RI Est	.40	Southn New Eng T	.71
Hubbell H Inc cIA	.32½	Southn Nw Eg T pfA	.95½
Hubbell H Inc cIB	.32½	Shunshine Min Co	.15
Hubbell H cIB	.32½	Zale Corp	.19
ICMRIty SBI	.40	Zale $.80pf	.20
Int Flvrs&Frag	.07		

c-Increased dividend. d-Reduced dividend. h-From income. j-From capital gains. b-Payable in Canadian funds. A, annual; Ac, accumulation; E, extra; F, final; G, interim; In, initial; Liq, liquidation; M, monthly; Q, quarterly; R, resumed; S, semi-annual; Sp, special.

Dividend News

Each day dividends declared by public corporations are listed in the *Wall Street Journal.* If any change in dividend policy occurred at a board of directors' meeting, it is reported separately. Otherwise, the dividends are listed alphabetically. There is a direct correlation between earnings and dividends. The average dividend payout of a company may be 50 per cent, and by studying the earnings trend an investor may be able to project an increase in dividend. Or the reverse may be true.

From the "Dividend News," we see that Addressograph Multigraph Corporation voted to indefinitely suspend the dividend. The reason is quite obvious. The company was operating at a deficit and dividends are paid out of earnings.

In the case of Allyn & Bacon, its semi-annual dividend was increased, reflecting an optimistic attitude on the part of the board of directors. Most corporations pay dividends quarterly and interest on bonds semi-annually. There are some corporations, however, that pay dividends monthly, semi-annually, and even annually. The payable date is the date the corporation mails the dividends to its stockholders.

The record date should not be confused with the ex-dividend date, which is far more important to a stockholder. As you can see, the ex-dividend date is listed at the end of the Dividend News. It lists securities that have to be held on September 16 in order to earn the dividend. If purchased on September 17, the buyer will not earn the dividend. If sold on September 17, the seller is entitled to the dividend. The list of stocks going ex-dividend on September 17 were reported in the *Journal* one day before putting all investors on notice that they had one last day either to sell or buy. If a company closed at $30 per share on September 16 and was going *ex* a 50¢ dividend on the 17th, it should open for trading the next day at 29½. If, however, it closes at 30 on the ex-dividend date (17th), the quotation in the *Journal* in the Net Change column will be + ½. The reason for this is that the dividend of 50¢ was reflected in the price of the shares on the day before at $30.

The record date is, then, important only to the corporation itself, and as a general rule a stock will go ex-dividend approximately four to five days before the record date. It takes that long for a corporation to record any changes in its stockholder list. Some publications list only the record date.

In the "Amount Paid" column in which the dividend is listed, a (c) next to the dividend signifies an increased amount. On the day a total of seven increases were declared for the Montgomery $1 Income Securities, thus increasing its monthly dividend.

Digest of Earnings Report

Corporations issue quarterly as well as annual reports and most financial publications carry these reports daily. The illustration here is a section of a typical list taken from the *Wall Street Journal* for September 17, 1974. The reader should not only scan the list for companies he or she owns, but also try to determine the general trend of earnings of all the corporations. Reading this list in conjunction with the Dividend News will

Digest of Earnings Reports

ALLIED LEISURE INDS (O)

9 mo July 31:	1974	1973
Shares ...	820,406	807,217
aShr earns ..	$.88	$.81
Revenues ..	b6,114,000	6,261,000
Income	719,000	659,000
Extrd item	d484,000	c288,000
eNet inco ..	235,000	947,000

a-Based on income before extraordinary items. b-Includes $500,-000 insurance recovery for business interruption. c-Tax-loss carry-forward credit. d-Debit; from fire loss. e-Equal to 29 cents a share in 1974 and $1.17 a share in 1973.

ASKIN SERVICE CORP. (A)

6 mo July 31:	1974	1973
Sales	$4,988,000	$5,699,000
Loss	a680,000	71,000
Loss dis op .	1,300,000	77,000
Net loss ...	1,980,000	148,000

a-Includes a loss of $515,000 on the discontinuance of stores.

BELL (W.) & CO. (O)

Year June 29:	1974	1973
Shr earns ...	$.46	$.45
Sales	24,932,540	21,580,127
Net income .	450,242	436,293
Shares	974,366	965,850

BENTLEY LABS INC. (O)

9 mo Aug 31:	1974	1973
aShr earns ..	$.68	$.54
Revenues ..	10,441,565	7,818,316
Net income .	1,458,344	1,160,171
aAvg shrs ..	2,155,913	2,162,200

a-Based on average common and common equivalent shares.

BERKLINE CORP. (O)

Year June 30:	a1974	1973
Shr earns ...	...	$.73
Revenues ·..	$56,317,000	57,549,000
Net loss	214,000	b1,126,000
Shares ...	1,496,034	1,542,000

a-Reflects pretax write-down of $430,000 in inventory of Waynline division that reduced certain products lines. b-Income.

GRANTREE CORP. (O)

Quar July 31:	1974	1973
Shr earns ...	...	$.05
Revenues ...	2,646,068	2,573,726
Net loss	58,470	a76,237
Shares	1,276,610	1,387,684
9 mo shr ...	.03	.18
Revenues .>.	7,778,573	7,388,140
Net income	b30,022	249,642

a-Income. b-Includes a gain of $67,829 on the sale of a subsidiary.

GREAT WESTERN UNITED (N)

Quar Aug. 31:	1974	1973
Revenues	$122,932,000	$70,696,000
Net income	14,932,000	1,172,000

The company reported share earnings of $6.27 in 1974 compared with one cent in 1973: fully diluted per share earnings were $5.45 in 1974. The company is in arrears on its preferred stock dividends.

HALCO PRODUCTS CORP. (A)

39 wk Aug. 1:	1974	1973
Shr earns ..	$.09	...
Sales	10,064,943	$6,349,671
Net income	93,822	d167,619
Avg shares .	1,044,443	671,226

d-Loss.

HARVEY GROUP (A)

26 wk Aug. 3:	1974	1973
Shr earns ..	a$.05	$.02
Revenues ..	20,049,000	19,180,000
Net cont op	100,000	b48,000
Loss dis op .	...	14,000
Income ...	100,000	34,000
Extrd cred	13,000	...
Net income	c113,000	34,000

a-Based on income before extraordinary credit. b-Equal to two cents a share. c-Equal to five cents a share.

HOLLY'S INC. (M)

Quar July 31:	1974	1973
Shr earns ..	$.45	$.37
Sales	4,303,292	3,439,105
Net income	210,269	175,844
9 mo shr .	.80	.72
Sales	11,347,379	9,347,677
Net income	383,904	350,295

MASTERS INC. (A)

Quar Aug 3:	1974	1973
Shr earns ..	...	$.29
Sales, etc .	$18,422,295	16,730,907
Loss bf tax	7,963	a672,368
Incu tax	c3,797	333,200
Net loss	4,166	a339,168
6 mo shr ..	...	.27
Sales, etc ..	32,867,029	29,171,753
Loss bf tax	667,968	a623,886
Inco tax ...	c327,200	306,000
Net loss	340,768	a317,886

a-Income. c-Credit.

McCORMICK & CO. (O)

Quar Aug 31:	1974	1973
Shr earns ..	$.35	$.29
Sales	52,002,000	41,794,000
Net income .	1,815,000	1,463,000
9 mo shr ..	.88	.73
Sales	144,266,000	123,222,000
Net income	4,535,000	3,697,000

MOHAWK DATA SCIENCES (N)

Quar July 31:	1974	1973
aRevenues	$43,314,000	$40,805,000
Loss cont op	2,746,000	1,214,000
Loss dis op	b600,000	97,000
Net loss ...	3,346,000	1,311,000

a-From continuing operations. b-Includes a provision of $425,000 for operating losses during the phase-out period of operations of discontinued subsidiaries.

NATIONAL PROPANE CORP. (Pa)

Quar July 31:	1975	a1974
Shr earns ...	$.04	$.04
Sales, etc ...	10,592,000	7,813,000
Net income	280,000	264,000

a-Restated.

NAUM BROS INC. (O)

Year June 30:	1974	a1973
Shr earns ...	$.35	b$.33
Sales	31,704,576	24,325,147
Income ...	279,342	257,443
Extrd chg ..	...	d169,198
Net income	279,342	c88,245

a-For 53 weeks. b-Based on income before extraordinary charge. c-Equal to 11 cents a share. d-From fire loss at a leased showroom.

---

help an investor further appreciate the correlation between earnings and dividends.

Who's News

Management changes can be a significant factor in the success of any company. Following these changes daily in the *Journal* can alert an investor to possible problems or to new possible areas of development. (See the illustration on page 118.)

New Product Development

One of the major elements of a growth stock, as we have seen, is the development of a patentable new product. The research laboratories of major corporations are constantly developing these new products. The *Wall Street Journal,* as well as other newspapers and magazines continually publish information regarding research and development.

Who's News

• • •

Commerce and Industry

Debron Corp. (St. Louis)—Marvin R. Boydstun, 54 years old, resigned as president and a director of this structural steel fabricator, taking early retirement. George W. Hall, chairman and chief executive, will assume the additional responsibilities of president, although that position won't be filled, the company said.

General Telephone & Electronics Corp.—Fred A. Martin was named regional vice president, marketing, in a newly created Northeastern sales area of GTE Sylvania Inc., a Stamford, Conn.-based subsidiary.

Allegheny Ludlum Industries Inc. (Pittsburgh)—Laurence E. Mullen was named to the new position of vice president, personnel and organization development, of this steelmaker.

Piedmont Natural Gas Co. (Charlotte, N.C.)—Lewis J. Odess, chairman of Pollution Control-Walther Inc., was elected a director.

FMC Corp. (Chicago)—Robert McLellan was named to the newly created post of vice president, international and government relations, for this diversified manufacturer.

Zayre Corp. (Framingham, Mass.)—Gerald Davis was named vice president-senior merchandise manager for this operator of discount department and apparel stores.

Howmet Corp. (Greenwich, Conn.)—Harvey P. Armintrout, formerly production manager and assistant works manager of the Wenatches, Wash., plant of Aluminum Co. of America, was named president of Eastalco Aluminum Co., a Frederick, Md.-based subsidiary of this diversified maker of gas-turbine parts.

Bourns Inc. (Riverside, Calif.)—Guy B. Entrekin Jr., senior vice president, operations, was elected to the newly created positions of executive vice president and chief operating officer of this manufacturer of electronic devices. Mr. Entrekin will continue as chairman of Precision Monolithics Inc., a subsidiary.

Pentair Industries Inc. (St. Paul, Minn.)—Peter J. King was elected president of this paper manufacturer. He succeeds Murray J. Harpole, who will continue as chairman. Mr. King was formerly vice president, finance and administration, at American Hoist & Derrick Co.

Singer Co. (New York)—Arthur J. Santry Jr., president and chief executive of Combustion Engineering Inc., was elected a director of this diversified manufacturer.

Finance

American Express Co.—Brooks Banker, executive vice president of this provider of insurance, checks and travel services, was elected to the additional newly created posts of vice chairman of Fireman's Fund Insurance Co. and of Fireman's Fund American Life Insurance Co., San Francisco-based subsidiaries. At Fireman's Fund, he will be responsible for corporate planning and development and for certain administrative areas.

News Items that Affect the Market

On September 17, 1974, the following articles appeared in the *Journal*. The market was reeling under incessant selling and had reached a twelve-year low. As previously mentioned, the Federal Reserve has a strong affect on the direction of the market, but how powerful can only be grasped by studying how stocks rallied over twelve points on heavy volume after the Fed's announcement. For months the Fed restricted the money supply in an attempt to curtail inflation. These articles were the first sign that some change in their policy might be developing.

Short-Term Fees Slide as Fed Acts To Loosen Credit

Treasury Bill Rates Plunge 7/8 Point; Heavy Buying By Foreigners Is Noted

A WALL STREET JOURNAL *News Roundup*

Short-term interest rates fell sharply yesterday as the Federal Reserve System, the nation's money manager, implicitly confirmed that it has eased its credit reins another notch.

The rate slide was aided by temporary, but massive, purchases of U.S. government securities by foreign central banks, presumably banks of oil-producing nations.

Treasury-bill rates experienced the most pronounced decline in the money market, plunging as much as 7/8 percentage point or so in resale trading.

The decline in bill rates, and advance in prices, was reflected in yesterday's regular weekly auction of new 13-week and 26-week bills.

The average return to investors on the 13-week bills declined to 8.185% at the latest auction from 9.099% at the prior sale. It was the lowest since 7.698% last July 29.

The average yield on the 26-week bills fell to 8.203% from 8.980% and was the lowest since 8.055% on July 29.

In the resale market, 13-week bills, due Dec. 12, closed at about 8.06% bid on some dealers' quotation sheets, down from 8.94% Friday. The companion 26-week issue, due March 13, fell to 8.42% bid from Friday's close of 8.86%.

Abreast of the Market
Industrials Rebound 12.59 From 12-Year Low In Heaviest Trading Session in Three Months

By VICTOR J. HILLERY

After its recent staggering slide to a 12-year low, the stock market cut loose yesterday afternoon in a sudden, surprise rally in the heaviest trading session in more than three months.

Brokers noted that yesterday the bid rate on three-month Treasury bills fell to 8.06% from 8.94% on Friday in the resale market. "The news reinforced the feeling that short-term interest rates can come down," commented Eldon A. Grimm, vice president of Birr, Wilson & Co. And Larry Wachtel, Bache & Co. vice president, observed: "When you bring something like this to a market as beaten down and oversold as this one you get these dramatic moves."

Short Interest Declined on the Big Board And Amex in Month Ended Last Monday

By a WALL STREET JOURNAL *Staff Reporter*

NEW YORK—Short interest fell on the New York and American stock exchanges in the one-month period ended last Monday.

On the Big Board, short interest was 18,-843,102 shares, down 749,880 shares from the June 14 level.

On the Amex, short interest was 3,381,187 shares, down 30,373 shares.

A short sale is the sale of borrowed stock. The seller expects a price decline that would enable him to purchase an equal number of shares later at a lower price for return to the lender. The short interest is the number of shares that haven't been purchased for return to lenders.

Fluctuations in short-interest levels of some stocks also may have been caused partly by arbitrage situations. Those are marked by the symbol (t) in the tables below, where the short interest in the issue exceeds 100,000 shares.

In a major method of securities arbitrage, a profit can be made in situations where a company's stock is to be exchanged for that of another, or for a new issue, as a result of a proposed merger. The profit opportunity arises when the various stocks sell at disparate prices.

An arbitrageur may make a small per-share profit by buying stock of one company and selling short the stock of the other concern involved in the prospective merger.

The tables below show the Big Board and Amex stocks in which a short position of at least 20,000 shares existed as of July 15, or in which there was a short-position change of at least 10,000 shares since mid-June.

NEW YORK STOCK EXCHANGE

SECURITY NAME	7-15-74	6-14-74	Shares-Warrants Listed
!Amer Tel&Tel wts75	1,028,023	1,019,620	31,313,679
ASA Ltd	74,302	55,242	4,800,000
Ahmanson (H.F.)	11,200	36,600	22,760,163
Alison Mtg Inv Tr	20,850	18,150	2,324,789
Amax Inc	39,475	30,463	23,859,440
Aluminum Co America	28,119	30,831	33,224,384
Amer Home Products	66,98	65,820	165,606,648
AMF Inc	67,299	29,899	19,130,359
tAmer Motors	141,489	165,390	29,545,222
tAmer Telephone	106,153	98,308	556,145,567
Amer Hospital Supply	39,698	43,536	35,298,191
Amfac Inc	3,900	21,700	10,836,404
AMP Inc	96,537	105,384	37,440,000
Arctic Enter	22,000	21,500	3,050,396
ARA Services	95,723	112,708	6,107,263
Atlantic Richfield	73,984	95,747	46,806,361
Avery Products	72,924	68,675	9,518,099
Avon Products	194,395	224,131	57,991,239
Balt Gas & Elec	14,990	2,125	24,529,111
Bandag Inc	21,360	23,840	12,584,871
Barnett Mtg Trust	47,200	46,375	2,121,498
Bausch Lomb	42,280	61,562	5,624,521
tBaxter Labs	105,187	124,157	29,860,435
!Black & Decker	224,939	258,415	40,161,070
Boise Cascade	24,143	37,444	31,152,642
Bristol Myers	37,403	49,807	31,982,496
Brunswick Corp	28,160	29,060	18,875,360

SECURITY NAME	7-15-74	6-14-74	Shares-Warrants Listed
tBuilder Investmt Grp	135,560	128,475	2,928,507
Citicorp	69,524	152,909	125,909,064
tBurroughs	137,879	142,125	39,067,854
Cabot Cabot & Forbes	23,080	19,900	2,991,587
Campbell Red Lake MN	28,275	28,964	7,999,000
Capital Holding	47,60	43,353	26,900,110
Caterpillar Tractor	27,160	29,150	57,199,535
Chase Man Mtg&RltyTr	96,545	49,840	4,884,368
Chesebrough Pond	40,257	41,457	15,915,313
tChrysler Corp WTS 76	448,601	475,971	1,800,000
Chrysler Corp	45,670	46,171	56,251,671
C.I.T. Financial	22,630	31,316	20,273,364
Citizens&So Rlty In	66,400	45,045	3,829,032
City Investing	53,563	2,150	22,960,274
CNA Financial	30,543	53,294	35,058,631
Coca Cola BottlingNY	110,115	110,834	16,216,165
Coca Cola Co	65,390	66,128	59,854,248
Colgate Palmolive	37,550	27,145	71,891,213
Colonial Penn Group	22,050	30,475	16,125,597
Combustion Engneerng	45,387	55,361	10,416,967
Commonwealth Oil Ref	22,990	31,015	13,949,961
Computer Sciences	73,200	72,500	14,861,276
tConsolid Edison of NY	143,800	203,200	61,554,082
Control Data	25,027	33,457	16,082,053
Crane Co	17,986	28,076	5,930,756
tCurtiss Wright	117,953	146,353	9,711,667
Damon Corp	29,25	6,515	7,006,727
Data General	22,790	23,969	7,995,072
Deere & Co	16,615	4,816	30,097,974
Deseret Pharma	200	20,600	2,940,960
Delta Air Lines	25,125	24,058	19,879,377
Digital Equip	83,193	96,645	11,937,310
tDisney Produtions	319,603	262,348	29,170,536
Diversified Mtg Inv	41,250	49,500	7,327,149
Dr Pepper	127,157	111,632	19,109,234
Dome Mines	32,885	26,880	5,840,004
Dow Chemical	25,448	27,066	97,665,190
Dun & Bradstreet	61,181	80,041	26,833,917
Duplan Corp	40,700	40,200	3,460,025
tDupont de Nemours	132,216	130,787	48,102,443
Eastern Airlines	22,453	13,138	18,848,977
tEastman Kodak	175,892	168,060	161,583,488
tJack Eckerd	30,659	41,909	18,705,223
Lilly Eli	47,680	39,540	69,434,940
Electronic Data Syst	36,325	40,275	12,370,267
Emerson Elec	42,814	74,158	52,529,792
Emery Air Freight	48,807	51,820	7,816,271
El Paso Co	39,113	40,413	27,929,352
Exxon Corp	24,391	53,084	226,602,256
Fairchild Camra	83,139	144,981	5,149,474
tFederal Nat Mtg	132,840	91,440	46,648,008
Fibreboard Corp	28,000	29,700	4,507,418
First Chicago	26,418	39,247	40,153,640
Fischbach & Moore	13,893	3,607	3,273,636
First Intl Bankshare	38,656	3,461	13,906,212
Fleetwood Enterprise	15,669	34,050	11,470,000
Flexi-Van Corp	27,384	25,985	5,804,011
Fluor Corp	33,011	40,266	14,711,672
Ford Motor	88,095	91,807	81,478,226
tGannett Co	117,124	110,774	22,210,648
Gardner Denver	28,070	31,920	16,535,225
Gen Amer Transport	34,405	33,307	11,945,252
General Electric	31,816	25,495	185,561,636
General Mills	37,060	35,470	23,692,963
General Motors	32,379	35,985	287,617,041
Gen Public Utilities	50,300	126,400	43,084,374
Gen Tel & Electronics	60,472	50,798	120,462,319
Genuine Parts	13,157	26,553	15,664,232
Georgia Pacific	20,267	33,754	54,917,388
Goodrich (BF)	21,286	16,006	14,558,266
Gould Inc	20,225	24,200	8,764,659
Great Amer Mtg Inv	50,900	36,900	4,454,343
tGrant (WT)	295,620	257,318	14,861,728
Guardian Mtg Invst	50,215	45,440	3,000,397
Guardian Ind	46,650	55,900	5,694,970
tGulf Resources Cheml	228,424	247,198	4,862,552
Gulf & Westrn Ind	82,662	96,613	21,751,153
Gulf & Westn Ind wts 78	82,570	89,295	6,922,172
Halliburton Co	34,987	43,340	19,210,846
Hammond Corp	23,200	32,800	3,498,922
Heller (Walt E) Int	23,166	20,494	11,057,392
Hercules Inc	29,012	27,369	41,803,080
Heublein Inc	36,829	12,944	20,955,953
Hewlett Packard	201,004	213,272	27,044,611

SECURITY NAME	7-15-74	Shares-Warrants 6-14-74	Listed
Holiday Inns	24,419	74,759	29,866,712
Homestake Mining	109,276	83,834	11,278,088
House of ʼFabrics	23,300	23,100	5,698,375
Hughes Tool	26,899	25,863	5,642,363
Ingersoll Rand	41,924	40,696	16,422,799
Interco Inc	28,227	9,257	10,969,574
Inter Business Mach	55,087	47,013	147,176,990
Int Flavors & Fragrnce	270,150	286,062	35,842,720
Inter Minerals & Chem	44,012	53,042	11,482,567
International Paper	30,723	17,410	44,946,159
Inter Tel & Tel	48,426	79,319	96,074,661
Itek Corp	59,297	46,362	2,968,121
tJack Eckerd	30,659	41,909	18,705,223
Jim Walt $160 cum cv pr	3,000	14,300	2,819,927
Johnson & Johnson	155,871	154,152	57,839,069
Kaufman & Broad	56,390	54,119	16,391,594
Knight Newspaper	29,695	26,445	10,415,824
KLM Royal Dutch	21,000	21,800	478,989
tKresge (S.S.)	229,653	280,347	119,876,852
tLTV Corp	393,002	497,792	9,007,533
Litton Industries	31,176	14,161	33,160,043
Long Island Lighting	27,300	1,000	22,588,607
Marcor Inc	66,200	31,054	29,260,631
Marriott Corp	72,432	80,484	31,140,731
tMartin Marietta	105,381	229,762	25,548,376
Masco Corp	30,664	31,119	12,233,675
Masonite Corp	37,125	46,425	16,225,196
Mattel Inc	54,521	57,395	16,861,874
Matsushita Elec Ind	8,962	56,962	7,098,879
tMcDonald's Corp	458,881	488,292	39,824,005
Melville Shoe	100	26,500	24,557,545
tMerck & Co	100,988	86,866	74,776,649
Merrill Lynch & Co	16,823	4,575	32,494,926
MGIC Investment	50,945	62,015	22,019,396
Minnesota Min & Mfg	67,132	78,683	113,835,317
Moly Corp	3,783	22,350	2,994,603
Monogram Industries	10,800	800	5,368,201
Monsanto Co	75,223	105,519	34,012,444
tMorgan (J.P.) & Co	188,274	146,184	36,691,755
Morris Philip	52,589	73,388	55,846,372
Morse Electro Prod	34,400	32,600	2,863,110
tMotorola Inc	101,609	160,931	28,089,368
Mountain States Tel	6,500	17,600	58,610,069
Nalco Chemical	44,300	1,400	19,971,432
National Chemsearch	33,995	35,695	11,654,556
Nat'l Semiconductor	112,629	135,595	11,836,245
Natomas Co	59,547	79,369	4,524,923
New England Tel&Tel	27,200	20,200	45,685,080
Northwest Airlines	19,957	45,732	21,604,136
Northwest Industries	22,441	26,141	7,453,532
Nthwestrn Steel&Wire	13,600	300	7,506,339
Northwest Ind wts 79	34,513	39,213	1,513,315
NVF Co	29,650	91,464	2,027,432
Occidental Petroleum	71,933	60,783	55,670,287
Owens Illinois	33,885	27,041	15,206,108
Owens Corning Fbrgls	13,650	24,696	14,903,790
tPan Amer World Airwy	247,645	162,935	41,050,579
Penney (J.C.)	49,002	56,380	58,836,133
tPenn Central	337,403	334,716	24,110,321
PepsiCo Inc	51,762	28,377	23,689,419
tPerkin Elmer	259,072	253,540	15,774,052
Pfizer Inc	31,497	22,407	70,532,485
Pizza Hut	42,490	40,015	3,294,788
Pittston Co	10,833	25,473	17,520,224
Polaroid Corp	271,978	246,200	32,859,525
Ponderosa System	60,780	99,427	4,757,475
Procter & Gamble	99,170	105,809	82,346,424
Pub Service Indiana	18,600	4,000	12,722,936
Pullman Inc	9,743	29,373	7,313,486
RCA Corp	20,329	11,644	74,610,271
tRamada Inns	101,741	109,641	25,215,017
Rapid Amer	37,349	10,635	6,872,042
Reliance Group	22,995	23,060	12,256,918
Republic Corp	29,350	28,750	10,965,374
Revlon Inc	27,510	27,910	13,329,751
Reynolds Metals	24,900	46,800	17,247,856
Reynolds Ind $2.25	21,100	11,000	7,042,477
Rockwell Intl	31,135	36,224	31,840,340
Rite Aid Corp	3,380	13,536	10,290,480
Robins (A.H.)	30,400	29,380	26,126,928
Royal Dutch Petr	2,167	28,917	18,880,803
Rubbermaid Inc	31,410	2,114	7,726,762
Ryder System	48,340	65,040	12,804,009
Santa Fe Industries	19,621	68,931	25,619,930
Savin Business Mach	55,100	58,100	3,025,703
Searle (G.D.) & Co	11,832	70,784	50,206,033
Sears Roebuck	02,069	73,278	157,490,863
St Regis Paper	20,641	42,650	21,724,033
Schering Plough	50,494	49,337	53,894,222
Schlitz (Jos.) Brewing	25,45	23,715	29,373,654
Schlumberger	52,184	48,384	37,800,384
Signal Cos.	40,113	16,972	21,042,183
Simplicity Pattern	80,736	80,102	13,579,139
Singer Co	61,994	48,141	17,152,848
tSony Corp. ADR	119,419	89,229	25,482,940
Southern Cal Edison	7,852	30,216	43,484,883

SECURITY NAME	7-15-74	6-14-74	Listed
Southen Railway	5,350	16,750	15,653,102
Sperry Rand	30,963	34,344	34,480,300
Sprague Electric	33,140	9,392	3,456,665
Stand Brands Paint	32,863	29,703	5,277,803
Tandy Corp	12,325	24,269	11,113,956
Tektronix Inc	62,508	66,866	8,679,447
tTeledyne Inc	106,607	70,798	32,317,712
Tenneco Inc	32,288	26,990	69,029,038
Tenneco Inc wts 1975	87,250	90,150	5,984,095
TelePrompTer Corp	33,775	31,075	16,510,050
Texasgulf Inc	21,770	13,460	34,560,000
Texas Instruments	191,677	180,363	22,937,550
Tesoro Petroleum	13,520	67,808	10,149,259
Tidewater Marine Ser	20,822	21,542	3,862,097
Trans Unic Corp	96,050	94,590	10,392,798
Trans World Airlines	28,857	33,753	12,699,233
Union Caʼbide	48,291	44,181	61,559,722
Union Corp	67,046	57,305	4,075,036
Union Oil Cal cv pr	20,700	600	8,185,816
Union Pacific	17,049	6,202	22,847,175
US Industries	14,684	1,700	29,978,016
US Steel	61,289	39,870	54,169,462
United Telecomm	14,550	25,440	42,033,718
Utah Intl	58,014	8,503	30,353,957
Upjohn Co	72,696	101,456	29,459,870
Va Elec & Power	200	11,400	50,976,981
Wang Labs	43,695	49,595	4,062,035
Warner Lambert	24,441	24,442	78,445,389
tWestern Air Lines	240,285	227,849	14,723,509
tWestern Union	316,732	210,313	13,818,320
Westinghouse Elec	73,949	13,636	88,514,274
Weyerhaeuser Co	80,405	125,797	128,005,627
Whittaker Corp	20,277	20,277	20,681,853
Winnebago Ind	349,534	412,114	25,216,086
Woolworth (F.W.)	13,020	2,000	29,360,731
Wyly Co	45,550	45,795	8,605,361
tXerox Corp	124,531	119,735	78,724,892
Zenith Radio	64,945	32,590	19,045,870

t-Possibly involved in arbitrage, depending on prices of securities involved.

AMERICAN STOCK EXCHANGE

	7-15-74	Shares-Warrants 6-14-74	Listed
Alaska Airlines	30,045	67,445	3,707,000
Amerada Hess wts '78	25,850	17,821	1,800,000
Aquitaine Co Can	13,000	3,000	21,838,000
Banister Contl Ltd	17,597	6,650	4,052,000
Bowmar Inst Corp.	267,235	263,445	1,996,000
Caressa Inc	40,769	40,000	2,820,000
Carrier Corp wts '76	29,150	42,800	1,125,000
CMI Inv Corp wts 76	223,625	232,920	495,000
Coffee Mat Corp	22,213	18,600	2,107,000
Coit Intl Inc	65,500	65,500	6,193,000
Compugraphic Corp	34,525	35,530	1,815,000
Condec Corp	38,566	36,989	2,249,000
Crystal Oil Co	39,490	40,390	1,600,000
Giant Yellowknife	94,966	58,135	4,303,000
Gould Inc wts	45,010	47,887	855,000
Hartz Mountain Corp	20,495	20,800	8,714,000
Houston Oil & Minrls	46,135	127,614	3,073,000
Husky Oil Ltd	101,429	96,029	9,699,000
Imperial Oil Ltd A	23,700	11,300	129,131,000
LTV Corp wts '78 115	50,596	51,800	1,594,000
Marinouque Mng Ind B	12,146	22,173	8,095,000
Marshall Industries	79,500	79,500	925,000
Natl Health Entprise	60,900	60,900	6,405,000
NJB Prime Inv SBI	24,900	15,700	1,200,000
Natural Gas wts '75	128,087	117,312	795,000
Plant Industries Inc	41,200	41,200	2,553,000
Pret Corp	21,400	21,400	2,870,000
Pulte Home Corp	20,000	20,000	2,033,000
Research Cottrell	13,250	26,440	4,176,000
Robintech Inc	28,104	34,467	1,445,000
Rollins Intnl Inc	22,000	23,135	3,874,000
Sambos Restaurants	39,650	29,714	11,838,000
Sys Engin Lab Inc	60,100	60,100	2,621,000
Syntex Corp	154,014	146,978	20,601,000
Technical Tape Inc	23,400	23,400	3,523,000
Telex Corp wts '76	22,925	26,054	963,000
Tiger Intl Inc wts 75	301,222	319,623	1,057,000
Wilshire Oil Co	21,690	20,485	7,327,000

121

Short Interest

Approximately the third week of each month the New York and American Stock exchanges release the "short interest" as at the fifteenth of that month. The short seller expects a price decline that would enable him to purchase an equal number of shares later at a lower price for return to the lender. The short interest is the number of shares that have not been purchased for return to lenders.

Financial newspapers report only those stocks on the New York Stock Exchange with short positions of at least 20,000 shares, or in which there was a short position change of at least 10,000 shares since the preceding month. The short position is important to an investor but even more so to a trader or technician since these sales represent stock that, in most cases, must be bought back. The technician, who is usually a trader of securities, maintains records of these short positions because should the market begin to rally he is aware that stocks with large short positions rally further and faster than other securities. He understands that short sellers are more nervous than the ordinary purchaser of stock and will hurry to cover their short positions if they sense a rally. The technician will try to time his regular sale so that he can sell out his long position to the short seller who is covering. Why do the exchanges allow short selling? It provides liquidity to the market. A short sale cannot be made unless the stock sold short is up from its last previous lower price. A short seller cannot sell a stock if it continues to decline without rising in price (uptick). In other words, the shares must be on the way up before he can sell short.

Arbitrage

Arbitrage is the simultaneous purchase and sale of the same securities, commodities, or foreign exchange in different markets to profit from unequal prices. True arbitrage is riskless and the profits very small. Many member exchange firms have arbitrage departments that concentrate solely on price of various stocks, commodities, or foreign exchange.

Examples

British pounds may be selling at a fraction higher in London than in New York, so a buyer simultaneously sells pounds in London and buys the same amount in New York. He then delivers the pounds purchased in New York to London and makes the profit on the exchange. The key elements are the *same commodity* and *done simultaneously*.

A member firm may be able to buy U.S. Steel on the Pacific Coast Stock Exchange for $44 and sell it for $44 3/8 on the New York Stock Exchange at the same time.

Hedging

Hedging is used to protect against a complete loss. It is the purchase or sale of a different security, or commodity, to counterbalance the first purchase or sale.

Example

After analysis, U.S. Steel looks attractive whereas Bethlehem Steel looks overpriced in relation to it. To hedge, buy U.S. Steel and sell Bethlehem Steel short.

Changes in Stock Holdings Filed at Big Exchanges

Changes in Stock Holdings Filed at Big Exchanges

The following officers, directors and large stockholders of companies reported changes in holdings under the Securities Exchange Act of 1934. Those identified as beneficial owners hold at least 10% of a company's equity securities. Unless otherwise noted, changes involved direct holdings of common stock and took place in July. Companies are listed where transactions generally aggregate 10,000 shares or $100,000.

NEW YORK STOCK EXCHANGE

AMFAC INC.—Gulf & Western Industries Inc., a beneficial owner, acquired 34,300 shares, increasing holdings to 2,093,300.

GENERAL HOST CORP.—Meshulam Riklis, a beneficial owner, privately sold 568,900 shares, eliminating holdings.

SIMMONS CO.—Gulf & Western Industries Inc., a beneficial owner, acquired 90,000 shares, increasing holdings to 763,900.

WHITE CONSOLIDATED INDUSTRIES INC.—Edward S. Reddig, chairman, acquired 10,000 shares, increasing holdings to 192,630.

WILLIAMS COS.—Kenneth F. Lundberg, a director, acquired 150,000 shares, increasing holdings to 152,000.

AMERICAN STOCK EXCHANGE

BOWMAR INSTRUMENT CORP.—William D. Meazell, a vice president and a director, acquired 10,000 shares and disposed of 1,000 shares, placing holdings at 50,300.

Prior to the Securities Exchange Act of 1934, large stockholders, officers, and directors could buy and sell shares without notifying anyone. Each Thursday the *Wall Street Journal* reports these changes, which should be reviewed by both investor and speculator.

A serious student of business, in addition to reading the monthly economic letters of major banks, may wish to study the table of statistics released each week in the magazine *Business Week*. See the illustration on p. 124.

The two largest industries in the United States are automobiles and housing. *Ward's Automotive* reports each week on the production of automobiles and shows production down 15 per cent from the preceding year

Business Week index

Copyright 1974 by McGraw-Hill, Inc.

1967 average **100**   Year ago **126.7**   Month ago **126.1**   Previous week **125.3r**   Latest week **125.5***

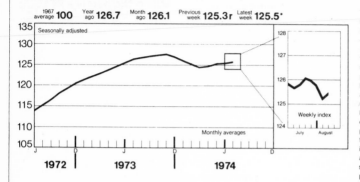

The index inched upward for the week ended Aug. 17, following three weeks of declines. After seasonal adjustment, bituminous coal output turned up strongly, reversing a substantial drop in the previous week. Auto assemblies increased significantly, as four plants scheduled Saturday operations while two lines remained on strike. Moderate gains occurred in steel, paper, electricity, and rail freight. Despite some overtime in four plants, truck output fell again because of a supplier strike. Small declines were posted in lumber, paperboard, intercity trucking, and crude-oil refinery runs.

Figures of the week

Production		Latest week	Previous week	Month ago	Year ago	1967 average
Raw steel/Amer. Iron & Steel Inst., thous. of net tons	Aug. 24	2,664	2,676 ≠	2,758	2,803	2,440
Automobiles/Ward's Automotive Reports	Aug. 24	106,932	86,222r ≠	124,333	124,252	142,438
Trucks/Ward's Automotive Reports	Aug. 24	34,363	32,793r ≠	52,332	48,988	30,490
Electric power/Edison Elec. Inst., millions of kilowatt-hours	Aug. 24	40,299	39,299 ≠	40,119	38,170	23,169
Crude oil, refinery runs/Amer. Pet. Inst., daily av., thous. of bbl.	Aug. 24	NA	12,537 ≠	12,608	13,001	9,815
Bituminous coal/Bureau of Mines, thous. of net tons	Aug. 17	13,875≠	12,205r	12,295	12,030	10,627
Paperboard/Amer. Paper Inst., thous. of tons	Aug. 24	573.9	552.4 ≠	572.3	578.6	438.8
Paper/Amer. Paper Inst., thous. of tons	Aug. 17	523.0≠	515.0r	541.0	514.0	402.8
Lumber/WWPA¹, SFPA², 225 mills, millions of feet	Aug. 17	187.9≠	198.2	204.0	211.4	186.4
Trade						
Rail freight traffic/Assn. of Amer. RRs, billions of ton-miles	Aug. 17	16.2≠	15.7	16.3	16.3	13.8
Intercity truck tonnage/Amer. Truck Assn. Inc., unadj., index	Aug. 17	103≠	103	103	109	100
Retail sales/Census Bur., unadj., in millions	Aug. 17	$10,431	$10,370	$10,417	$9,527	$6,035
Department store sales/Census Bur., unadj., in millions	Aug. 17	$1,014	$995	$979	$973	$527
Prices						
Industrial raw materials, 13 spot commodities/BLS, Tues. index	Aug. 20	221.1	225.8r	229.1	191.8	100
Foodstuffs, 9 spot commodities/BLS, Tues. index	Aug. 20	266.2	272.2	254.8	241.9	100
Finished steel composite/Iron Age, lb.	Aug. 26	12.346¢	12.346¢	12.346¢	9.363¢	6.464¢
Copper/electrolytic, del., Metals Week, lb.	Aug. 24	86.6¢	86.6¢	86.6¢	60.1¢	38.6¢
Aluminum, primary ingot major U. S. producer, Metals Week, lb.	Aug. 24	36.0¢††	36.0¢	33.5¢	25.0¢	25.0¢
Wheat/No. 2 hard, Kansas City, Grain Market Review, bu.	Aug. 24	$4.40	$4.38	$4.45	$4.99	$1.68
Cotton/strict low middling 1-1/16 in., USDA, lb.	Aug. 28	48.19¢	49.79¢	56.60¢	75.69¢	25.20¢
Gold/Wed. final setting, London open mkt., troy oz.	Aug. 28	$154.350	$155.500	$156.000	$107.300	$35.000
Finance						
500 stocks composite/S&P, price index	Aug. 28	71.64	75.00	81.43	102.60	91.93
AA corporate bond yield/S&P	Aug. 28	8.96%	8.75%	8.76%	8.04%	5.66%
Treasury bill rate/new issue, 91 days, Fed. Res.	Aug. 26	9.908%	8.846%	7.698%	8.668%	4.321%
Long-term government bond yield/10 years or more, Fed. Res.	Aug. 24	7.30%	7.35%r	7.12%	6.74%	4.85%
Commercial, industr., and ag. loans†/Fed. Res., in millions	Aug. 21	$130,568	$130,295r	$129,953	$111,305	$64,471
Free reserves/Fed. Res., in millions	Aug. 21	–$3,017	–$2,735r	–$3,297	–$1,932	$195

Monthly figures		Latest month	Month ago	Year ago	1967 average
Exports/Comm. Dept., seas. adj., in millions	July	$8,307	$8,357	$5,865	$2,586
Imports/Comm. Dept., seas. adj., in millions	July	$9,036	$8,613	$5,829	$2,241
Budget surplus or deficit(–)/Treas. Dept., in millions	July	–$3,472	$7,052	–$4,506	–$8,790
12 leading indicators composite/Comm. Dept. seas. adj., index	July	179.2	176.1r	165.6	100
Help-wanted advertising/Conference Board, seas. adj., index	July	119	116	131	100

≠ Used in computing Business Week Index (chart); other components (not listed) are machinery, defense & space equipment.
* Preliminary, week ended Aug. 17, 1974   † Reporting member banks   r Revised   NA Not available
1 Western Wood Products Association   2 Southern Forest Products Association
†† This series has been changed to reflect the greater volume of aluminum trading at the major U. S. producers' price.

Reprinted with the permission of Business Week, © *(1974).*

or from 124,252 to 56,932 units, and off 25 per cent from 1967, which *Business Week* uses as an average. As *Business Week* observes, auto assemblies increased significantly to 106,932 units from the preceding week or 86,222 units but should be followed carefully to see if production continues to increase. General Motors, the industry leader, sold below $40 per share for the first time since 1960 during the week these statistics were released.

Figures on housing starts are not compiled in *Business Week* but are published in the *Wall Street Journal* and many other daily financial sections of local newspapers. Housing starts fell from over 2,500,000 in 1973 to an annualized rate of less than 1,200,000 in 1974. The housing industry, during 1974, entered a severe slump because of extremely high interest rates for mortgages.

The reader does not have to be reminded of inflation during the past several years, with wheat, among other commodities, rising from $1.68 a bushel to $4.40 a bushel, representing over a 160 per cent increase since 1967. The price of gold soared over 300 per cent.

In finance, inflation reflected itself in the increased yields of Treasury bills (91 days), rising from 4.321 per cent to 9.908 per cent, AA Standard & Poor's corporate bond yields rose from 5.66 per cent to 8.96 per cent.

With everything else rising, what happened to the stock market? Standard and Poor's 500 stock index fell from 91.93 to 71.64, or a decline of over 20 per cent from 1967 to mid-1974.

As we learned from the technician, there is more to the stock market than statistics and the underlying influence since the mid-1960s has been inflation. What is inflation? What causes it?

Money, Prices, and Interest Rates

Money stock in the chart on page 126 refers to the money supply, which is made up of all the currency in circulation, plus demand deposits. The General Price Index is an index of prices the consumer pays for commodities.

Inflation is the result of an excessive expansion of the money stock. From 1952 until 1963 (refer to chart) the money stock rose gradually from approximately $124 billion to $150 billion. At the same time the General Price Index rose from 88 (based on a scale of 100 in 1958) to 107. Stated another way, the money stock rose 20 per cent during the period from 1952 until 1963 and the General Price Index rose the same percentage. During these eleven years inflation was gradual, rising at less than 2 per cent per year.

From 1963 until mid-1974 the money stock grew from $150 billion to $279 billion, while at the same time the General Price Index rose from 107 (base of 100 in 1958) to 167.09.

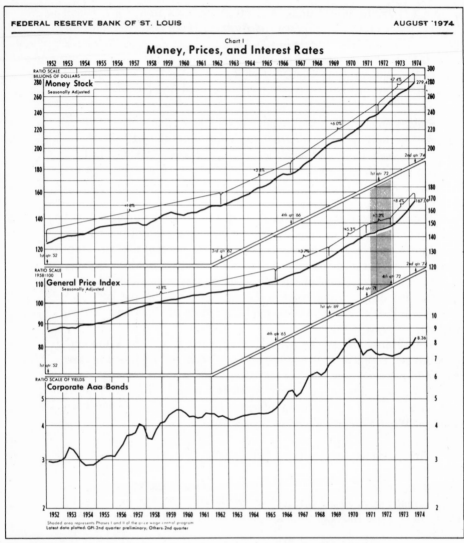

This is strong evidence that as the money supply in the hands of the public increases, the general price level of the cost of living increases. Why and how did the money stock grow?

The Federal Reserve may expand the money supply by (1) lowering reserve requirements, (2) lowering discount rates, and (3) buying government debt instruments in the open market. It is this last operation that was the primary cause of increasing the money supply. We now know how, but why?

During the period of rapid growth in the money supply, America was was engaged in a costly war in Vietnam. There are three methods of financing government expenditures: (1) by taxation, (2) by borrowing from the public, and (3) by inflation. Unlike the Korean War, during which individual income taxes were increased and corporations paid an excess profits tax, the Vietnam war was financed by what is technically called monetization of debt, or as we know it, by expanding the money stock. These resulting large budget deficits, if allowed to continue, cause inflation.

INFLATION AND INTEREST RATES

There is a direct correlation between inflation and interest rates. (see chart). During the period of rapid money growth, the yields on AAA corporate bonds rose from slightly over 4 per cent to well over 8 per cent. Interest rates do not fluctuate. The true rate of return remains approximately 3 per cent. Interest rates rise because there is an inflation premium added to the normal rate of return. As inflation grows, interest rates rise. In Brazil, interest rates touched 40 per cent in 1974 because inflation was over 35 per cent.

Interest is, in reality, made up of two elements, a normal rate of return and inflation. Savers will not lend or invest unless they receive a rate of return that compensates them for the anticipated rate of inflation. Inflationary policies involve heavy risk of creating an inflationary boom that could lead to a severe recession.

In addition to the *Wall Street Journal,* an investor may wish to subscribe to other newspapers and magazines that specialize in financial information. A list follows.

1. *Commercial and Financial Chronicle*
2. *Journal of Commerce*
3. *Barron's*
4. *Forbes*
5. *Business Week*
6. *Investment Dealers Digest*
7. *U.S. News and World Report*

Brokerage houses maintain libraries containing all the latest information on corporations. Most carry the following services:

1. Standard & Poor's
2. Moody's
3. Value Line

Because most business publications find it easier to publish good news rather than negative information the reader must recognize that the recommendations made by such publications must be investigated in detail. They are excellent sources of information but the final decision must rest with the investor.

It is then not recommended that either an investor or a speculator base his buying and selling on any service. These recommendations should be used as an information tool and not be viewed as all-knowing or completely objective.

In addition to all the above available information, an investor may write for the economic letters from several of the major banks in the country:

1. First National City Bank
2. Chase Manhattan Bank
3. Morgan Guarantee Survey
4. Federal Reserve Bank of St. Louis

An investor should also write for the annual reports of the corporations he is studying to add to the published sources at his disposal. There is no shortage of original source material and it is surprising how much of this information is available at no charge. It will not take long for the reader to find the newspapers, magazines, and economic letters best suited for his use in developing a keener sense of cause-and-effect relationships in the stock market.

QUESTIONS

1. Do you believe that only shareholders should read the financial news?
2. Why do newspapers list the ten most active stocks of the day on each exchange, including the Over-the-Counter Market?
3. What information can you learn from the stock quotations listed daily?
4. How does an over-the-counter trade differ from a trade on a listed exchange?
5. Define the terms "bid and "asked." What is the difference between the two prices called?
6. If an investor wishes to buy bonds and doesn't know what the prevailing interest rates are, how can he learn quickly? Give at least two examples.
7. Define the following terms: (a) dividend record date, (b) ex-dividend, and (c) dividend payable date.
8. Is it important for an investor to know what the average dividend payout is? Why?
9. How often do corporations issue earnings reports? Are these reports mandatory? Explain.
10. How often is the short interest released? To whom is this list most important? Why?
11. Define arbitrage. Give an example.
12. What is hedging? Illustrate.
13. Is it necessary for large stockholders, officers, and directors to report their securities purchases and sales? If so, why?
14. What is inflation? What causes it?
15. Is there a correlation between inflation and interest rates?

8

PUT AND CALL OPTIONS

Why should puts and calls be the least understood operation of the securities market? Perhaps it is the brokerage community itself that is the cause of the secrecy. In 1884 a panic caused a brilliant Wall Street speculator, Russell Sage, to renege on many of his put and call contracts. Since that time and up until the 1960s, most brokerage firms did not write or buy options, no doubt as a result of this previous traumatic experience. Registered representatives are not trained in this field and most, therefore, ignore it completely.

A *put* is an option to *sell* a specific stock, in 100 share lots, at a specific price within a specified time limit.

A *call* is an option to *buy* a specific stock, in 100 share lots, at a specified price within a specified time limit.

A *warrant* is an option to buy a specific stock at a specific price for a specified period of time. The differences between a warrant and a call are:

1. Warrants are issued by corporations.
2. Warrants are usually for much longer periods of time, sometimes even perpetual.

Options are used daily in the real estate business and their use in this area perhaps most closely parallel to their use in stock dealings. Suppose that a corporation wishes to build a plant in one of two areas but has not yet made a decision about which place it will choose. For a comparatively small amount of money, the corporation ties up both pieces of property by buying options on both for the period of time needed to make the decision. When the decision is made the corporation exercises its option on the piece of property it wants and lets the other option expire. A small price to pay for ensuring that the land would not be sold before the decision was made.

Options are used in baseball and football to give the owners the power or right to choose their players. If they exercise the option, they hire; if they let the option expire, the player is free to sign with another team. Hollywood studios take out options on actors and actresses and publishing houses have options on writers. In put and call options, the choice belongs to the holder of the option to exercise his contract before the expiration date. By doing nothing, he allows his option to lapse.

There are an estimated 25 million shareholders in the United States and probably not 25,000 understand options and option writing. These things not difficult to learn and can be very vaulable tools in an investing career.

Most put and call dealers belong to the Put and Call Brokers and Dealers Association, Inc., which regulates the dealers. It has rules of conduct, minimum financial requirements, and standard option contracts. None of these existed in 1884. In addition, each option either purchased or written (sold) must be exercised through a member firm of the New York Stock Exchange which guarantees the options. This increases the assurance that the option will be honored. I have been dealing in options since 1950 and I know of no instance in which an option contract has not been honored. Option contracts are negotiable, and on the back of each contract is the name of the stock exchange firm where the individual or institution that sold the contract has his account.

The option dealer is in effect a middleman since he arranges for the purchase and the sale of the contract between the buyer and the seller. His business is to find a seller (writer) of an option contract if there is a demand for either a put or a call. His profit, like any middleman's, is the difference between what he pays for an option and what he sells it for.

Option Contracts

Option contracts are written for periods of thirty days, sixty days, ninety-five days, six months ten days, and sometimes for as long as one year. The thirty-day and the sixty-day contract are not popular, and most contracts are written for ninety-five days or six months ten days. These options are considered securities under the Internal Revenue Code and may be taken as capital gains.

Premium

The money premium paid for the option entitles the holder to exercise his contract at any time during and up to the expiration date. This premium is not applied to adjust the price of the stock.

To illustrate:

An option is bought on U.S. Steel for ninety-five days at $40 per share for a $400 premium. At any time during the ninety-five day period the holder may call (exercise) his option on 100 shares of U.S. Steel at $40 less any dividend that was paid on the stock during this period. If the expiration date is approaching and Steel is selling or $43, the holder will still execute his option. He can then sell the stock at $43 and recover some of the premium he paid. If, however, the stock is selling for $36, he will allow his option to expire.

An option never expires on a holiday. If the exchange is closed for an unexpected holiday, the contract will expire on the next business day.

The Writer or Seller of Options

As stated previously, for every buyer of an option there must be a writer or seller. Why does he write options? Who can write options? What can he expect to earn? What risks does he face?

A writer of options is usually a sophisticated market investor or institution who wishes to either accumulate a portfolio or make additional money on an already existing portfolio. Anyone can write options. It is one of the most interesting facets of the securities market.

The buyer of a call pays a premium in money at the time he purchases the contract.

He believes that a certain stock now selling at $35 will rise quite rapidly to $50 and wishes to speculate but either does not have, or does not choose to risk, $3,500. So he buys a call (option to buy) on 100 shares for a $300 premium for a 95 day period at $35 per share plus approximately $12 for federal and state taxes. No taxes are paid on puts. The speculator now knows that he will lose only $312 even if the stock drops to $20 per share. If the stock rises to $50, his profit will be $1,500 less the cost of his option, or over a 300 per cent return on his money.

To illustrate:

		Costs	Receipts
Cost of 95-day option		$ 312	
Bought 100 shares $35		3,500	
Commission (approx.)		60	
Sold 100 shares $50	$ 5,000		
Less commission (approx.)	70		$ 4,930
		$ 3,872	−3,872
Profit			$ 1,058

If the stock falls below the option price, the buyer will not exercise his option and his loss will be the cost of the option, and no more. However, if the stock does not rise to $50 as hoped but only to $38, the buyer should exercise his option and recover part of the premium paid. In this case he would have lost about $120, or the total of the commission.

The buyer of a *put* option believes that the market will fall. He purchases a put option at $35. His position is the exact opposite of the holder of the call option. He can make money only if his particular stock falls in price. If the buyer pays $300 for a 95 day Put and exercises his option when the stock drops to $25 his profit will be $1,000 less the cost of the option and the buying and selling commissions.

To illustrate:

		Costs	Receipts
Cost of 95 day Put option		$ 300	
Sold 100 shares at $35	$ 3,500		
Commission (approximate)	60		$ 3,440
Bought 100 shares at $25	$ 2,500		
Commission (Approximate)	50	2,550	
		$ 2,850	$ 3,440
			—2,850
Profit			$ 590

The holder of the Put option made $590 or almost 200 per cent on his investment of $300.

Using Puts and Calls for Trading

Most options, as we mentioned, are purchased for ninety-five days or for six months and ten days, and the stock market is never so accommodating that the stock will keep rising or falling steadily up to the last day of the contract. There can be several up and down movements in the market during the period and traders (speculators who buy and sell often) try to take advantage of them. To illustrate: On March 30, an individual buys a call (option to buy) on PDQ at $35 per share, anticipating a market price of $50. His contract expires on June 30th. PDQ starts to rise and within a month is at $50. The holder of the option may exercise at any time during the option period but he still has two months to go on his contract. Should he hold or should he exercise the option? Or is there another alternative?

If he holds and the stock rises higher than $50, his profits increase. However, when he purchased the option he expected the stock to rise only to $50. If he continues to hold and the stock falls back to $40, the holder can still exercise his option but his profit will have shrunk.

If he exercises the option, he makes over $1,000, which is over 300 per cent on his money. But what of the elapsed time? Could he have done something with the remaining two months?

He could trade against the option. The trader calls his broker and enters a short sale on PDQ at $50. This is an entirely different transaction and requires that the trader put up the necessary money to cover this trade. When the order is executed, the trader has now locked in his profit. If the stock falls, he makes as much money on the short sale as he loses on his option. If the market rises, he loses as much money on the short sale as he makes on the option. Why should the trader pay commissions to lock in his profits when he could simply have exercised his option? During the next month PDQ drops back in price to $42. The trader now covers his short position. His option still has one month before expiration and during this period PDQ again rises to $50, at which point the trader exercises the option. Let us examine his profits:

			Costs	Receipts
Cost of call option			$ 300	
Sold short 100 shares	$50	$ 5,000		
Less commission		70		$ 4,930
Bought 100 shares	$42		4,200	
Plus commission			65	
Exercised call	$35		3,500	
Plus commission			60	
Sold 100 shares	$50	$ 5,000		
Less commission		70		4,930
			$ 8,125	$ 9,860
				—8,125
Total profit				$ 1,735

The trader's profits have increased substantially as the result of using the unexpired time remaining on the option. He may never have made the short sale without the protection of the call option. Since the stock market is often quite volatile, nimble traders may make many trades against their options.

These illustrations pertain to call options but the same procedures, in reverse, may be used by the holder of put options.

Using Puts and Calls to Protect a Short Sale or a Purchase at Time of Commitment

An individual wants to buy a stock selling for $35 because he feels that it will go to $50 but he is worried that adverse circumstances might affect the price of the stock in the meantime. If these circumstances materialize, the stock could drop to $25. The trader, as a result, buys stock at $35 and simultaneously buys a put option at the same price for $300. If the stock falls, his loss is limited to the cost of the put plus the commissions. If, however, the stock rises to $50, he sells it and allows his put option to expire.

To illustrate:

		Costs	*Receipts*
Bought 100 shares at $35		$ 3,500	
Commission		60	
Cost of put option		300	
Sold 100 shares $50	$ 5,000		
Less commissions	70		$ 4,930
		$ 3,860	$ 4,930
			—3,860
Profit			$ 1,070

The investor made over 25 per cent on this transaction. He invested almost $3,900 and made a profit of over $1,000. If he had not bought the put option, he probably would not have bought the stock and thus would have lost his profit.

In the same set of circumstances, except that the trader sells short with the stock at $35, he can buy a call option to protect him in the event that the stock goes up in price.

Buying Puts and Calls to Protect a Profit

In the first example a speculator buys a call option at $35, expecting it to rally to $50. It does rise to $50 in a month and upon reexamining his position he feels that the stock can continue to rise but does not want to risk his profit. He also doesn't have the necessary capital to go short against his option. He can buy a put option to protect the profit in his call option. If the stock falls in price, whatever he loses on his call option he makes back on his put option. An interesting result occurs if the stock continues its rise to 70. The call option is exercised at $35 and sold for $70, or at a gross profit of $3,500 less the cost of the call and the put plus commissions, or at a profit of approximately $2,650.

With a little imagination you can see that put and call options can be used in many profitable ways.

Put and call options, the contracts themselves, are considered securities. All securities held *less* than six months and 1 day are considered short-term capital gains. If there are no offsetting losses, then the amount of the gain is added to ordinary income. If a security is held longer than six months, then the taxpayer has two choices, both of which are far better than the tax treatment for short-term capital gains. The first choice is that the investor may add one-half of his long term capital gain to his ordinary income and pay taxes on this figure. The second is that he may pay a flat percentage of 25 per cent on the total long term capital gain. This tax preference is given to every investor but is subject to certain limitations. The possibility of changes in the tax laws make it advisable for an investor to coordinate his activities with his accountant.

Using Options for Long Term Capital Gains

If a speculator bought a six-month ten-day option on a stock at $35, he would be faced with a different problem when he chose to exercise his option. If, of course, the stock declines, he still allows his contract to lapse; if it rises to $50 and if more than six months have elapsed, he should not exercise his option. He can and should sell the contract back to the put and call dealer for $5,000 less the cost of commissions paid in and out. No additional money is needed. As a result of this transaction, the investor now has a long-term capital gain that has considerable tax advantages over a short-term gain.

If the option is exercised, the stock would be considered as bought the day the option contract was called. If the stock is sold on the same day, the gain would be considered short term. The following example illustrates the tax advantages of *selling* the option and not *exercising* it. We assume a 50 per cent tax bracket.

If exercised:

		Costs	Receipts
Cost of 6-month 10-day option		$ 450	
Bought 100 shares $35		3,500	
Commission		60	
Sold 100 shares $50	$ 5,000		
Commission	70		$ 4,930
		$ 4,010	$ 4,930
			− 4,010
Profit (short-term gain)			920
50% tax bracket			—460
Net profit			$460

If option is sold:

	Costs	Receipts
Cost of 6-month option	$ 450	
Sold option to dealer -		
dealer sells stock	$ 5,000	
Dealer exercises option	3,500	
	$ 1,500	
Less commissions	130	$ 1,370
	$ 450	$ 1,370
		−450
Profit (long-term gain)		920
25% tax		230
Net profit		$ 690

In this example the same individual pays $230 less tax by selling the option; or stated another way, he has increased his earnings by 50 per cent.

How to Make a Long-Term Capital Gain by Going Short

The tax law states explicitly that all short sales result in short-term capital gains. A speculator can remain short for over six months and still not receive the benefit of a long-term gain. However, if a speculator buys a put option for six months and 10 days at $35 and holds the option for over six months, he may sell the option back to the put and call dealer. Any gain is then considered long term.

Averaging Down or Up with Puts and Calls

An individual buys 100 shares of a stock at $35 and watches it drift down to $25. He can buy another 100 shares at $25, thus averaging his cost at $30 per share. However, he may not wish to, or is not able to, buy another 100 shares. He buys a call option at a cost of $250 for ninety-five days at $25 per share. The stock rises to $37 and he decides to exercise his option for 100 shares and then sell his 200 shares. The transaction would appear as follows:

			Costs	Receipts
Bought 100 shares	$35		$ 3,500	
Plus commission			60	
Cost of call option			250	
Cost of 100 shares	$25		2,500	
Plus commission			50	
Sold 200 shares	$37	$ 7,400		
Less commission		115		$ 7,288
			$ 6,360	$ 7,288
				−6,360
Profit				$ 925

The investor did not risk $2,500 plus commission to buy another 100 shares, but instead accomplished the equivalent with $250. He was able to turn a potential loss into a profit. If the stock fell further, his loss on the second 100 shares would be limited to $250. A short seller of a stock can reverse this procedure if he sells short at $35 and the stock rises to $50 by buying a put option.

What Are the Effects of Dividends, Stock Dividends, Stock Splits, and Rights During the Term of the Option?

Dividends.   Most corporations pay dividends quarterly; therefore, within the period of ninety-five days at least one dividend and perhaps two would have been paid. The option contract is automatically reduced by the amount of the dividend.

Example: If a dividend of 60¢ on a $35 stock was paid during the holding period of the option, the contract is automatically reduced to $34.40 per share. This new price applies to holders of both put and call options. The *writer* of the call option, not the *holder* of the option, receives the dividend. If the buyer exercises his option, he receives the dividend through a reduction in the price of the option. The holder of the put option, on the other hand, pays for the dividend through a reduction in the price of the option.

Stock Dividends

If a stock dividend of 10 per cent is paid during the holding period, the owner of the option can now call 110 shares of stock at the original price of the contract. And, again, conversely, the holder of the put option can now put or sell 110 shares at the original contract price.

Stock Splits

A corporation splits its stock by issuing additional shares of stock to its shareholders. If it is a two for one split and the holder owns 100 shares, the corporation issues an additional certificate for 100 shares. The owner does not own a larger share of the company as a result, only more shares. If a speculator holds an option for 100 shares at $35 and the stock splits two for one, his option is good for 200 shares at $17.50 per share. The holder of a put option could now sell or put 200 shares at $17.50 per share.

Stock Rights

At times corporations issue "rights" to their current shareholders to subscribe to additional shares below the market price. On the day the stock sells ex-rights, the first price the rights sell for is reduced from the price of the option.

$$\text{VALUE OF RIGHTS} = \frac{\text{Current Market Price of Stock Less the Exercisable Price of Rights}}{\text{Number of Rights Necessary to Buy Each Share Plus One}}$$

(Prior to the stock selling ex-rights)

To illustrate: American Telephone announces that it will allow its shareholders to buy additional shares of stock at $40 per share. A holder of ten rights can buy one additional share. One right is issued for each share owned. If American Telephone is selling for $51 per share the day the rights are admitted to trading, what is the value of each right?

$$\text{Value of Rights} = \frac{\$ 51 - \$ 40}{10 + 1} = \frac{\$ 11}{11} = \$1.00$$

$$\text{Value of Rights} = \$ 1.00$$

Ex-rights means that the individual who purchases the security on that day *does not* receive the rights to the lower-priced shares. If he bought them the day before, he would be entitled to the rights. The price of the stock usually declines by the same amount the rights initially sell for. If, for example, the rights open on the day the stock sells ex-rights for $1.00, then the price of both the put and call options are reduced by $1.00. This is the same way in which regular dividends are handled.

Writing Options

In 1884, when Russell Sage was bullish and expected a substantial market advance, he wrote put options. If the price of the stock advanced, the holder would allow his option to expire and Mr. Sage would earn the premium. He was speculating that the market would act as he predicted. We know it did not, and he lost a large fortune. Is the writing of options speculative? Yes. But if certain principles are followed, option writing can be both instructive and profitable.

Types of Options that are Written

1. A call option—an option allowing the holder to demand delivery from the writer of 100 shares of stock during the life of the contract at a specified price.
2. A put option—an option allowing the holder to sell to the writer 100 shares of stock during the life of the contract at a specified price.
3. A straddle option—a combination of a put and a call option that allows the holder or holders to exercise either option for 100 shares of stock or both options against the writer, during the life of the contract at a specified price. Until now we have examined only the buying or writing of straight put and calls, but since the majority of option writing is negotiated in straddles, let us examine this type of option.

To illustrate: Mr. A calls his broker and places an order to buy two calls on PDQ at $35 for $300, each for 95 days. The broker relays the bid to the put and call dealer. It is up to the dealer to find a writer for this bid. Most experienced writers do not like to write straight calls, because the premiums received do not return an adequate yield for the risk involved. In addition, if the writer is bullish when he writes puts, the writer of call options should be bearish when he writes calls. The put and call broker must now find a writer who is bearish and will accept the premium offered. This is not an easy task. In order to complete Mr. A's order for two calls and find a writer willing to guarantee delivery of the options, the put and call dealer has devised an ingenious method called "conversion."

The dealer offers the writer $450 to write a *straddle,* combining one put and one call, at $35, expiring in ninety-five days on 100 shares of PDQ. The writer accepts. The put and call dealer now has one call and one put, but he needs two calls. How can he change a put into a call? The answer is by conversion. What is conversion? It is a method that enables the put and call broker to exchange a put with a New York Stock Exchange member for a call. The following procedure ensues:

1. The put and call dealer will deliver to a member firm of the New York Stock Exchange a put against which the New York Stock Exchange firm will purchase 100 shares of PDQ.

2. The New York Stock Exchange firm (against this riskless position) then issues a call option to the put and call dealer.
3. The put and call dealer then pays the firm interest for the use of its money.

As the demand for calls or puts increases, the demand for conversion money also increases. The rate of interest the put and call dealers pay varies with the money market conditions. Rarely do rates reach the level at which any one other than a member firm of the New York Stock Exchange could profitably participate in the conversion business. The payment of commissions precludes a non-member from converting puts into calls, or calls into puts.

Let us examine the possibilities for the straddle writer. If the option is called, the following takes place:

			Costs	Receipts
Bought 100 shares	$35		$ 3,500	
Plus commission			60	
Premium received				$450
Called on 100 shares	$35	$ 3,500		
Less commission		60		$ 3,440
			3,560	$ 3,890
				−3,560
Net Profit for 95 days				$ 330

This is a return of approximately 10.6 per cent quarterly, which translates into over 40 per cent on an annual basis if successfully carried out during the balance of the year.

If the option is put, the following occurs:

			Costs	Receipts
Bought 100 shares	$35		$ 3,500	
Commission			60	
Premium received				$450
Put on 100 shares	$35		3,500	
Less dividend		$60		
Plus commission		60		
			$ 7,060	$450
			−450	
Cost 200 shares			$ 6,610	
Cost 100 shares			$ 3,305	

In this case the writer reduced the average cost of owning 200 shares. Writing straddles can then be a method of building a portfolio. A writer should write straddles or puts only if he is willing to buy additional shares of the same company.

Premiums Paid

The premiums paid by the put and call dealer vary considerably from stock to stock and from day to day. Premiums on straddles seldom fall below 40 per cent on an annualized basis and can sometimes exceed 100 per cent. Most options are written on stocks listed on the New York Stock Exchange, with considerably less written on the American Exchange and still fewer for over-the-counter issues. It isn't that there is no demand for options on these other exchanges, but simply that the writers do not wish to assume the additional risk.

A *Strip Option* is a straddle with an additional put. If a writer is extremely bullish, he can receive an extra premium for the additional put, thereby increasing his yield if the stock is called.

A *Strap Option* is a straddle with an extra call. The writer may, instead of writing two straddles, decide that he wishes to own a maximum of 300 shares. If the stock falls he is only obligated to buy an additional 100 shares. The writer receives the premium for the straddle plus an extra premium for the call.

Neither the strip nor the strap options are popular, but there are occasions when writers or sellers of options are willing to assume these additional risks.

ADVANTAGES AND DISADVANTAGES OF OPTION BUYING

Advantages

1. Limited loss
2. Unlimited profits
3. Can be used to ensure profits
4. Can be used to average
5. Can be used to facilitate trading
6. Can be used for tax advantages

Disadvantages

1. Stock must rise or fall more than the cost of the option before buyer can make a profit.
2. Option good only for limited period.
3. Onus is on buyer to judge when is the best time to execute option.

4. More difficult to buy options than stocks.
5. If buyer executes option early, the remaining time on contract is a lost asset.

METHODS OF WRITING OPTIONS

1. Write "naked" puts if you are bullish.
2. Write "naked" calls if you are bearish.
3. Write straddles if you are bullish or bearish.
4. Write strips if you are bullish.
5. Write straps if you do not wish to write two straddles and want to limit your obligation to buy only 100 additional shares.

A writer writes naked when he does not own the stock to deliver against the option. He is also naked when he writes a put option and is not short in the stock he wrote the option against. Whenever a straddle is written, the writer is always naked on one side of the option.

Writers include individuals, institutions, pension funds, and some mutual funds that either wish to earn a higher return on their portfolio or to accumulate securities below the current market price. The minimum capital suggested is $100,000, with no limitation on the maximum amount. There are some individuals who write options with less than $100,000, but they cannot diversify properly or spread their risk over a period of several months.

Example—Two Assumptions

1. Most options written are straddles (one put and one call).
2. Put and call dealers convert puts into calls by using the method just described, convert calls into puts.

Since a New York Stock Exchange firm receives interest only on its capital, it rarely, if ever, risks any of this capital to increase its yield. If you recall, the firm bought 100 shares of PDQ at $35 and issued a call option to the put and call dealer in exchange for a put option and interest on the amount the dealer had invested. Therefore, if PDQ rises and the stock is called, the firm delivers the stock. If the stock is called a month prior to the expiration date, the member firm earns its interest for the full period since it received the interest when it issued the call option.

If, however, the price of PDQ falls below the option price, the buyer of the calls on 200 shares allows them to expire. The NYSE firm waits until the last possible moment (options expire at 3:15 p.m. New York Time) to exercise its put option. The firm wants to be absolutely sure that the call option cannot be exercised after they have put the stock to the writer of the straddle. The amount lost on the 100 shares of PDQ is made up by the amount gained on the Put.

The experienced writer should always ask the put and call dealer if he is converting. If the answer is yes, the writer can invest his capital by writing straddles over a period of time and will know exactly when he is obligated to buy more stock against his outstanding contracts. The writer with $100,000 can diversify by writing approximately $8,000 per week over a three-month period. Therefore, his put options will not all fall due at the same time. Regardless of how bullish an individual is on the market, bear markets strike suddenly.

ADVANTAGES AND DISADVANTAGES OF WRITING (SELLING) OPTIONS

Advantages

1. The writer can earn substantial return on capital.
2. He can spread risk.
3. He can possibly obtain tax advantages.
4. Put and call business is stimulating to an investor.
5. The writer is the recipient of many bids on stocks he has never heard of. He can investigate and sometimes discover new growth companies.

Disadvantages

1. Writer assumes substantial risk in writing naked puts and calls and straddles.
2. Gains can be limited to the amount of the premium.
3. Few brokers fully understand options.

THE CHICAGO BOARD OPTIONS EXCHANGE

Because the demand for puts and calls grew so rapidly, the Chicago Board of Trade decided to open an exchange devoted exclusively to options on securities.

Advantages of CBOE over Put and Call Dealers

1. It provides a central market place to buy and sell options.
2. The buyer or writer of options has a choice of several expiration dates and often a choice of different option prices.
3. Prices for all options are listed daily in financial publications.
4. Volume of all trades is shown daily.
5. All buyers and writers have the advantage of a two-way auction market.
6. Buyer of option and seller of option can close out their options anytime they wish and receive a current market price.

Chicago Board Options Exchange

Friday, August 23, 1974

Closing prices of all options. Sales unit is 100 shares. Security description includes exercise price.

Option & price	— Oct — Vol.	Last	— Jan — Vol.	Last	— Apr — Vol.	Last	Stock Close
Am Tel 50	42	⅛	151	½	b	b	43⅛
Am Tel 45	281	13-16	263	1 13-16	778	2¼	43⅛
Atl R .. 90	151	1	66	2¾	61	3⅞	76½
Atl R .. 100	69	¼	b	b	b	b	76½
Avon ... 60	83	1-16	b	b	b	b	23½
Avon ... 50	2	⅛	a	a	b	b	23½
Avon 45	10	⅛	55	¼	b	b	23½
Avon ... 40	105	⅛	1	⅝	b	b	23½
Avon .. 35	76	⅜	88	¾	10	1 9-16	23½
Avon .. 30	600	⅞	50	1¾	42	2⅝	23½
Beth S . 30	193	2⅛	93	3¼	33	4	30⅛
Beth S . 35	54	11-16	39	1⅜	b	b	30⅛
Bruns . 15	183	3-16	349	7-16	98	¾	9
Bruns .. 10	192	11-16	120	1⅛	261	1½	9
Citicp .. 40	178	⅞	84	9-16	b	b	26⅛
Citicp .. 35	222	7-16	119	1⅛	b	b	26⅛
Citicp .. 30	223	1 7-16	98	2⅝	52	3⅞	26⅛
Eas Kd 120	28	⅛	b	b	b	b	75
Eas Kd 100	258	½	102	1½	35	3	75
Eas Kd 90	606	1 9-16	202	3⅞	59	5½	75
Exxon .. 90	172	¼	b	b	b	b	68⅝
Exxon . 80	290	15-16	89	2¼	70	3¾	68⅝
Exxon ..70	181	3½	54	6	10	7½	68⅝
Ford 50	100	¼	19	13-16	b	b	39⅜
Ford ... 45	103	¾	29	1½	19	2⅜	39⅜
Ford .. 40	108	2⅛	23	3⅛	3	4	39⅜
Glf Wn 25	40	⅜	58	⅞	b	b	20¼
Glf Wn 20	149	1 9-16	80	2¼	59	2¾	20¼
Gt Wst 20	193	⅛	122	⅛	b	b	6¾
Gt Wst 15	173	⅛	115	⅜	b	b	6¾
Gt Wst 10	323	⅜	324	⅝	659	1	6¾
I B M 270	225	5-16	b	b	b	b	190
I B M 240	129	1¼	94	5⅛	b	b	190
I B M 220	499	4½	97	11	7	15⅞	190
I B M 200	491	11⅝	62	19½	25	25¼	190
I N A .. 35	a	a	b	b	b	b	
I N A .. 40	83	1-16	b	b	b	b	20⅜
I N A .. 30	12	⅛	6	¼	b	b	20⅜
I N A .. 25	2	5-16	37	¾	74	1 3-16	20⅜
I T T .. 30	59	1-16	b	b	b	b	18⅜
I T T .. 25	48	¼	25	11-16	b	b	18⅜
I T T .. 20	290	1 1-16	142	1⅞	67	2½	18⅜
In Har . 30	68	1-16	b	b	b	b	20¼
In Har 25	72	5-16	107	¾	58	1 1-16	20¼
Kerr M 65	223	½	17	1½	14	2½	48⅞
Kerr M 75	42	⅛	b	b	b	b	48⅞
Kerr M 85	21	1-16	b	b	b	b	48⅞
Kerr M 55	95	2	15	3⅞	a	a	48⅞
Kresge . 35	108	⅛	29	11-16	b	b	25¼
Kresge 30	62	¾	70	1⅞	51	2¾	25¼
Loews .. 25	137	3-16	b	b	b	b	13⅞
Loews .. 20	59	¼	154	7-16	b	b	13⅞
Loews 15	323	13-16	98	1 7-16	95	1 13-16	13⅞
M M M 75	85	¼	12	1	a	a	58
M M M 65	48	1⅜	19	3	a	a	58
Mc Don 60	4	⅛	123	7-16	b	b	31
Mc Don 50	276	¼	122	⅞	b	b	31
Mc Don 40	536	1¼	231	2½	71	4	31
Merck .. 80	106	⅛	2	¾	b	b	57⅝
Merck ..70	118	13-16	18	1¾	3	3⅛	57⅝
Merck ..60	147	3¼	85	4¾	13	6¼	57⅝
Monsan 60	305	2⅝	124	4¾	26	6⅜	55½
Nw Air 25	112	5-16	52	15-16	b	b	17
Nw Air 20	233	1⅛	93	1 15-16	107	2⅝	17
Pnz U .. 25	48	⅛	a	a	b	b	17½
Pnz U 20	171	13-16	100	1 13-16	13	2⅜	17½
Pnz U .. 15	109	3¼	32	4¼	b	b	17½
Pnz U 250	1	5-16	b	b	b	b	17½
Polar .. 80	207	1-16	b	b	b	b	19⅝
Polar .. 70	324	1-16	b	b	b	b	19⅝
Polar .. 60	144	1-16	7	1-16	b	b	19⅝
Polar .. 45	94	⅛	12	7-16	b	b	19⅝
Polar .. 40	149	⅛	89	½	b	b	19⅝
Polar .. 35	249	5-16	95	13-16	b	b	19⅝
Polar .. 30	287	½	200	1 5-16	b	b	19⅝
Polar .. 25	1202	1⅜	281	2½	146	3½	19⅝
R C A . 20	62	⅛	31	5-16	b	b	12⅞
R C A .. 15	283	7-16	50	1	118	1 7-16	12⅞
Sears .. 90	3	1-16	b	b	b	b	55⅛
Sears .. 80	34	⅛	113	½	12	1½	55⅛
Sears . 70	117	⅝	107	1⅛	32	2⅝	55⅛
Sperry ..40	67	5-16	59	¾	b	b	28⅛
Sperry . 45	39	⅛	b	b	b	b	28⅛
Sperry . 35	330	¾	70	1¾	68	3	28⅛
Tex In 120	19	⅛	b	b	b	b	73⅝
Tex In . 90	194	⅞	53	3	3	4¼	73⅝
Tex In . 80	163	3⅜	40	6	22	8¼	73⅝
Tex In 100	b	b	43	1⅛	b	b	73⅝
Upjohn 75	175	15-16	165	2⅜	13	3¾	57⅜
Upjohn 85	133	⅜	75	1⅛	b	b	57⅜
Upjohn 65	491	3	87	5¾	40	7¼	57⅜
Weyerh 35	66	1 1-16	14	2¼	23	3¼	30⅝
Weyerh 40	13	⅛	2	1 1-16	b	b	30⅝
Weyerh . 45	35	⅛	a	a	b	b	30⅝
Xerox 120	73	⅛	20	½	28	1⅛	77¼
Xerox 100	172	11-16	108	1⅝	119	3½	77¼
Xerox .. 90	275	1⅝	78	3¾	43	5½	77¼
Xerox .. 80	339	4¾	141	7⅜	96	9¼	77¼

Total volume 26,898. Open interest 400,762.

a—Not traded. b—Unavailable.

Disadvantages of CBOE

1. Only call options are traded on the CBOE—no puts or straddles are handled.
2. Only a small percentage of the stocks listed on the NYSE are traded on the CBOE.
3. No stocks traded on the American Stock Exchange or the Over-the-Counter markets have call options on the CBOE.

As the Chicago Board Options Exchange market grows, almost all the current disadvantages will be eliminated and both the writer and the buyer will be able to meet in a central market place to buy and sell options.

CHICAGO BOARD OPTIONS EXCHANGE DAILY LISTING

The Chicago Board Options Exchange listing gives the following information each day:

1. Closing prices of all options
2. Complete list of all options available to trade
3. Price or prices at which various options can be exercised
4. Volume on each option for each expiration date
6. General direction of stock market

To illustrate: The first option listed on the CBOE is American Telephone, and the option can be exercised at $50. Notice that there are three different options at $50—one expiring in October, another in January, and the last in April. These are three separate and different options on the same stock. The only difference is the expiration date. Usually the longer the expiration date, the larger the premium paid for the option. The October option closed at 1/8 on 42 trades of 100 shares each. Since American Telephone closed at 43 1/8, the option price of $50 is almost seven points above the stock's closing price. Therefore, the option has little value.

The option expiring in January sold 151 trades, 100 shares each unit, at ½. A speculator will be willing to pay more for this option since the expiration date is three months later than the expiration date of the first option.

Listed directly under the $50 option is the American Telephone $45 option. This price is less than two points away from the closing price of the stock and is worth more. In this case, 281 trades closed for 13/16, expiring in October, 263 trades for 1 13/16, and 778 trades at 2¼. Again, the longer the expiration, the larger the premium.

If you look down the list to Avon, you will see options trading at $60, $50, $45, $35, and $30. The CBOE starts to trade in the new options only when the stock price reaches a new level. As a stock drops in price or rises in price the CBOE will open another option. The CBOE determines whether this level is every five or ten points, which usually depends on the price and volatility of the stock. Avon evidently suffered a precipitous drop in price since the exchange listed the $60 option price a little over six months ago. The longest option price is nine months, and Avon's October option still had a little over two months before expiration.

There are four option periods expiring January 30th, April 30th, July 31st, and October 31st. As each period expires, it is eliminated from the CBOE listing and a new contract is opened for another period nine months in the future. On November 1st, instead of listing October, January, and April, the exchange will list January, April, and July.

If you continue down the list, you will notice that in almost every situation each new option listed for the same stock is at a lower price. This situation undoubtedly signifies a bear market, with prices falling quite rapidly. Kerr McGee resisted this trend and rose from $65 to $85 before it declined to below $50.

It is quite obvious that the vast majority of call options will not be executed in this market atmosphere. It is also equally obvious that the writers of these options, if they wrote them naked, will not have to worry about delivering stock. If, on the other hand, they own the security they wrote the option against, then they suffer the loss on this security less the price of the option received. The American Stock Exchange now trades in options that are not included on the CBOE. The popularity of option buying and writing is now increasing at a rapid rate.

Although option buying and option writing is not recommended for every investor or speculator, he should understand the basic principles of this little understood but highly useful tool.

QUESTIONS

1. Define the terms "put," "call," and "warrant."
2. Describe and define an option dealer.
3. Are put and call options securities? Of what significance is this?
4. Is it necessary to have a writer or a seller of options for every buyer? Explain.
5. Describe at least three ways in which puts and calls can be used.
6. Explain and give an example of how a dividend, a stock dividend, and a stock split is adjusted to the option price.
7. Define the term "straddle." Why did it become popular with writers of options?
8. Explain the term "conversion."
9. List some of the pros and cons of option buying.

10. What does writing naked mean? Give an example.
11. Who usually writes options?
12. List some of the advantages and disadvantages of writing options.
13. What is the Chicago Board Option Exchange?
14. Does a listed exchange for options give the buyer any advantage?
15. When does the CBOE allow the same stock to be traded at a different price?
16. In what different periods do CBOE options expire?
17. Do you feel that every speculator and investor should understand options? Why?

9

MUTUAL FUNDS, CLOSED END FUNDS, NO LOAD FUNDS, AND PENSION FUNDS

Most Americans prefer to do their own investing. Right or wrong, experienced or inexperienced, they will no doubt continue to operate in this manner. However, a large number of the over 30 million shareholders seek the help of men who devote their full time to investments. Without realizing it, many investors, in turning over their savings to banks and insurance companies, have taken the first step in managing their money. These banks and insurance companies then invest this money and pay the investor interest.

Personally managed investment requires some background in finance and economics. It is not necessary to have a degree in the subject, but it does require that an investor spend a great deal of time reading and analyzing financial data. He must have the ability to make his own decisions not only on what to buy and when to buy it, but on what to sell and when to sell it. And finally, one of the toughest tests an investor has to meet is the courage to admit he has made an error. Only time and experience can develop these talents, but when an investor has acquired the ability to manage his own portfolio, the results can be very gratifying.

It is almost impossible for an investor to be completely independent. He cannot possibly do all his own research and investigation. He needs assistance. Reading financial publications regularly is one recognition of this need. Newspapers, magazines, economic letters, and brokerage reports are some of the tools he must utilize.

For many people who do not have the inclination, the time, or the background to handle their own investments, mutual funds stand ready to provide the service. Mutual funds have been the recipient of billions of dollars of this investment money.

A mutual fund is an open-end investment company, usually a corporation, but it may be a trust, without a fixed capitalization, which constantly sells and buys its own shares in the Over-the-Counter Market. In essence, investors pool their money in order to obtain management and diversification.

These funds are regulated by the Investment Company Act of 1940. All mutual funds are registered under this act.

Commonly Used Terms

1. Public Offering Price is the price at which shares are first offered to the public. After this initial offering, shares are then sold for the net asset value minus commission, if any.

2. Net Asset Value is the total of a fund's securities and other assets less the total liabilities, divided by the number of shares outstanding. It is the same as book value. The Investment Company Act of 1940 requires a mutual fund to compute its net asset value at least once each day at the close of the New York Stock Exchange. Some funds compute the N.A.V. twice each day.

3. Bid Price of a Fund is the net asset value per share. This price is computed daily and appears in the newspapers.

4. The Asked price is the bid price, or the net asset value plus the commission or sales charge.

5. Sales Charge of a Fund, under the Investment Act of 1940, must be stated as a percentage of the offering price. If the sales charge is 8 per cent and the asked price is $15, the sales charge per share will be $1.20.

6. Dividends are paid out of the income from the securities invested in a fund's portfolio.

7. Capital Gains Distribution represents a payment to the shareholders of the gains made on the sale of a fund's securities. These gains, when available, are usually paid once a year. They should not be considered part of the dividend return but as a return of capital. In order for the shareholder to keep his investment intact, he should reinvest this capital gains distribution.

8. Redemption Privilege takes into consideration one of the three ideals of an investment—liquidity. Mutual funds redeem their shares at the current net asset value. In most instances there is no redemption charge. These shares are sold back to the fund and not to anther shareholder. Actually, open-end investment companies or mutual funds constantly sell and buy back shares in their company. With these funds they build a portfolio of securities enabling a small investor to establish diversification. A mutual fund may own a hundred securities that an individual could not buy except by pooling his resources with others. The investment principle of diversification spreads the risk over many securities.

Advantages of Mutual Funds

1. They provide diversification.
2. They provide professional management.
3. They enable an investor to reinvest his dividends.
4. They encourage individuals who would not ordinarily buy shares to become investors.
5. They enable an investor to take advantage of dollar cost averaging.
6. Some mutual funds offer investors a conversion privilege. They manage several different funds involving income stocks, growth stocks, etc., and they often allow an investor to switch from one fund to another without an additional sales charge.
7. Withdrawal plans funds allow investors to receive monthly payments from their accounts. These withdrawals are made out of principal and dividends.
8. Some funds provide life insurance with periodic investment plans. An investor is then assured that all payments will be made in the event of death.

Disadvantages of Mutual Funds

1. Sales charge is high, approximately 8 per cent.
2. An investor has no control over which securities are bought and sold.
3. An investor, if he must sell early, will usually suffer a loss as a result of the sales charge.
4. Funds charge a management fee averaging about ½ of 1 per cent of the total net assets.
5. Some contractual plans, in which an investor agrees to buy shares periodically over a five- or 10-year period charge the major portion of the sales charge in the early years. If an investor stops buying, he receives no refund on these sales charges.

Types of Mutual Funds

1. Balanced Funds
2. Growth Funds
3. Specialized Funds
4. Bond Funds
5. Income Funds
6. Foreign Investment Funds
7. No Load Funds

8. Money Market Funds
9. Closed-end Funds

Balanced funds attempt to diversify their portfolios by maintaining a balance of bonds, preferred stocks, and common stocks. These funds are not aggressive and follow the major investment objective of safety of principal.

Growth funds are aggressive and concentrate mainly on common stocks. Many of these companies are in new industries and are relatively unknown. Gains can be rapid if management is right, but losses are part of the growth stock risk.

Specialized funds specialize in one specific industry. It could be computers, chemicals, steels, utilities, etc. The principle of diversification is abandoned by these specialized funds in order to attain maximum capital gains. An investor must be extremely careful in selecting the right fund, because industry favor in the stock market waxes and wanes.

Bond funds specialize in building a portfolio of corporate or municipal bonds. They are conservative in nature and appeal to an investor seeking both safety of principal and income.

Income funds invest primarily in high-yield common stocks and appeal to investors who are seeking income and are willing to assume the risks of common stock ownership.

Foreign investment funds appeal primarily to investors seeking geographical diversification. The securities of Japanese, German, French, English, Dutch, and other foreign corporations are purchased by these funds. It is difficult for an investor, regardless of how sophisticated he is, to thoroughly analyze a foreign company. These funds enable him to spread his risk.

No load funds do not assess their customers a sales charge. In 1971 funds that invoked sales charges totaled 90% of all mutual fund sales, with the no load funds making up the difference. The reason should be obvious. No load funds do not maintain sales forces or large merchandising operations. Nevertheless, they have been growing at an impressive rate. In 1972 they accounted for over 13 per cent of sales and just under 17 per cent in 1973. One of the disadvantages of buying mutual funds is removed as a result of charging no commission. Various studies show that there is little difference in the performance of load and no load funds.

In 1974, a new concept of selling money market instruments boosted their share to over 38 per cent of all fund sales. Investors withdrew their funds from banks and placed them in these funds in order to take advantage of the high interest rates. Treasury bills and certificates of deposit have minimum amounts that can be purchased, and these minimums are usually beyond the limits of the small investor. These new funds enable him to realize higher-yields by buying the money funds. The only cost is the management fee.

The no load funds were growing at over 25 per cent per year even before these new money market funds were sold and will probably resume this growth pattern once the need for money market instruments abates.

Closed-end funds are usually corporations that specialize in managing investments and not in selling a product or a service. They have a fixed number of shares and if the company is public these shares may be bought and sold on an exchange at standard commission rates. A closed-end fund is not a mutual fund, since its shares are fixed. A mutual fund is an open-end investment company. There is no limit to the number of shares it can sell.

Closed-end funds are similar to mutual funds in that they both offer an investor diversification and management.

Examples of Closed End Funds

1. Lehman Corporation
2. Madison Fund General Public Service
3. Tri-Continental

All are traded on the New York Stock Exchange.

Advantages of Closed-end Investment Company

1. Commissions are less than the sales charge of a mutual fund.
2. Investor can sometimes buy these shares below net asset value.
3. Speculators may buy and sell on margin.
4. Speculators may go short.
5. The speculative principle of leverage may be used by purchasing the "dual funds."

Disadvantages of Closed-end Investment Company

1. The investment principle of dollar cost averaging cannot be used because these institutions do not generate a steady flow of money.
2. A closed-end fund may offer additional shares to its own shareholders or to the public. These shares may be sold at a premium or a discount from net asset value.
3. An investor can possibly buy these shares at a premium and sell them at a discount.

A closed end investment company does not have an open registration to sell additional shares in the same manner as a mutual fund. Therefore, such companies do not have a continuing flow of money and cannot dollar cost average. To raise additional money they must file a registration statement with the SEC, and at the time of the issuance of these new shares its stock may be selling at a premium or a discount. It is then entirely possible for an investor to pay a premium during a buoyant market and for some reason be forced to sell when the shares are selling at a discount from their net asset value. The proper timing of the purchase and sale of these securities then becomes an additional problem to the investor.

Dual Funds and the Principle of Leverage

A special type of closed-end investment company has been developing over the past ten years. A dual fund offers two types of securities, income and capital shares. The two types of stocks are issued in equal dollar amounts.

The owner of the income shares is entitled to all net dividends and interest paid to the fund on both classes of securities. He does not participate in any capital appreciation. The owner of the capital shares profits from the capital gains on all the shares held by the fund. In addition, any decrease in the value of the fund up to 50 per cent affects only the owners of the capital shares. Any losses in excess of 50 per cent are shared by the income shareholders.

Leverage is defined in physical terms as the mechanical advantage or power gained by using a lever. Financial leverage is usually gained by using borrowed money. A speculator who buys stock in his margin account, which enables him to borrow money from his broker, is using the principle of leverage. If the margin requirements are 50 per cent, his losses or gains are twice what they would be if he bought the stock outright.

In the case of dual funds, the leverage factor exists for both classes of stock. Income shareholders are giving up their chances for capital gains by accepting the income on twice their investment. Capital shareholders are giving up their right to income in the hope of participating in twice the gain. Management sets a call date at which time the income shares are recalled. Until that time neither class of shares are redeemable by the company. The fund then may become an open-end investment company.

Closed-end Bond Funds

Bonds usually pay interest twice a year, but many investors need income on a more regular basis. During the past few years insurance companies and banks have sold shares in companies they manage for the sole purpose of buying debt instruments. Massachusetts Mutual Income Shares and Pacific American Income Shares are two of these bond funds. They pay dividends quarterly. The investor owns shares in these companies, and although the company receives interest from its investments, the shareholders receive dividends from the company.

These bond funds may sell at a premium or a discount from their asset value. If interest rates rise, the price of the shares will fall because investors will demand a higher return on their money. Falling interest rates will cause the shares to increase in price because the portfolio of bonds will rise to reflect lower interest rates. As the net asset value of the bond fund increases, the market value usually follows.

Important Provisions of the Securities Act of 1933

1. As we know securities must be registered with the SEC before they may be offered for sale accompanied by a current prospectus. A prospectus must be updated every sixteen months.
2. Any solicitation of shares must be accompanied by a prospectus for open-end investment company shares. It is extremely important to understand that the SEC does not pass on the merits of an investment but tries to make sure that all significant facts are contained in the prospectus to enable an investor to make a decision.

A Prospectus Contains Some of the Following Information

1. Type of company—open end or closed end
2. Offering Price
3. Commissions
4. Redemption features
5. Computation of Net Asset Value
6. Objectives of the company

The Securities Exchange Act of 1934, as mentioned earlier, sets forth regulations for all exchanges, brokers, and dealers. The act was amended in 1939, setting up the National Association of Security Dealers. The N.A.S.D. sets "Rules of Fair Practice" that regulate the sales of investment company shares.

The securities industry is very closely regulated but investment companies are scrutinized even more so, at every level of authority, from the securities acts of 1933 and 1934, through the Investment Company Act of 1940, the Federal Reserve Board, and finally to the National Association of Security Dealers.

Some Important Provisions to Protect the Investor

1. An N.A.S.D. member who computes the rate of return on investment company shares by adding the capital gain distribution to the dividend is in violation of the Rules of Fair Practice.
2. Commissions on mutual funds are scaled down as purchases increase. If a sale is made in dollar amounts just below the point at which the sales charge is reduced, it is contrary to the Rules of Fair Practice.

3. The principal underwriter may not offer anything of material value beyond the discounts or concessions set forth in the prospectus to a member or a registered representative.
4. No N.A.S.D. member shall profit himself by withholding a customer's order to buy shares of an open-end investment company.

The Investment Company Act of 1940 provides rules of investment company procedure but does not entail supervision by any federal or state agency.

Some Important Provisions of the Investment Company Act of 1940

1. It prohibits investment companies from purchasing securities on margin. Some investment companies are permitted to make short sales.
2. A majority vote of the stockholders is required before an investment company may change any of its policies.
3. The act prohibits open-end investment companies from issuing senior securities (preferred stocks and bonds). Closed-end funds are not so restricted.
4. The Internal Revenue Code affords advantageous tax treatment beneficial to shareholders if certain requirements are met. The following are some of these requirements:

   a. The investment company must be a domestic corporation.

   b. At least 90 per cent of its gross income must be from dividends and interest from securities the investment company holds.

   c. It must distribute to its shareholders not less than 90 per cent of its net income during any taxable year.

The effect of this income tax provision is to avoid the "double taxation" of dividends. Before a regular corporation pays a dividend, it pays federal income taxes. Then when the investor receives the dividend, he pays taxes again. If an investment company falls within the rules of Subchapter M of the Internal Revenue Code, it does not pay federal income taxes. Only the investor pays taxes on the amount received.

Dividends to an investor are treated as ordinary income, but he may exclude $100 from the total of all dividends received from domestic corporations. Any capital gain, if held longer than six months and one day by the investment company and then distributed to the investor, is taxed as a long-term capital gain.

The exceptional growth of Real Estate Investment Trusts in the early 1970s owed its success to Subchapter M of the Internal Revenue Code. Other companies, such as Mesabi, which receives most of its income from royalties, conformed to the requirements of a "regulated investment company" and avoided paying double taxes.

Funds are listed by name, net asset value, offering price, and net change. No dividends are listed. The payment of dividends from income

Mutual Funds

Friday, September 13, 1974

Price ranges for investment companies, as quoted by the National Association of Securities Dealers. NAV stands for net asset value per share; the offering includes net asset value plus maximum sales charge, if any.

	Off. NAV NAV Prc. Chg.			Off. NAV NAV Prc. Chg
Adm Gwth	3.16. 3.46— .05		Div Shrs	2.27 2.49— .04
Adm Incm	2.86 3.13— .03		Ntwide	6.68 7.31— .08
Adm Insur	6.55 7.18— .06		NY Vent	7.58 8.30— .10
Adviser Fd	3.46 3.78— .03		C G Fund	6.06 6.55— .14
Aetna Fnd	4.75 5.19— .15		Century Sh	6.77 7.40— .12
Aetna InSh	10.61 11.60— .01		Chalng Inv	6.00 6.56— .11
Afutur (v)	4.85 4.85— .14		**Channing Funds:**	
AGE Fund	3.58 3.65+ .04		Amercn	.86 .94— .01
Allstate	6.53 7.02— .14		Balanc	7.15 7.81— .09
Alpha Fnd	7.48 8.17— .14		Bond Fd	7.24 7.91— .03
Amcap Fd	2.91 3.18— .07		Eqty Gth	4.76 5.20— .09
Am Birthrt	9.55 10.49— .03		Eqty Prg	1.70 1.86— .03
AmDiv Inv	5.75 6.28— .12		Fnd Amr	4.74 5.18— .10
Am Equity	3.07 3.36— .06		Growth	3.03 3.31— .05
American Express Funds:			Income	5.09 5.56— .04
Capital	4.05 4.43— .12		Prov Inc	2.86 3.13— .04
Income	6.41 7.01— .06		Special	1.05 1.15— .01
Invest	5.60 6.12— .08		Venture	4.49 4.91— .09
Spec Fnd	4.05 4.43— .13		Charter Fd	7.22 7.89— .15
Stock Fd	4.64 5.07— .11		**Chase Group of Boston:**	
Am Grwth	3.32 3.63— .04		Fnd Bost	4.46 4.87— .07
Am Ins Ind	3.21 3.51— .04		Front Cp	2.82 3.08— .05
AmInv (v)	2.90 2.90— .07		ShTr Bos	5.01 5.48— .08
Am Mutual	6.08 6.64— .08		Special	3.54 3.87— .05
AmNat Gw	1.54 1.68— .03		Chem Fnd	6.31 6.90— .16
Anchor Group:			**CNA Management Funds:**	
Growth	4.50 4.93— .12		Liberty	3.11 3.40— .05
Income	5.48 6.01— .02		Manhtn	2.06 2.25— .06
Reserv	10.20 11.18+ .01		Schus Fd	x4.44 4.85— .21
Spectm	2.78 3.05— .05		Schus Sp	4.26 4.66— .10
Fund Inv	4.70 5.15— .11		TMR Ap	4.46 4.87— .11
Audax Fnd	4.57 5.00— .03		**Colonial Funds:**	
Wa Natl	7.18 7.87— .15		Convert	7.25 7.92— .05
Axe-Houghton:			Equity	1.73 1.89— .04
Fund A	3.69 4.01— .02		Fund	7.51 8.21— .11
Fund B	5.69 6.18— .06		Growth	3.66 4.00— .09
Stock Fd	4.49 4.91+ .01		Income	7.65 8.36— .03
Axe Scie	3.13 3.40— .02		Ventur	1.67 1.83— .03
BLC Gwth	6.40 6.99— .15		ColGth (v)	8.53 8.53— .15
Babson (v)	6.99 6.99— .22		**Commonwealth Trust:**	
Bayrock	4.31 4.71— .06		A & B	.70 .75 ..
Bayrok Gr	3.48 3.80— .05		C	1.00 1.08— .01
BeacHI (v)	6.08 6.08— .06		Cmpass Gr	3.88 4.24— .03
Beacnl (v)	6.87 6.87— .09		Comp Cap	3.32 3.64— .06
Bondsk Cp	3.16 3.45— .05		Comp BdSt	6.34 6.89— .12
Berksh Gw	2.24 2.45— .05		Composit	5.29 5.75— .21
Bos Found	6.50 7.21— .18		Concrd (v)	6.28 6.28— .08
Brown Fnd	1.83 1.89— .10		Consol Inv	6.25 6.75— .25
Burnm (v)	7.01 7.01— .12		Constlatn	3.66 3.66— .09
Calvin Bullock Funds:			ContMt (v)	5.95 5.95— .08
Bullock	8.37 9.16— .13		Coutry Cap	7.96 8.61— .14
Canadn	8.12 8.89+ .07		Crown Dal	4.00 4.37— .08

and distributions of capital are separate. An investor should refer to the fund's prospectus for the history of dividends paid.

Some investment companies manage many different types of funds, thus enabling an investor to buy one type (growth) during his peak earning years and switch to another type (income) when his income begins to abate. The letter "v" next to a company indicates that the fund is a no load fund. The net asset value and the offering price are the same.

Mutual funds, like securities, must be studied by an investor to determine which one is best qualified to fill his needs. The size and the management capabilities vary greatly. Many studies of funds are made periodically by financial services, and an investor should study these reports carefully before deciding which fund to buy.

Closed-end vs. Open-end Investment Companies

1. Public Offering.   A closed-end offering can be presented for sale only once unless a new registration statement is filed with the SEC.

An open-end offering to the public is continuous. The prospectus must be brought up to date at least once every sixteen months.

2. Who Redeems Shares?   A closed-end fund does not redeem its own shares. The owner must sell on the open market.

Under the Investment Act of 1940, an open-end fund must make payment within seven days.

3. What Price is Received at Redemption?   A closed-end fund may be selling at a premium or discount at the time of sale.

The price of an open-end is usually at net asset value. Sometimes a redemption charge of 1 per cent or 2 per cent is deducted.

4. What is the Relation of Purchase Price to Net Asset Value?   A closed-end purchase price may exceed or be less than the net asset value. The price often depends on investor psychology.

An open-end purchase price is based on the net asset value plus the sales charge.

5. Principle of Dollar Cost Averaging.   Closed-end funds do not generate a continuous flow of money since shares are only issued once. A fund should maintain buying reserves to take advantage of market dips.

Theoretically the flow of money in open-end funds is continuous, thus enabling the funds to buy more shares during market dips. However, during some market sell-offs the public holds back on investing and even sells more than it buys.

Managed Accounts with Brokerage Firms

There are some investors who prefer to have their accounts managed by a firm. They reason that many of these firms spend millions of dollars in research and that they should take advantage of this specialized inform-ation. Many firms have branch offices in major cities throughout the world and can therefore act quickly on events affecting the market. Some firms charge an advisory fee; others do not. Those firms that charge a fee reason that they are being paid for the assets managed and are not just generating commission income for the firm.

Disadvantages of a Managed Account
with a Brokerage Firm

1. The client may feel that the firm is not objective. A major source of income to the firm is generated from commissions and some investors may feel the advisor is making recommendations solely to create commissions.
2. Discretionary accounts sometimes cause problems between the investor and his broker. Often the advisor is charged with mis-managing the account if losses occur.
3. The brokerage firm sometimes hesitates to take quick losses when it makes an error in the fear that it may be accused of overtrading the discretionary account.
4. The investor may feel other accounts are receiving priority.

Because of these disadvantages, many brokerage firms do not seek or encourage investment advisory accounts. Others, however, feel they have successfully overcome these disadvantages. If an investor is interested in having a brokerage firm manage his funds, he should request a history of the firm's record before making a decision.

Many investors maintain that brokerage houses cannot be totally objective but may still wish to retain an investment counselor. Independent advisors and banks offer their services to the investor for a fee. Banks, brokers, attorneys, accountants, and personal friends are excellent sources to contact when looking for an investment counselor. It is always best to find a person with whom you can openly discuss your entire financial situation, whose judgment and experience you feel that you can trust, and who has earned the respect of the people with whom he does business.

Many of these counselors are registered with the Securities and Exchange Commission and often perform a broader service for their clients. In addition to securities, he may handle a client's entire investment portfolio.

Advantages of an Independent Advisor

1. An advisor is able to spend considerable time on each individual portfolio.
2. He receives a fee for his services and is not dependent on commissions.
3. Advisors are able to act quickly when they receive important information.
4. They understand how to work with stockbrokers, accountants, and lawyers.

Disadvantages of an Investment Advisor

1. Investment advisors charge fees that vary depending on the amount of the portfolio. A small investor pays a higher fee.

2. Some will only accept accounts of $100,000 or more, and others restrict their services to even larger accounts.
3. The annual fee to an investment advisor is usually ½ of 1 per cent, which he receives regardless of performance.

Banks

Banks offer investment advice together with custodian services through registered investment advisors in their employ. Investors often select banks as custodians or trustees because they are institutions with theoretically unlimited life. They can service a trust for its entire life, whereas an independent advisor may not outlive the trust.

Banks are regulated by state and federal laws and are subject to "prudent man" behavior. Under law the bank must always answer the question, "Would a prudent man have acted the same way in the same circumstances?" Aware of this fact, banks are generally more conservative in managing portfolios and seldom look for quick short-term gains. Banks receive a fee for their services regardless of performance. In addition they do not have the capacity for the individual attention offered by the investment advisor.

Other Investment Advisors

There are many investment advisory services that supply weekly or monthly letters to their subscribers. In addition, they also solicit advisory accounts, which they manage for a fee. Some of these advisory services have impeccable reputations; others are considered hucksters.

PENSION FUNDS

The Employee Retirement Security Act of 1974

This bill, passed by Congress in 1974, brings many of the aspects of the operation of private pension funds under government supervision for the first time. This new bill primarily deals with the *funding* of pension plans, which are the actual payments into the fund.

It is estimated that there are over 30 million stockholders in this country but the estimate is vastly understated. Every employee included in a pension plan is a stockholder, and soon this number will include the majority of people working. This law was passed for their benefit. Corporations, in the management of these pension funds, must now follow the "prudent man" rule the same as the banks.

Vesting

Vested benefits are benefits not contingent on the employee's continuing in the service of the employer. In some pension plans, payment of benefits will begin only when an employee reaches the normal retirement date; in other plans, payment of benefits will begin when an employee actually retires.

An employer has three alternatives in vesting employees:

1. 100 per cent vesting after ten years.
2. 25% vesting after five years, then 5 per cent for each additional year up to ten years, and 10 per cent a year vesting until 100 per cent vested in fifteen years.
3. 50 per cent vesting whenever age and years of service equal 45 and then be increased by 10 per cent each year for the following five years. However, each employee with ten years' service, regardless of age, must be at least 50 per cent vested, with an additional 10 per cent per year thereafter. Prior service counts toward vesting.

Management Responsibility

The bill established personal liability for management of the funds by fiduciaries using the "prudent man" rule. These rules are spelled out in the bill and anyone managing pension funds should be aware of and knowledgeable about them.

Result of Merger With Other Plans

Funding and vesting of each employee's accrued benefit after a merger must be at least equal to what it was before the merger.

Pension Accounts for Individuals Not Covered by Pension Plan

This legislation establishes, for the first time, a provision for individual employees not covered by pension plans to set up their own retirement accounts. The amount is limited to 15 per cent of earned income up to $1,500.

Keogh Plan

For the self-employed, the bill moves the limit on Keogh plan contributions up to 15 per cent of income or $7,500 annually, whichever is lower, except that a minimum of $750 is allowed.

Impact of New Pension Law on Corporate Earnings

When this bill passed, there were some dire predictions that it would bankrupt many corporations. The main fear was that corporations would not have enough money to pay into the fund the "unfunded vested benefits" and that even if they did the future payments would reduce their earnings substantially. Earnings estimates were reduced substantially by many analysts in most cases. Initial surveys, however, do not bear out these negative predictions. Each corporation has to be analyzed individually to determine the extent of its maximum liability under this law.

QUESTIONS

1. What is a mutual fund? What is its purpose?
2. Define the following terms: a. public offering price; b. net asset value; c. bid and asked price; d. capital gains distribution; e. redemption privilege.
3. List some of the advantages and disadvantages of mutual funds.
4. Describe some of the different types of mutual funds.
5. Do no-load funds have sales forces?
6. What is a closed-end fund? How do they differ from mutual funds?
7. What are some of the advantages and disadvantages of closed-end funds?
8. Describe a dual fund. Define leverage. Is leverage inherent in the purchase of a dual fund?
9. What is a prospectus and what information is contained in it?
10. What are some of the "rules of fair practice" enacted by the Securities Exchange Act of 1934?
11. What are some of the provisions of the Investment Company Act of 1940?
12. Explain the importance of Subchapter M of the Internal Revenue Code.
13. Besides buying either an open-end or a closed-end fund, how else can an investor have his money managed?
14. In corporation pension plans, what does the term "vesting" mean?
15. Under the Employee Retirement Security Act of 1974, may an individual, not covered by a corporate pension plan, set up his own retirement plan? If so, what are its limitations?
16. Does an investor and analyst have to take into consideration the "unfunded vested benefits" in analyzing a corporation? Why?

10

MAJOR ERRORS IN SPECULATING AND INVESTING

Speculation implies a high degree of risk. An experienced speculator is willing to assume this risk if he has considered all the possibilities. He is not a wild plunger. Dividends hold little interest for him and the long-term views of the economy or the company hold even less. He recognizes that changes within a company may cause its stock to rise or fall. But he has the ability to make quick decisions and is not afraid to take a loss.

He usually trades in securities listed on the New York Stock Exchange because it affords him greater liquidity and he is able to utilize the ticker tape reports. He buys on margin, which gives him greater leverage, and it isn't important whether he makes his profit buying a stock or selling it short.

New issues, (companies that have sold stock to the public for the first time), special situations, puts, calls, arbitrages, or hedges are all within his purview. He will buy a cyclical stock (a company whose products rise and fall with the economy) when he thinks its earnings are due for a rise and sell it when he feels the cycle is nearing its end.

A speculator, in short, places no restrictions on his trading activities. The vast majority of investors, however, rarely speculate, although most have tried.

Speculating and Investing Errors

1. Using long-term analysis for short-term speculating
2. Taking small profits
3. Letting losses run
4. Adopting break-even psychology
5. Averaging down
6. Utilizing stock market "tips"

7. Pyramiding incorrectly
8. Overtrading an account

1. Long Term-Analysis Used for Short-Term Speculating

Many speculators, including accountants, lawyers, and businessmen who have developed more than a working acquaintance with corporate financial statements, study a corporation's report and decide for themselves on proper valuation of the security. Not only do they place a value on the stock, but they assume the market will react, almost immediately, by moving up. The trend of the market as a whole, the industry group the security belongs to, and the direction of the price movement of the stock purchased is of secondary importance to them. They have made a lengthy study of the company based on long-term considerations and expect the stock to move up shortly after purchase.

It is difficult to estimate the immense losses taken by apparently intelligent men who continually buy stocks in this manner. They are using long-term analysis to try to make short-term profits. The pure fundamentalist must be prepared to wait, sometimes for more than two years, before the market gets around to "properly" evaluating his undervalued security.

A fundamentalist is interested in values; a technician, in trends. If a stock has fallen from $30 per share to $20, its long-term potential may be quite good but for the short term it may continue to fall to $15 or less. Because a stock is a good value at $20 per share does not mean that it cannot decline further over the short term and become an even better buy. An investor who thoroughly analyzes the corporate financial statements and makes his purchase based on these facts is studying past history to project the future. Many changes may be taking place within the company that are not yet reflected in the statements he is studying. If an investor bought the stock at $20 hoping for a short-term profit, he might wait and watch for six months while it drops to $15. During that period of time adverse conditions are probably affecting the corporation that have not yet been reflected in its reported earnings and financial statement. When this news is released, the disillusioned speculator sells his stock and takes a 25 per cent loss.

Understanding financial statements is an essential tool of stock market speculating and investing but there are many additional factors to consider.

2. Taking Small Profits

Once the speculator has taken his position he has made the first of the necessary decisions that go toward making a profit. If the stock moves up in price, there are several possibilities open to him such as buying more or selling out what he has at a profit. Buying more stock requires the knowledge of how to successfully pyramid, discussed later in this chapter. Few speculators buy additional stock as it rises in price. Instead, they are very nervous with the profit they already have. It takes courage to hold on to a stock with a profit since the market fluctuates constantly, and with each downturn more and more speculators with profits sell their shares.

Xerox, Syntex, Polaroid, and many other growth stocks had astronomical advances during the 1960s, but these advances were never straight up. Some of the declines were quite precipitous. During each decline many speculators thought the bubble had burst; and, indeed, in some instances they were right. Many companies were considered growth stocks one year by Wall Street and avoided the next.

When the speculator initiates his trade, he should attempt to set a price at which he is willing to take a profit. If he buys an established company, he may be willing to settle for a smaller profit than he would if he buys a young growth company. It is a most unfortunate fact in the marketplace that most of us settle for small profits because of the fear of losing what has already been gained. The bromide issued by many in Wall Street, "You never go broke taking a profit" has its corollary, "You never get rich taking small profits".

3. Letting Losses Run

Probably the hardest thing for a speculator to learn in the stock market is to take small losses rather than hold on and hope for a change in trend. The many speculators who buy and sell securities will, if they have kept records, learn, however, that they have taken small profits and let their losses run. They may even find that they have made as many good trades as they have bad, but the losses exceed the profits.

When he initiates a trade, the trader might immediately place a stop loss order (order to sell at a specified price) at a price below his purchase. He has now made the most difficult decision beforehand. He knows exactly the amount of the loss he is willing to take. A good trader may lose on 50 per cent or more of his trades but his gains far exceed his losses. He realizes that some of the reasons for such a large percentage of losses are that he may have bought at the wrong time or he may have misread the technical position of the stock and bought when he should have been selling. He is not afraid to admit he has made a mistake. Charts will help the trader study break-out points and false penetrations of these areas.

When a trade is opened, the speculator is usually hopeful that he will make a profit. If the stock falls, his mood changes. He should be aware that he must take small losses and trade for large gains but he rationalizes his position. He decides to wait for a rally and then sell. If the stock does not rally, his loss is large.

Yet it is still the rare speculator who will accept small losses. Many unsuccessful traders settle for quick gains. Psychologically, they have not approached the market with the idea of making money.

An astute speculator sets selling points, both up and down, before opening trades. If the profit potential is small, he does not open the trade. He looks for a profit potential of at least three times the possible loss.

If an unsuccessful speculator were to examine his long-term transactions, those held in excess of six months, he would undoubtedly discover that most of them incurred losses. A *good* speculator finds himself locked into gains, not losses.

4. Break-even Psychology

"If I ever get even I'm going to sell". This is another phrase constantly repeated by traders and investors alike. They buy a stock and suffer as they watch it fall in price. It might take six months, one year, or even longer for the stock to rally to the price paid. The same type of trader who sold the stock to the break-even investor originally is now buying it back. He now expects the stock to break out, immediately after all the break-even selling is absorbed. It is best to avoid selling when there no longer is a loss. Place a stop loss order a few points below the break-even point. If the stock falls again, the loss is limited. However, if it rises, which it often does in these circumstances, you may realize what could be a substantial gain.

Chartists pay special attention to these break-even points, and if they are short of capital they wait until the stocks break through these points before they buy. Technicians understand that it is a human trait not to want to admit a mistake in judgment, and that breaking even is not a mistake to the unsuccessful trader.

The break-even syndrome has elicited another stock market lament. "Sell when I buy and buy when I sell" the trader who says this is lured into the market at the wrong time and should reexamine his reasons for buying and selling. His lament is correct. His approach and psychology to the market must be changed if he is to become a successful trader.

The break-even trader probably bought at the lip of the saucer then sat with the stock during its decline and subsequent rise back to the other lip (See following illustration).

Bought here — Sold here at break-even point

5. Averaging Down

The speculator who does not take a small loss commits one error. When he buys more stock on the way down, he commits his second error. He reasons that if the stock was a good buy at $20 per share, it must now be a better buy at $15. He hopes for a market rise, not to make money, but to break even. The trader, by refusing to take a small loss and compounding this error by committing more money just to break even, does not intend to make money trading. He only hopes to.

At $13 a share, the trader buys another 100 shares. He now owns 300 shares at a total cost of $4,800, or an average of $16 per share. At $10 per share, his fear prevails and he sells out. If the trader bought his stock on 50 per cent margin, he lost a substantial part of his working capital.

Averaging down suggests that the stock will reverse its pattern and rally back to the price at which it was originally bought. This happens too rarely. Many fortunes have been lost by people who thought that they could violate the rule against averaging down. In less than two years, for example, Avon Products fell from $140 to $20 per share. The company prior to this debacle was considered one of the great growth companies in America and was owned by over 240 investment trusts. Averaging down on Avon would have meant financial disaster to an investor or a speculator. You may be wondering at this point asked if averaging at the bottom of a long reaction, or even better, after a strong bear market, would be advisable. The assumption here is that no stock was bought during the decline, now that it has hit it must be all right to buy. The answer to this question is contained in the Avon example. Many people must have thought Avon had bottomed out at $100 and bought more stock. Surely at $80 they believed it could go no lower. And who is bearish enough to suggest that it could ever go below $50? Vast fortunes have been lost in Avon averaging on the way down.

6. Stock Market Tips

Anyone who has ever been in a Wall Street brokerage office for any period of time cannot avoid listening to the almost incessant stream of information and rumor. The information is rarely unemphatic. The bearer of the information speaks with authority about the status of a corporation. He does so because he believes in the information he is passing along. The news is usually on the positive side regarding a substantial earnings increase, a dividend increase, a stock dividend, or even a stock split. All of these events are construed as constructive to the price of a stock. Some of this information is found in the newspapers but a considerable portion is circulated by telephone. The amount of financial data being circulated is enormous and no amount of capital would be sufficient to buy all the securities suggested. The purpose of this immense bulk of information is to help you buy into a "good thing."

Americans usually are optimistic about the future. It is against their nature to be pessimistic. Therefore, the vast majority of news is bullish. Rarely do rumors circulate about a company that will report lower earnings or lower the dividend or in general be in difficulty. That type of news usually comes suddenly and unexpectedly. Except when the market is suffering through a period of panic, rumors are usually optimistic.

What about tips in general? Are there any conclusions that can be drawn from the welter of data that flows back and forth across the country? It is an interesting fact that from the time a stock begins to move up in price to the time it stops going up, there is a stream of advice suggesting that the stock be bought. But when the stock begins to fall, rarely will anyone be advised to sell. After a precipitious drop in price, the advice is to switch to another security. Tips usually start at the beginning of an advance and can be extremely useful to speculators. This observation has given rise to the adage, "Buy on rumor, sell on news." Therefore, tips should not be arbitrarily discarded, but instead should be investigated for their credibility. Besides investigating the salient financial data of a corporation, the technical position of the company's stock should be studied. The majority of stock market tips will be eliminated in this manner, and that is probably the difference between the successful speculator and the individual who consistently incurs large losses. The successful speculator investigates as thoroughly as possible by checking all the sources he can. He does not buy on impulse. He would rather miss a move in the stock than buy the wrong stock at the wrong time.

When a speculator hears information that is bearish, he realizes that it is more reliable than bullish news. As we have mentioned, most speculators buy securities and rarely, if ever, go short on a stock. The bearish tip is usually more accurate because of the unwillingness of brokerage firms and newspapers to disseminate gloomy news. There is always the possibility that the negative predictions will turn out to be wrong. Prior to the Securities Acts of 1933 and 1934, unscrupulous insiders, taking advantage of this unwillingness to make bad news public, would sell to the unwary public.

A speculator keeps busy checking out the reliability of tips or market information. He keeps accurate records of the sources of his information and of exactly what was recorded in order to check on its accuracy later. A speculator who remains in Wall Street for many years usually has eliminated all but a few of his sources of information.

7. Pyramiding Incorrectly

Pyramiding involves buying more stock as it rises in price, usually on margin. It is, in essence, the opposite of averaging down. In both methods, any substantial decline entails large losses. For this reason, pyramiding is a dangerous form of speculating if each additional purchase is as large as the original buy or if the pyramiding is as heavy as the speculator's margin account will permit.

Pyramiding Applied Correctly

There are times when pyramiding is the proper course of action. In this case the procedure is probably better referred to as "buying on a scale up." A speculator who wishes to accumulate 500 shares does not buy them all at once. He starts by purchasing 200 shares. If the market drops, he takes his small loss, following the golden rule. He again purchases 200 shares of the stock when he feels it is ready to move up again. As the stock moves up, he checks his chart and sees that the stock has broken through the top of the 200-day moving average. He decides to buy more and places an order for 200 additional shares. The stock continues to rise and is now 5 points above the original purchase. The speculator buys another 100 shares and now has accumulated his 500 shares, without being totally margined. His account appears as follows:

Bought 200 shares	$20	$ 4,000
Bought 200 shares	$22	4,400
Bought 100 shares	$25	2,500
Cost of 500 shares		$ 10,900
Average price per 100 shares		$ 21.80

The speculator can decide to place a stop loss order at $23 1/8, thus assuring himself that the transaction will not end up in a loss. If the stock continues to rise, he can keep raising his stop loss orders or leave the original one in at $23 1/8, depending on how he interprets the technical pattern of the stock's move.

Pyramiding can be a very dangerous speculative tool but if used correctly and in a conservative manner it can result in substantial profits.

8. Over-trading An Account

A speculator who constantly sits in a broker's office falls prone to a weakness called over-suggestibility. If he has capital to invest, he is usually searching for a good investment opportunity. When he receives market information he acts without checking either the fundamentals or the technical status of the stock—and buys. Shortly after, if the stock drifts downward, he sells and takes a small loss. If he follows this pattern consistently, he eventually will have to make a large profit to recover from so many small losses. Because he does not want to disregard the information he receives, he acts hastily.

Constant buying and selling is one of the costliest errors a speculator can make. A good speculator will plan to miss a few stock moves and investigate each situation before he places an order.

A trader, consciously or subconsciously, "tunes out the market" when it becomes bearish. He does not want to be lured into buying stocks during the downturn. He knows if he stays around and listens to all the market news he will undoubtedly buy into some situations. He can defend himself by avoiding the boardroom. He doesn't listen to rumor.

A speculator also can be susceptible to mental fatigue if:

1. He devotes too much time to his account.
2. He places too much hope on the outcome of each trade.
3. The pressures weigh on his mind as each trade remains open.
4. He is indecisive about what action to take.
5. He fears the possibility of a loss.
6. He has doubts about whether he has acted wisely.

There are probably other elements that add to the strain and fatigue on a speculator. He hovers between the two opposite poles of hope and fear. Nowhere will you find individuals more sanguine and ebullient than in Wall Street during a bull market, with the possible exception of the winning team in the World Series or the Super Bowl; on the other hand, the mood of hope and buoyancy can swiftly turn to fear and despair when the market turns bearish.

If a speculator, regardless of how strong, remains under this tension for a long period, he will succumb to mental fatigue. His judgment becomes impaired, and his responses slow down as he increasingly oscillates between hope and fear.

If a speculator is bullish, he will open a trade by buying. Fatigue would manifest itself in this situation only if the trader had already reached the state of over-suggestibility. While the trade remains open, however, the cumulative effect of the strain can cause the trader to make many speculating errors. He may average down, instead of taking a small loss. He may sell out at the break-even point just before the stock starts on a strong upward move. He knows he is making poor decisions but continues to make them. The strain and fear increase. His eagerness to make money makes him impatient. He becomes over-suggestible and consequently overtrades his account.

The student of the stock market might well ask, "Is anyone suited to speculating?" No one can answer this question but an individual himself. During a bull market many new traders are lured into stock market speculating and it is only then that they can answer the question. Before any move is made in this direction, the following advice is suggested:

1. Before speculating, spend as least six months trading on paper.
2. Intend to make money; do not merely hope to.
3. Become an omniverous reader of financial data. Good traders are able to predict effects from causes.
4. Write reasons for every purchase and sale. Bad trading habits can be isolated in this manner.
5. Have faith in your own ability. Wall Street has different geniuses every year.
6. Do not sell short in a bull market. Stay with the trend.
7. Be able to take many small losses.
8. Have courage to hold stocks showing profits.
9. Be able to resist most Wall Street rumors.
10. If signs of fatigue and strain appear, stop trading. Take a few weeks off.

Additional Errors in Speculating

1. A trader buys only securities that are fast moving. A speculator buys only stocks that have high volume and are moving up in price. If the stock does not move, the speculator sells. Purely and simply, he is a gambler. He does not measure his risks and only envisions profits. He does not study the financial structure of the company to establish value or the technical patterns to establish timing. He buys solely because the stock is extremely active on the tape.

2. Inheritors of stocks. If it was good enough for my father to hold, why should I sell? In spite of economic changes, many legatees refuse to sell securities that they should no longer be holding. They become emotionally involved and refuse to listen to advice from qualified counselors.

3. Many investors avoid the top-quality companies. They argue that large companies cannot continue their growth and therefore completely overlook them in their analysis. Their portfolios contain none of the industry leaders and they wonder why they are not doing well in the market. It is suggested that a portfolio place its greatest emphasis on quality. Speculators searching for growth stocks usually avoid the leaders in an industry. Investors should not.

4. Some individuals begin as investors and end up as speculators. It is difficult to be both investor and speculator at the same time. What usually happens is that the speculator wins out and sells out all the investment stocks, leaving himself with a number of little-known companies. It is suggested that an investor allocate a certain portion of his capital to trading (10 per cent to 15 per cent) in order to keep in close contact with the market and keep the balance of his securities in a safe deposit box.

5. Some investors overdiversify their portfolios. It is an established

fact that the quickest way to increase or to lose your capital is to invest it all in one stock. Therefore, diversification is a basic principle of investing. Many investors, however, spread their risks too thin and find themselves with only a few shares in several dozen companies. They probably could not name all the securities they own and have long since given up reading the annual reports and following the daily progress of their holdings. Their losses will undoubtedly be greater than their gains. It is suggested that either this type of investor sell at least half of his holdings and concentrate on the more successful companies he holds, or sell everything and buy mutual funds.

6. Bonds and preferred stocks are safer than common stocks. Bonds and preferred stocks have fixed yields and fluctuate with interest rates. Therefore, they are as speculative as common stocks. Inflation has become part of our daily lives and although the preferred dividend or the interest on the bond may be very secure, the stock or the bond can still experience a sharp decline. Fixed income securities are dangerous investments in an inflationary environment and cannot be viewed with safety. Should inflation abate, these fixed income securities will rise in price. A portfolio should contain elements of both fixed income securities and common stocks for diversification.

7. Speculators want to make a quick profit. Many traders often accumulate capital for a few weeks or a month that they plan to place eventually in a long-term investment, but they do not want to see the capital remain idle. As a result, they search for a "mover." The usual result is a substantial loss. It is recommended that the trader put his money in the bank until he needs it for the investment.

Bull Market End

1. Optimism is pervasive.
2. Price-earnings ratios are high.
3. New common stock issues are flooding the market.
4. Brokerage firms are expanding.
5. The stock market is one of the chief sources of conversation.
6. Mergers are prevalent.
7. Many corporations are declaring stock dividends and stock splits.
8. Margin accounts have high debit balances.
9. The Federal Reserve has raised the discount rate for its member banks at least twice.
10. Many financial writers are publishing reports of a "new era of prosperity."
11. Some financial men are warning that the boom is getting out of hand.
12. The stocks that make up the Dow Jones Industrial Average are selling at approximately twenty times earnings.
13. Bond yields exceed stock yields by at least 3 per cent.

14. It is difficult to find a stock on the New York Stock Exchange selling under $10 per share.
15. Volume on the more speculative American Stock Exchange is at an all-time high.
16. Over-the-counter stocks are rising rapidly in price.
17. Mutual fund sales far exceed redemptions.
18. Corporations are extending their cash positions in order to finance growth. Financial statement ratios are deteriorating.
19. Many financial analysts are projecting higher earnings and are generally bullish.
20. Sales of second homes, second and third cars, boats, and airplanes are at their peaks.
21. Interest rates are in an accelerated rise.
22. The Federal Reserve is talking of restraining the money supply.
23. Banks are expansive in their lending policies.

Bear Market End

1. Pessimism is pervasive.
2. Only the highest-quality corporations can sell bonds and even they have difficulty selling stocks.
3. Brokerage offices are closing.
4. Corporations declare fewer and fewer stock dividends and stock splits.
5. The number of mergers declines and many that are made are of the "shotgun" variety.
6. Brokerage firms are sending "sell-out telegrams" to cover margin accounts in trouble.
7. Writers and commentators warn that Armageddon is close at hand.
8. The Dow Jones Industrial Average sells between seven and ten times earnings.
9. Bond yields are high but now stock yields have risen to meet them.
10. Many stocks on the New York Stock Exchange are selling below $10 per share.
11. Volume on the American Stock Exchange has declined significantly.
12. The Over-the-Counter Market has collapsed and many over-the-counter brokers have gone out of business.
13. Mutual fund redemptions exceed sales (the dollar cost averaging principle notwithstanding).
14. Corporations are selling assets to stay liquid. Financial statement ratios begin to have more significance to investors and analysts.
15. Many financial analysts are extremely cautious and seldom make unqualified recommendations.
16. A wave of corporate bankruptcies, including several large banks, washes over the economy.
17. Forced sales of second homes, second cars, boats, and airplanes take place. Personal bankruptcies increase.
18. Interest rates are high but have stopped climbing.

19. Banks are stringent in their credit policies.
20. The Federal Reserve begins to loosen the money supply.

QUESTIONS

1. Define speculation. Contrast it to investing.
2. How would you overcome using long-term analysis for short-term profits?
3. "You can never go broke taking a profit" is usually associated with which major error in trading?
4. Explain break-even psychology. Why is it considered an error in trading and investing?
5. Why is averaging down the antithesis of taking small losses? Why is averaging down so dangerous?
6. Should all stock market tips be ignored? Why are most tips bullish rather than bearish?
7. After receiving a market tip from a "reliable source," what steps should a speculator take before investing?
8. Explain pyramiding. Give an example of the correct and the incorrect method of pyramiding.
9. What does overtrading an account mean? How can a speculator overcome this tendency?
10. If you wished to learn to speculate (trade) in the stock market, what should you do and learn first?

GLOSSARY

ACCOUNTANT'S OPINION—An opinion rendered by a certified public accountant after auditing books of a corporation.

ACCRUED INTEREST—Interest accrued or earned on a bond since the last interest payment was made. The buyer of the bond pays the market price plus the interest earned to the date of purchase.

ADVANCE-DECLINE RATIO—The measurement of the number of advances or declines in the market.

ANNUAL REPORT—The formal report issued yearly by a corporation. The annual report includes the balance sheet, the profit and loss statement, the statement of changes in financial position, the accountant's report, and the president's letter to the stockholders.

ARBITRAGE—The simultaneous purchase and sale of the same securities, commodities, or foreign exchange in different markets to profit from unequal prices.

ASKED—The price at which a person will sell a security.

ASSETS—Everything that a corporation owns or is due to it. Some assets such as cash, accounts receivable, and inventories are called current assets, whereas buildings, plant, and equipment are known as fixed assets.

AVERAGES—Averaging is a way to measure the trend of stock prices. The Dow Jones Industrial Average is made up of thirty securities listed on the New York Stock Exchange. Standard & Poor's 500 stock average covers a broader cross-section of the market.

AVERAGING DOWN—Buying additional shares of a stock as the price declines.

BALANCE SHEET—The balance sheet is a condensed financial statement listing the company's assets, liabilities, and capital as of a given date. It shows what the company owns, what is owed to it, what it owes, and the ownership interest of the stockholders.

BAR CHART—A chart in which each bar represents the trading range of a stock within a specified period of time, usually a day, a week, or a month.

BARRON'S CONFIDENCE INDEX—A ratio of Barron's ten highest-rated corporate bonds to the Dow Jones forty composite bond yield average.

BEAR—A person who believes the market will decline.

BEAR MARKET—A declining market.

BEARER BOND—A bond that does not have the owner's name registered on the books of the issuing company. The interest and principal are payable to the holder.

BID—The price at which a person will buy a security.

BID AND ASKED—(see Quotation).

BIG BOARD—This is the popular term for the New York Stock Exchange.

BLUE CHIP—A nationally known company. Its products and services are widely accepted. It has a long record of earnings and dividends.

BOARD OF GOVERNORS OF FEDERAL RESERVE BANK—The seven-man Board of Governors is chosen by the President of the United States for a term of 14 years for each member.

BOND—Basically, a promissory note of a corporation, usually issued in denominations of $1,000. The bond itself is evidence of the debt of the corporation, which promises to pay the bondholders a specified amount for interest and to repay the loan at a fixed and determinable future time. The holder of the bond is a creditor of the corporation. In many cases bonds are secured by collateral.

BOOK VALUE—Assets equal liabilities plus capital. Capital is then equal to assets minus liabilities. The shareholders of a corporation own the capital of the corporation. To arrive at the book value, add all the assets of a corporation (less any goodwill or other intangible assets), less all the liabilities, plus the liquidation value of any preferred stock outstanding. The sum arrived at is then divided by the number of shares outstanding. This value may or may not have any significance to market value.

BREAK-EVEN PSYCHOLOGY—Holding a stock through a long decline and selling when it returns to the purchase price.

BROKER—An agent who handles the public's orders to buy and sell securities, commodities, or other property for a commission.

BULL—A person who believes the market will rise.

BULL MARKET—A rising market.

CHICAGO BOARD OF EXCHANGE—The CBOE is a market devoted exclusively to options on securities.

CALL OPTION—An option to buy 100 shares of a specific stock at a specified price for a specified number of days.

CALLABLE—A bond issue or a preferred stock issue that may be redeemed by the issuing corporation under definite conditions before maturity. These conditions are set forth in the prospectus at the time of original issue.

CAPITAL GAIN OR CAPITAL LOSS—This gain or loss results from the sale of a capital asset. Stocks, bonds, and commodities are considered capital assets. Under current federal income tax laws, a capital asset, if held six months or less, is a short-term capital gain or loss, and if held in excess of six months is a long-term capital gain or loss. The tax rates on short-term and long-term capital gains are materially different. An investor should consult his accountant for specific information.

CAPITAL STOCK—The shares representing ownership of the business. These shares include preferred as well as common stock.

CAPITALIZATION OF A CORPORATION—The total amount of all securities issued by a corporation. Capitalization may include bonds, debentures, preferred stocks, common stock, capital paid in excess of par, and retained earnings.

CASH FLOW—The net income of a corporation plus amounts charged (bookkeeping entries) for depreciation, depletion, or other write-offs not involving an actual outlay of dollars.

CERTIFICATE—The actual piece of paper that evidences the ownership of stock in a corporation. Special paper is used to discourage forgery. If signed by the owner, it becomes a negotiable instrument the same as a check made out to cash. Care should be taken before a stockholder endorses his certificates.

COMMON STOCK—Securities that represent ownership in a corporation.

CONGLOMERATE—A corporation that owns or controls many other corporations in widely varied industries.

CONVERTIBLE BOND OR PREFERRED STOCK—A security that may be exchanged by the owner for common stock, usually in the same company, in accordance with the terms of the issue.

COUPON BOND—A bond with interest coupons attached. The coupons are clipped as they come due and are presented by the holder for payment.

COVERING SHORT—Buying back a security previously sold short.

CUMULATIVE PREFERRED—A preferred stock providing that if one or more dividends are omitted, the omitted dividends must be paid before any dividends may be paid on the common stock.

CURB EXCHANGE—The old name of the American Stock Exchange, the second largest exchange in the country.

CURRENT ASSETS—Those assets of a corporation that are expected to be realized in cash, or sold, or consumed during the normal operating cycle of the business, usually one year. They include cash, accounts receivable, and inventories.

CURRENT LIABILITIES—Money owed by the corporation due and payable within one year.

CURRENT RATIO—Ratio of current assets to current liabilities.

DAY ORDER—An order to buy or sell, which is good only for the day it is entered.

DEBENTURE—A promissory note backed by the general credit of a corporation and not secured by any mortgage or lien on any specific property.

DEFICIT FINANCING—A situation in which the government spends more money than it receives.

DEPLETION ALLOWANCE—Certain natural resources, such as oil and gas, and timber and metals, which are essential to the productive capacity of the country. The government allows a corporation to deduct certain charges against earnings in order to provide incentive to find these needed resources.

DEPRECIATION—An asset has an estimated useful life. The tax law provides that this asset may be written off over this useful life as a charge against earnings.

DIRECTOR—The corporate by-laws stipulate the number of directors the corporation should have. These directors are elected by the shareholders and establish company policy. They appoint the president, vice-presidents, treasurer, etc. One of the main duties of a director is to formulate dividend policy.

DISCOUNT BOND OR PREFERRED STOCK—A bond or a preferred stock that sells below its par value.

DISCOUNT RATE—The rate of interest a regional bank of the federal reserve charges member banks on their promissory notes.

DISCRETIONARY ACCOUNT—An account in which a customer gives a broker discretion to buy or sell within specified limits. The broker usually determines what, when, how much, and at what price to buy and sell.

DIVERSIFICATION—The principle of spreading investment risk over many different companies in different fields.

DIVIDEND—A payment, determined by the board of directors, to be distributed pro rata among the shares outstanding. Preferred stock usually receives the same fixed dividend. Common stock dividends vary with the fortunes of the company. If business is good, dividends may be increased, and if business is poor, the dividend may be omitted.

DOLLAR COST AVERAGING—A system of buying securities at regular intervals with a fixed dollar amount. It enables an investor to buy more shares of a security when the price is depressed. Thus temporary downturns in the market benefit the investor if he can continue to buy in bad times as well as good.

DOUBLE TAXATION—The federal government taxes corporations on their profits. The board of directors may decide to pay a dividend that, when received by the shareholders, is again taxable to them.

DOW THEORY—A theory of predicting trends in the stock market by analyzing the market performance of thirty industrial and twenty transportation stocks. The theory states that the market is in a basic upward trend if one of these averages advances above a previous important high, followed by a similar penetration of the other average. The opposite holds true in a declining market. It does not predict how long this trend will continue or whether the penetration of the averages is false or not.

EQUITY—The ownership interest of a preferred or common stockholder.

EX-DIVIDEND—This term means "without dividend." The buyer of a stock selling ex-dividend does not receive the recently declared dividend. Dividends are usually paid quarterly.

FEDERAL RESERVE SYSTEM—A system of banking headed by a seven-man Board of Governors appointed by the President of the U.S. and consists of 12 Regional Reserve banks (banker's banks) and over 6,000 commercial banks.

FISCAL POLICY—The federal budget represents the fiscal policy of the government. If the government's receipts are greater than its expenditures the government is operating at a surplus. Should the reverse be true, the government is using deficit financing.

FISCAL YEAR—Any date other than December 31 (calendar year) on which a corporation chooses to end its business year.

FIXED ASSETS—Assets of a relatively permanent nature, not intended for resale, and used in the operation of the business.

FLOOR OF THE EXCHANGE—The trading areas of the New York Stock Exchange and the American Stock Exchange where stocks and bonds are bought and sold.

FLOOR BROKER—A member of the stock exchange (owns a seat) who executes orders for his firm on the floor of the exchange.

GENERAL PRICE INDEX—An index of prices the consumer pays for commodities.

GOOD 'TIL CANCELLED ORDER (GTC) OR OPEN ORDER—An order placed by a broker to buy or sell at a specified price that remains open until it is executed.

GOVERNMENT BONDS (DEBENTURES)—Obligations of the U.S. government and regarded as the highest-grade issues in existence.

GROWTH STOCK—The stock of a company whose earnings are growing at a relatively faster rate than the gross national product.

HEDGING—A protection against a complete loss. It involves the purchase or sale of a different security or commodity to counterbalance the first purchase or sale.

HORIZONTAL INTEGRATION—A method of growth by which a corporation extends the same services or products in other areas.

INCOME STATEMENT—A statement listing the revenue, expense, and income of a corporation.

INDENTURE—The written agreement under which bonds and debentures are issued, which sets forth the interest rate, maturity date, and other agreed-upon terms.

INDEX—An index is a measurement device, a statistical yardstick expressed in terms of percentages of a base year or years. For example: The Federal Reserve Board's index of industrial production is based on 1967 as 100. If the index stood at 120, it would mean that industrial production was 20 per cent higher than the base period of 1967.

INFLATION—Inflation usually results from continuous deficit financing. Prices and wages continually increase.

INTEREST—The amount paid to the lender for the use of his money. A corporation pays interest on its bonds to its bondholders.

INTEREST COVERAGE (BONDS)—The number of times the earnings of a corporation covers its interest payments.

INVESTMENT BANKER (UNDERWRITER)—A broker who offers new securities of a corporation to the public. In practice, several investment bankers form a syndicate to distribute or sell the securities to individuals or institutions.

INVESTMENT COMPANY—A company or trust that sells shares to the public and invests its capital in other companies. There are many types but the principal ones are the open-end funds (mutual funds) and the closed-end funds.

INVESTMENT COUNSELOR—A person whose principal business consists of acting as investment advisor to clients.

INVESTOR—An individual whose main purpose is to obtain a safe return on his capital. His concerns are safety of principal, liquidity, dividend income, and to some extent, capital appreciation.

LETTER OF INTENT—A letter issued by an investment banker to a corporation outlining the salient points of the prospective underwriting of the corporation's securities.

LEVERAGE—The effect of magnifying gains or losses. It can be used by purchasing the shares of a corporation whose debt is quite large. If the corporation does well, interest is paid on the debt and the balance is reported as earnings to the shareholders. If business is poor, the earnings of the corporation may disappear. Investors may use leverage by borrowing and buying on margin. Both losses and gains will be magnified.

LIABILITIES—All the claims of the creditors of a corporation.

LIMIT ORDER—An order to buy or sell a stated amount of a security at a specified price.

LIQUIDITY—Liquidity refers to the marketability of a security. The ability of an investor or speculator to easily buy and sell.

LISTED STOCK—The stock of a corporation that is traded on the securities exchange.

LOAD—The part of the offering price of an open-end investment company. It covers the sales commissions and costs of distribution. The load is usually incurred only on the purchase. In most cases there is no cost to sell.

LONG-TERM CAPITAL GAIN OR LOSS—A security held more than six months receives special tax treatment when sold and is considered a long-term holding.

LONG-TERM LIABILITIES—Debts of the corporation such as bonds, mortgages, and other debts not maturing within one year.

LOW-PRICED CONFIDENCE INDEX—A measurement by *Barron's,* a weekly newspaper, of low-priced stocks.

MARGIN—The amount a customer may borrow to buy securities. He borrows from the brokerage firm, which in turn borrows from the banks. The Federal Reserve regulates the amount that can be borrowed. It has varied from 40 per cent to 100 per cent of the purchase price.

MARKET ORDER—An order to buy or sell a stipulated number of shares of a security at the most advantageous price.

MATURITY—The date on which a bond, a note, or a debenture becomes due and is to be paid.

MEMBER BANKS—A commercial bank that is a member of the Federal Reserve System.

MEMBER CORPORATION—A securities brokerage firm organized as a corporation with at least one member of the New York Stock Exchange who is a director and a holder of voting stock in the corporation.

MERGER—A merger is effected when one corporation buys out another corporation.

MONETARY POLICY—The policy the Federal Reserve follows in establishing its control over commercial banks.

MONEY STOCK—The money supply, which is made up of all the currency in circulation plus demand deposits.

MUNICIPAL BOND—A bond issued by a state or a county, city, town or village. Interest paid on municipal bonds is exempt from federal income taxes and state and local taxes within the state of issue.

MUTUAL FUND—An open-end investment trust. A corporation that sells stock to the public on a continuing basis and purchases securities with the proceeds.

NATIONAL ASSOCIATION OF SECURITY DEALERS—An association of brokers and dealers in the over-the-counter securities business. The association is dedicated to, among other objectives, adopting, administering, and enforcing rules of fair practice and rules to prevent fraudulent and manipulative acts and practices. In addition, it promotes just and equitable principles of trade for the protection of investors.

NASDAQ—An electronic system that provides brokers and dealers with price quotations on securities traded over-the-counter.

NET ASSET VALUE—This term is generally used in connection with investment companies. Each day an investment company totals its assets by adding the market value of all securities owned. All liabilities are deducted and the balance is divided by the number of shares outstanding. The resulting figure is the net asset value.

NEW ISSUE—A security sold by a corporation for the first time. The proceeds from the sale, after deducting the commissions, is remitted to the corporation.

ODD LOT—An amount of stock less than a round lot (100 shares). Some inactive stocks sell in roundlots of ten shares, in which case an odd lot would be from one to nine shares. The differential between the odd-lot price and the effective round-lot price is 1/8 point.

ODD-LOT DEALER—A member firm of the exchange that buys and sells odd lots of stocks.

ODD-LOT RATIO—The ratio of odd-lot purchases to sales.

OFFER—The price at which a person will sell a security.

OPEN-END INVESTMENT COMPANY—(see Mutual fund).

OPEN MARKET OPERATIONS—The Federal Open Market Committee buys and sells United States government securities to inject reserves into the banking system.

OPEN ORDER—(see Good 'til canceled order).

OPTION—A right to buy or sell specific securities at specified prices within a specified time.

OVER-THE-COUNTER—A market for securities made up of dealers who may or may not be members of a securities exchange. The buying and selling is primarily handled by telephone. Many thousands of companies cannot meet the requirements of a regional exchange and are traded in this market.

PAPER PROFIT—An unrealized profit on a security still held. Until a stock is sold, an investor has only a paper profit.

PAR—In the case of common stock, par is a dollar amount assigned to the share by the company's corporate charter. Par value has little significance as far as the market value of the stock is concerned. Par value on bonds and preferred stock is important, since the par usually represents the dollar value upon which dividends and interest are figured.

PINK SHEETS—Sheets on which quotes on over-the-counter securities are listed daily.

POINT AND FIGURE CHART—A chart in which price changes are plotted only when the movement up or down is big enough to accommodate the point scale a technician is using.

PORTFOLIO—The holdings of securities by an institution or individual. Portfolios usually contain bonds, preferred stocks, and common stocks of many different companies.

PREEMPTIVE RIGHTS—Certain rights a stockholder has, under law, among which is the right of every shareholder to maintain his same percentage of ownership.

PREFERRED STOCK—A class of stock representing ownership, with a prior claim on the company's earnings. Usually entitled to dividends at a specified rate when declared by the board of directors and before payment of a dividend on the common stock. Usually also entitled to priority over the common stockholders in the event of liquidation. May be cumulative, convertible, or participating.

PRICE-EARNINGS RATIO—The price of a share of stock divided by the earnings per share for a twelve-month period.

PRIME RATE—The interest rate banks charge their largest and strongest customers.

PRINCIPAL—A dealer buying and selling for his own account. Term can also be applied to a person's capital or to the face amount of a bond.

PROMOTER—The individual who starts a corporation, and who usually receives compensation by buying stock in the corporation below the original price or by receiving options on the stock.

PROSPECTUS—The abbreviated form of the registration statement a corporation has filed with the SEC in order to sell securities to the public.

PROXY—Written authorization given by a shareholder to represent him and vote his shares at a shareholders' meeting.

PRUDENT MAN RULE—Investing funds in a security if it is one that a prudent man of discretion and intelligence, who is seeking a reasonable income and preservation of capital, would buy.

PUT OPTION—An option to sell 100 shares of a specific stock at a specified price for a specified number of days.

PUT AND CALL BROKER—The option dealer is a middleman. He arranges for the purchase or the sale of options between a buyer and a seller. His profit is the difference between what he pays for an option and what he sells it for.

PYRAMIDING—Buying more stock as it rises in price. A speculator usually uses borrowed money.

QUOTATION—A quote is the highest bid to buy and the lowest offer to sell a security in a given market at a given time.

QUICK RATIO (ACID TEST)—Ratio of cash plus temporary investments plus receivables to current liabilities.

RECESSION—A decrease in Gross National Product for two consecutive quarters coupled with an increase in unemployment. Inventories are unusually high in relation to sales. Retailers do not reorder when all their merchandise is sold, causing manufacturers to curtail production. When inventories again adjust to sales, the recession has bottomed out.

RECORD DATE—The date on which you must be registered as a shareholder on the stock book of a company in order to receive a declared dividend.

REGIONAL BANK, OR RESERVE BANK—One of the twelve central banks established by Congress in 1913.

REGISTERED BOND—A bond that is registered on the books of the issuing corporation in the name of the owner. It is transferrable only when endorsed by the registered owner.

REGISTERED REPRESENTATIVE—Formerly called a "customers' man." He is a full-time employee who has met the requirements of the exchange as to background and knowledge of the securities market.

REGISTRANT—The corporation that files a Form S-1 with the SEC in order to sell securities to the public.

REGISTRATION—Before a company may publicly offer new securities, they must be registered under the securities act of 1933.

RESERVE REQUIREMENTS—The requirement set by the Federal Reserve for its member banks. A 10 per cent reserve would require each bank to have $1.00 dollar on hand for each $10.00 of customers' deposits.

RIGHTS—When a company wants to raise more funds by issuing additional securities, it may give its stockholders the opportunity ahead of the public to buy the new securities in proportion to the number of shares each owns. The certificate evidencing this privilege is called a "right."

ROUND LOT—A unit of trading. On the New York Stock Exchange the unit of trading is generally 100 shares in stock and $1,000 for bonds. For some inactive stocks, the unit of trading is ten shares.

SEAT—A membership on the exchange is called a "seat." Prices and requirements of obtaining a seat vary with each exchange.

SECURITIES AND EXCHANGE COMMISSION—The SEC was established by Congress to help protect investors.

SECURITIES—May be either a certificate of ownership (common or preferred stock) or a certificate of debt (bond).

SHORT COVERING—Buying back stock previously sold short.

SHORT SALE—Selling stock not owned, hoping to buy it back at a later date in order to make a profit.

SHORT POSITION—On the New York Stock Exchange a tabulation is issued once a month listing all issues on the exchange in which there was a short position of 20,000 or more shares.

SHORT-TERM CAPITAL GAIN OR LOSS—The profit or loss or a security held for six months or less.

SINKING FUND—A fund accumulated periodically by payments from a corporation to pay off a debt at maturity.

SPECIALIST—A member of the New York Stock Exchange who has two functions. First, he operates to maintain an orderly market insofar as reasonably practicable in the stocks in which he is registered as a specialist. Second, he acts as a broker's broker. On all limit orders the specialist keeps a record for the brokers and will execute the order when the stock hits the limit price.

SPECULATION—The investment of funds by a speculator with safety of principal a secondary consideration.

SPECULATOR—A person who is willing to assume a relatively large risk in the hope of gain. His main concern is appreciation of his capital and not safety of principal.

SPIN-OFFS—A spin-off occurs when a corporation distributes shares of a company it owns to its stockholders.

STOCK DIVIDEND—A dividend paid in securities rather than cash.

STOCK SPLIT—The division of the outstanding shares of a corporation into a larger number of shares.

STOCKHOLDER OF RECORD—A stockholder whose name is registered on the books of the issuing corporation.

STOP LIMIT ORDER—A stop order that becomes a limit order after the specified price has been reached.

STOP ORDER—An order to buy at a specific price or to sell below the current market.

STRADDLE—A combination of a put and a call option.

STANDARD & POOR'S INDEX—An average consisting of 500 stocks, including 425 industrials, 25 railroads, and 50 utilities of varying quality.

STRAP OPTION—A combination of one put and two call options.

STREET NAME—Securities held in the name of a brokerage firm instead of the customer's name are said to be carried in "street name."

STRIP OPTION—A combination of two put options and one call option.

STOCKHOLDERS' EQUITY—The proprietorship interest or net worth of a corporation.

SUBSIDIARY—A corporation is considered to be a subsidiary of another corporation if that other corporation owns 50 per cent or more of its voting stock.

TAPE READING—The ability to read and interpret the ticker tape.

TAX-EXEMPT BOND—(see Municipal bond).

TAX-FREE INCOME—Interest received on bonds issued by a state, city, or municipality.

TECHNICIAN—A person who uses charts to help make decisions on what stocks to buy and when to sell.

TICKER—The instrument that prints prices and volume of security transactions in cities and towns throughout the United States and Canada within minutes after each trade takes place on the floor of the exchange.

TIPS—Ostensibly "inside" information on corporation affairs.

TRADER—A person who buys and sells for his own account for short-term capital gains (see Speculator).

TRADING POST—One of twenty-three trading locations on the floor of the New York Stock Exchange at which stocks assigned to that location are bought and sold. Approximately seventy-five stocks are traded at each post.

TWO-DOLLAR BROKER—Members on the floor of the New York Stock Exchange who execute orders for other brokers having more business at that time than they can handle themselves, or from firms whose exchange member is not on the floor.

UNDERWRITER—(see Investment banker).

UP-TICK—A term used to designate a transaction made at a price higher than the preceding transaction. Also called a "plus tick." A stock may be sold short only on an up-tick or on a "zero-plus" tick. A "zero-plus" tick is a term used for a transaction at the same price as the preceding trade but higher than the preceding different price. If a stock trades at 41, then at 41 1/8 and again at 41 1/8, the first trade at 41 1/8 is an up-tick and the second trade at 41 1/8 is a zero-plus tick.

VERTICAL INTEGRATION—A method of growth by which a corporation attempts to control more of the components that go into the production of its products.

VOTING RIGHT—A stockholder's right to vote his stock in the affairs of the company.

WARRANT—A certificate giving the holder the right to purchase securities at a stipulated price within a specified period of time or sometimes perpetually.

WRITER OF OPTIONS—A person who, for a premium, guarantees to either deliver or buy securities.

YIELD—The return on an investment.

INDEX

A

Account, opening of new, 8-9
Accountants:
  opinion of, 174
  role of, 15
Accounting statements (*See also* Financial statements)
  annual report, 19-20
  balance sheet, 15, 16-19, 24-25 (*fig.*)
  statement of income, 15-16, 23 (*fig.*)
Accrued interest, 174
Acid test (*See* Quick ratio)
Addressograph Multigraph, 109-10, 116
Advance-decline ratio, 174
  as chartists' influence, 103
Adverse opinion, as CPA evaluation, 19-20
Advice:
  banks, 159
  brokerage firms, 157-58
  independent advisors, 158-59
  other, 159
Aldrich, Nelson, 76
Allied Stores, 109, 110
All or none order, 12
Allyn & Bacon, 116
Amerada Hess, 109, 110
American Airlines, 110
American Depository Receipts, system of, 4
American District Telegraph, 74
American Motors Company, 39

American Stock Exchange (ASE), 5, 6, 7, 9, 103, 110, 114, 122, 144, 146, 172
  history of, 4-5
American Sugar, 109, 110
American Telephone and Telegraph Company, 58, 65, 92, 112, 138, 144
America's Fastest Growing Companies, 38
Annual report, 174
  significance of, 19-20
Appreciation potential, as element of ideal investment, 63
Arbitrage, 122, 174
Ascending bottom, chart pattern, 98
Ashland Oil Company, 113
Asked price:
  definition, 112, 174
  of fund, 149
Assets, 174
  on balance sheet, 16-17
"At a specified price," 9
At the close orders, 11
"At the market," 9
At the opening order, 11-12
Authorized shares, definition, 17
Automatic Fire Alarm Company, 74
Averages, 174
Averaging down:
  definition, 174
  as error, 166
  with puts and calls, 136-37
Averaging up, with puts and calls, 136-37
Avon Products, 41, 67, 146, 166

B

Balanced funds, 150, 151
Balance sheet, 16-19, 24-25 (*fig.*), 174
  definition, 15
Banking Act (1935), 79
Bank of America, 79
Bank of England, 1
Banks:
  Federal Reserve, 76-79
  as investment advisors, 159
  regional, 79
Bar chart, 175
Barron's Confidence Index, 104, 127, 175
Basic trend of market as a whole, as chartists' influence, 102
Bearer bond, 175
Bear market, 87, 92-93, 175
  chart patterns, 99-100
  general characteristics, 172-73
  and writing options, 142-43
Bethlehem Steel, 123
Bid, definition, 112, 175
Bid and asked, 175
Bid price, of fund, 149
Big Board, 2, 175
Blackout period, 83-84
Blue chip stock, 175
Board of Governors, Federal Reserve Banks, 77, 81, 84, 175
Bond dealers, New York Stock Exchange, 4
Bond funds, 150, 151
Bond market, direction of, 83
Bond quotations, reading financial news of, 112-13
Bonds:
  definition, 175
  interest coverage ratio, 36-37
Book value, 67-68, 175
Book value per share, as significant statistic, 34-35
"Breakaway gaps," 100
Break-even psychology:
  definition, 175
  as error, 165
Broker, definition, 175
Broker-client relationship, 8-12
Bull market, 87, 175
  chart patterns, 98-99
  definition, 92
  general characteristics, 171-72
  and writing options, 142-43

Business Week, 123, 125, 127
  index facsimile, 124
"Buying on a scale up," 168
Buy low! Sell high! method, 64-65
Buy order, 9-10

C

Call, definition, 129
Callable, definition, 176
Call option:
  definition, 176
  writing of, 139-41
Capital gains:
  definition, 176
  long term: going short, 136
  long term: using options, 135-36
  options as, 130
  short term: put and call options as, 134-35
Capital Gains Distribution, definition, 149
Capitalization ratio, 27-28
Capital loss, 176
Capital paid in excess of par, definition, 19
Capital stock, 176
Capital structure, of corporation, 12
Cash flow, 69, 176
Certificate, definition, 176
Certified Public Accountant (CPA), kinds of evaluations on reports, 19-20
Chartcraft, Inc., 96
Charting methods:
  differences between, 97-98
  internal market trends as influence, 102-4
  meaning of chart formations, 98-102
  point and figure, 96-97
  pros and cons, 98
  similarities, 97
  vertical bar, 94-96
Chase Manhattan Bank, 79, 128
Chevrolet, 39
Chicago Board of Exchange, 176
Chicago Board Options Exchange (CBOE):
  advantages over put and call dealers, 143
  daily listing, 144, 145 (*fig.*), 146
  disadvantages, 144

Chicago Board of Trade, 143
Civil War, 14
"Clean opinion," (*See* Unqualified opinion)
Closed-end bond funds, 151, 153-54
  advantages and disadvantages, 152-53
  vs. open-end, 157
Commercial and Financial Chronicle, 127
Common stock, 176
  as income security, 51
Common stock and surplus, as term in ratio, 27, 28
Conglomerate, 176
  definition, 42
Conversion, definition, 139-40
Convertible bond, 176
Convertible debentures, 49-50, 51
Corporate bonds, as income securities, 48
Corporate earnings:
  as factor in market fluctuation, 88
  impact of new pension law on, 161
Corporation:
  capitalization of, 176
  facets for inquiry by investors, 12-13
Coupon bond, 176
Covering short, 176
Cumulative preferred, definition, 176
Curb exchange, 177
Currency, elasticity of, 84-85
Current assets, 177
  definition, 16, 17
Current liabilities, 177
  definition, 17
Current ratio, 22, 26, 177

D

Day order, 177
Debentures, 177
  as income security, 49-50
Deficit financing, 85, 177
Deflation, and inventory accounting, 22
Depletion allowance, 177
Depreciation, 177
Descending top, chart pattern, 99
Digest of earnings report, interpretation of, 116-17
Director, definition, 177

Disclaimer of opinion, as CPA evaluation, 20
Discount bond, 177
Discount rate, 177
  changes in, 83
"Discounting member bank's paper," 79
Discretionary account, 177
"Disintermediation," 84
Diversification, 177
Dividend news, interpretation of, 115-16
Dividend payable date, definition, 116
Dividend record date, definition, 116
Dividends, 177
  "double taxation" of, 155
  during term of option, 137
  of fund, 149
  paid since and current rates, 52-57 (*T*)
Dividends per share and dividends payout, as significant statistic, 33-34
Dollar-cost averaging (D.C.A.) method, 64, 65, 157, 178
  major weakness of, 65-66
Double and triple bottoms, chart pattern, 99
Double and triple tops, chart pattern, 100
Double taxation, definition, 178
Dow, Charles H., 89
Dow Chemical, 65
Dow Jones Industrial Averages, 35, 84, 91 (*T*), 93, 96, 103, 104, 171, 172
  history and bases of, 89-90, 92
Dow Jones News Service, 81
Dow Jones Transportation Average, 90
Dow Theory, The, 90
Dow Theory, 40, 94, 178
  summary of, 92-93
Dual funds, 152, 153
Dual trading, 6
DuPont, 39, 65
Durant, William C., 39

E

Earnings per share, 69
Earnings per share-common stock, as significant statistic, 32-33
Earnings summary, importance of, 12
Eastman Kodak Company, 39, 65

Employee Retirement Security Act (1974, 159
"Equipment trust" certificates, 48
Equity, 178
Erie Canal, 1
Exchange of stock or bonds, as growth method, 42, 43-44
Ex-dividend, 178
  definition, 116
"Exhaustion gap," 101
Expansion, types of, 41-42
Ex-rights, definition, 138
Exxon Corporation, 65

F

Federal Open Market Committee (FOMC), 84, 85
  changes in operations during blackout, 83-84
  report on meeting, 81-82
Federal Reserve Act, 77, 79-80
  and credit control, 78-79
Federal Reserve Bank of New York, 84
Federal Reserve Bank of St. Louis, 128
Federal Reserve Banks, 48
Federal Reserve Board, 154
Federal Reserve Operations, 77
Federal Reserve policy, as factor in market fluctuation, 87
Federal Reserve System, 171, 172, 173, 178
  chain of command, 77
  effect on market, 118
  elasticity of currency, 84-85
  enemies of policy, 80-81
  Federal Open Market Committee, 84
  history, 76
  market conditions indicating policy change, 82-84
  money, prices, and interest rates, 125, 126 (*T*)
  powers of, 78-79
  reserve requirements, 80
  ways of expanding money supply, 126-27
Fill or kill order, 11
Financial analysis, limitations of, 71
Financial news:
  economic letters available, 128
  inflation and interest rates, 127-28
  publications, 127
  reading and understanding stock quotations, 107-27

Financial news (cont.)
  Wall Street Journal sections, 106-107
Financial statements (*See also* Accounting statements)
  notes to, 20-22
  key ratios in analysis of, 22, 26-37
First In-First Out (FIFO) inventory accounting, 21-22, 40
First National City Bank, 128
Fiscal assets, 178
Fiscal policy, 178
Fiscal year, definition, 178
Fixed assets, definition, 16, 17
Floor broker, 178
Floor of the Exchange, 178
Floor partners, 3
Forbes, 127
Ford Motor Company, 5, 39, 40
Foreign affairs, as factor in market fluctuation, 88
Foreign investments funds, 150, 151
Franklin National Bank, 82
Free from care, as element of ideal investment, 63

G

Gallup poll, 89
Gaps, as stock measures, 100-101
General Motors, 9, 10, 11, 39, 41-42, 65, 96, 125
  as one stock index, 93-94
General Price Index, 125, 178
General Telephone Company, 42
Good for Week or Month or a Specific Date order, 11
Good 'til cancelled order, 11, 178
Government bonds, 178
Government fiscal policy, as factor in market fluctuation, 88
Great Depression, 51
Grinnell Corporation, 74
Growth:
  by acquisition, 42-44
  from within, 42
Growth companies:
  characteristics of, 38
  how to find, 41-42
  methods used for growth, 42-44
  outstanding examples, 39-41
Growth funds, 150, 151
Growth stocks, 44, 179
  different rates, 45 (*T*), 46
  disadvantages, 46-47

H

Hamilton, William, 90
Harris poll, 89
Head and shoulders formation, chart pattern, 99-100
Hedging, 123, 125, 179
Helter-skelter expansion, 42
Herold, John S., 38
Holmes Electric Protective Company, 74
Horizontal expansion, 41
Horizontal integration, 179
Housing industry, effect of inflation on, 125

I

Income funds, 150, 151
Income investing:
    disadvantages, 51, 58-59
    investors' characteristics, 47
    types of securities, 47-51
Income statement, 179
Indenture, 179
Independent advisor, advantages and disadvantages of, 158-59
Index, 179
Industrial Revolution, 14
Industry approach, to securities, 66-67
Inflation, 125, 179
    as enemy of Federal Reserve policy, 80-81
    and income investment, 51, 58-59
    and interest rates, 127-28
    and inventory accounting, 22
Interest, definition, 179
Interest coverage (bonds), 179
Interest coverage (bonds) ratio, 36-37
Interest rates, and inflation, 126-28
Internal Revenue Code, 130, 155
International Business Machines (IBM), 34, 39, 92, 96
Inventories:
    FIFO, 21-22
    LIFO, 21-22
"Inventory turnover," (*See* Sales to inventory ratio)
Inverted head and shoulders bottom, chart pattern, 98-99
Investment banker (Underwriter), 179
Investment companies:
    definition, 179
    percentage of cash held by, 104

Investment Company Act (1940), 149, 154, 157
    important provisions, 155-57
Investment counselor, 179
Investment Dealers Digest, 127
Investments:
    additional errors, 170-72
    elements of ideal, 61-66
    major errors in, 162-70
Investor psychology, as factor in market fluctuation, 88
Investors:
    definition, 179
    and income investing, 47-59
    SEC Act requirements of importance to, 12-13

J

Journal of Commerce, 127

K

Kennedy, John F., 73
Kent cigarettes, 39
Keogh plan, 160
Korean War, 127

L

Last In-First Out (LIFO) inventory accounting, 21-22, 40
Leadership, as chartists' influence, 102
Lehman Corporation, 152
Letter of intent, 179
Leverage, 153, 179
Liabilities, 180
    on balance sheet, 17
Limit orders, 10, 180
Liquidity, 180
    as element of ideal investment, 62
Liquidity ratio (*See* Quick ratio)
"Listed" bonds, 62
Listed stock, 180
Litton Industries, 42
Load, definition, 180
Loan demand, 83
Long-term analysis, used for short-term speculating, 163
Long-term capital gain, 180
Long-term debt, as term in ratio, 27, 28

Long-term liabilities, 180
  definition, 17
Losses, allowing small as error, 164-65
Low-priced confidence index, 93, 180
Low-priced stock activity, as chartists'
  influence, 103

M

Madison Fund General Public Service,
  152
Managed accounts, 157
  disadvantages, 158
Management:
  as factor in securities choice, 70
  following changes in, 117, 118
  new, study of, 75
  responsibility of in pension plans,
    160
  success of as growth characteristic,
    38, 40-41
Margin, 180
Margin requirement, 78-80
Marine Midland Company, 58
Marketable denomination, as element
  in ideal investment, 64
Market order, 180
Market trends:
  internal, as influence on chartists,
    102-4
  investors' awareness of, 89
Markup, definition, 112
Massachusetts Mutual Income Shares,
  153
Maturity, 180
McGee, Kerr, 146
"Measuring gap," 100-101
Member banks, 180
Member corporation, 180
Mental fatigue, and speculation,
  169-70
Mergers, 74, 180
Mesabi, 155
Minnesota Mining and Manufacturing
  (MMM), 39
Monetary policy, 180
Money market funds, 151
Money stock, 180
Moody's, 38, 48, 50, 113, 114, 127
Morgan Guarantee Survey, 128
Moving average, 21, 22
Municipal bonds, 180
  as income securities, 48

Mustang, 39, 40
Mutual funds, 181
  advantages, 150
  definition, 148-49
  disadvantages, 150
  interpreting listing of, 155-57
  types, 150-53

N

"Naked" options, writing of, 142
National Association of Security Deal-
  ers (NASD), 110, 155, 181
  Rules of Fair Practice, 154
National Association of Security Deal-
  ers   Quotation   Bureau
  (NASDAQ), 5, 181
National Science Foundation, 42
"Net amount," 111
Net asset value, 181
  definition, 149
Net change, definition, 112
Net income to net worth ratio, 30
Net income to sales ratio, 29
Net working capital assets per share,
  68
New issue, 181
"New lows" approach, to securities, 67
New product, as growth characteristic,
  38, 39, 41
New product development, interpret-
  ing, 117
News items, effect on market and
  examples, 118, 119-20
New York-Carlisle DeCoppet & Com-
  pany, 103
New York Curb Exchange (*See* Amer-
  ican Stock Exchange)
New York Stock Exchange(NYSE), 4,
  5, 6, 7, 8, 9, 10, 13, 64, 67, 84,
  103, 110, 114, 122, 130, 139,
  140, 141, 142, 144, 149, 152,
  162, 172
  function of, 2
  history of, 1-2
  membership in, 2-3
  types of seat holders, 3-4
New York Stock Exchange Rule (405),
  8
No load funds, 150, 151, 152
Not Held orders, 11
Number of days sales in receivables
  ratio, 31-32

O

Odd lot, definition, 181
Odd-lot dealer, 181
  New York Stock Exchange, 3
Odd-lot ratio, as chartists' influence,
  103-4
Offer, definition, 181
Olin Corporation, 74
Open-end investment company, 181
  vs. closed-end, 157
Open Market operation, 181
Open order, 178, 181
Option contracts, 130
Options:
  advantages and disadvantages of
    buying, 141-42
  advantages and disadvantages of
    writing (selling), 143
  CBOE, 143-46
  definition, 181
  effect of dividends during term of,
    137
  effect of stock dividends during term
    of, 137-38
  effect of stock rights during term of,
    138
  effect of stock splits during term of,
    138
  methods of writing, 142-43
  premiums paid for, 130-31
  types written, 139-41
  use for long-term capital gains,
    135-36
  various uses of, 129-30
  writer's or seller's risks, 131-32
Orders:
  handling of by broker, 9
  types of, 9-12
Over-The-Counter Markets (OTC), 5,
  51, 149, 172, 181
  reading financial news of, 110-12
Over-trading an account, as error,
  168-70

P

Pacific American Income Shares, 153
Pacific Coast Stock Exchange, 122
Paper profit, 181
Par, definition, 181
Payment of bond interest, 75
Pension funds, 159-61

"Pink sheets," 5, 182
P.J. Lorillard Company, 39
Point and figure chart, 96-97, 182
  compared to vertical bar chart, 97-98
Polaroid Corporation, 46, 67, 164
Portfolio, definition, 182
Preemptive rights, definition, 182
Preferred dividend arrearages, 75
Preferred stocks, 176, 177, 182
  as income securities, 50-51
Premium, paid for options, 130-31
Price-earnings ratio (P.E. ratio), 109,
  182
  as significant statistic, 35-36
Prices of recent issues, interpretation
  of, 113-14
Prime rate, 182
  direction of, 82-83
Principal, definition, 182
Principles of consolidation, as financial
  statement note, 20, 21
Profits, taking small as error, 163-64
Promoter, definition, 182
Prospectus, definition, 182
Proxy, 182
"Prudent man" rule, 159, 160, 182
Public offering price, definition, 149
Purchase for cash, as growth method,
  42, 44
Put, definition, 129
Put and call broker, 182
Put and Call Brokers and Dealers
  Association, Inc. 130
Put and call options (*See also* Options)
  averaging down or up with, 136-37
  buying to protect a profit, 134-35
  premiums paid by dealer, 141
  trading uses, 132-33
  use to protect short sale or purchase,
    133-34
Put option:
  definition, 182
  writing of, 139-41
Pyramiding, 183
  correctly applied, 168
  incorrect, as error, 167-68

Q

Qualified opinion, as CPA evaluation,
  19
Quick ratio, 26-27
  definition, 183
Quotation, definition, 183

R

Rambler, 39
Ratios:
  on financial statements, 22, 26-37
  limitations of, 37
Real Estate Investment Trusts, 155
Realistic maturity date, as element in
  ideal investment, 63-64
Recession, 183
Record date, 183
Redemption Privilege, of fund, 149
Regional banks, 79, 183
Regional exchanges, 6
Registered bond, definition, 183
Registered representative, 183
  role of, 8
Registrant, 183
Registration, definition, 183
Reserve Bank (*See also* Federal Reserve
  System), 183
Reserve requirements, 183
Reverse saucer, chart pattern, 100
Revolutionary War, 1, 14
Rhea, Robert, 90
Rights (*See also* Stock rights), 183
Rohn & Haas, 39
Romney, George, 39
Roosa, Robert V., 77
Round lot, definition, 183

S

Safety of principal, as element of ideal
  investment, 62
Sage, Russell, 129, 139
Sales charge, of fund, 149
Sales per share of stock ratio, 36
Sales to fixed assets ratio, 29
Sales to inventory ratio, 30-31
Saucer formation, chart pattern, 99
Schering Corporation, 46
Scotch Tape, 39
Sears, Roebuck, 41
Seat:
  cost of on NYSE, 2
  definition, 183
Securities (*See also* Income investing,
  Undervalued securities)
  definition, 183
  government, agency and miscellane-
  ous, 114

Securities (cont.)
  technical approach to trading:
    basic chart formations and mean-
    ing, 98-102
    internal market trends as in-
    fluence, 102-4
    methods, 94-98
    pros and cons, 98
  value questions, 15
Securities Exchange Act, (1933, 1934)
  9, 14, 20, 167
  important provisions for investor
  protection, 154-55
  provisions and amendments, 6-8
  requirements of importance to inves-
  tors, 12-13
Securities and Exchange Commission
  (SEC), 3, 6-8, 152, 154, 157,
  158, 183
Sell order, 10
Shares outstanding, definition, 17
Short covering, 184
Short interest, interpretation of, 122
Short position, 184
  as chartists' influence, 103
Short sale, 103, 184
Short sale order, 10
Short term capital gain, 184
Short term capital loss, 184
Sinking fund, definition, 184
Small capitalization, as growth charac-
  teristic, 38, 39-40, 41
S-1 form, as information source, 12
Specialist:
  definition, 184
  NYSE, 3
Specialized funds, 150, 151
"Special situation":
  definition, 73-74
  factors, 74-75
Speculation, 184
  additional errors, 170-72
  advice on, 170
  major errors in, 162-70
Speculator, definition, 184
Spin-offs, 74, 184
Squibb, 74
Stability of income, as element of ideal
  investment, 62
Standard & Poor's Guide, 38, 48, 114,
  125, 127
  bond ratings, 49, 50
Standard & Poor's Index (SPIA), 93,
  184

Statement of income, definition, 15-16, 23 (*fig.*)
Stock dividends, 184
  during term of option, 137-38
Stock Exchanges:
  American, 4-5
  New York, 1-4
  over-the-counter market, 5
  regional, 6
  third market, 5-6
Stockholder of record, definition, 184
Stockholders' equity, 184
  definition, 17
Stock market tips, listening to as error, 166-67
Stock quotations, reading and understanding, 107-26
Stock rights, during term of option, 138
Stocks, support levels of, 104
Stock splits, 184
  during term of option, 138
Stock transactions, printing and interpretation of, 2
Stop limit order, 184
Stop orders:
  definition, 184
  use of, 10, 11
Straddle option:
  definition, 184
  writing of, 139-41
Strap option, 141
  definition, 184
Street name, 63, 184
Strip option, 141
  definition, 184
Subsidiary, definition, 185
Support levels, of stocks, 104
Sylvania Electric Corporation, 42
Syntex, 164

T

Tape reading, 101-2, 185
Tax-exempt bond, 185
Tax-free income, 185
  as element of ideal investment, 63
Technician, 185
Tender offer, 74
Texas Instruments, 39
Third market, 5-6
Ticker, 185
  early installations, 2

Tips, 185
  listening to as error, 166-67
Traders, 185
  NYSE, 3
Trading post, definition, 185
Tri-Continental, 152
"Truth in securities laws," (*See* SEC Acts)
Two-dollar brokers, 185
  NYSE, 3
"two-tier market," 47, 67

U

Umbrella pattern, 100
Undervalued securities:
  basic approaches to, 66-67
  elements of ideal investment, 61-66
  factors for study, 67-70
    examples of securities which pass tests, 70-73
  special situations, 73-75
Underwriter:
  definition, 185
  identity of, as important, 12
Unfunded vested benefits, 161
Unique service, as growth characteristic, 38, 39, 41
U.S. Congress, 85, 159
U.S. Monetary Commission, 76
U.S. News and World Report, 127
U.S. Steel, 96, 122, 123, 130, 131
U.S. Supreme Court, 74
U.S. Treasury Bonds, as income securities, 47-48
U.S. Treasury Department, 88
Unqualified opinion:
  as CPA evaluation, 19
  example, 20
Unsecured bonds (*See* Debentures)
Up-tick, definition, 185

V

Value as collateral, as element in ideal investment, 64-65
Value line, 127
Vertical bar charts, 94-96
  compared to point and figure, 97-98
Vertical expansion, 41-42
Vertical integration, 185
Vesting, 160

Vietnam War, 127
Volume, basic technical rules of, 95
Voting right, 185

W

Wall Street Journal, The, 67, 83, 89,
    90, 92, 103, 106, 110, 116, 125,
    127
  bond quotations, 111 (*fig.*)
  changes in stock holdings, 123
  digest of earnings report, 117
  dividend news, 115
  explanatory notes, 109 (*Fig.*)
  government, agency and miscellan-
    eous securities, 114
  over-the-counter market, 111 (*fig.*)
  prices of recent issues, 114 (*fig.*)
  trading volume, 108 (*fig.*)
  Who's News, 118 (*fig.*)

Ward's Automotive, 123
War of 1812, 14
Warrant, 185
  compared to call, 129
Wilson, Charles, 93
Working capital ratio (*See* Current
    ratio)
World War I, 16, 77
World War II, 66, 79
Writer of options, 185

X

Xerox Corporation, 39, 46, 164

Y

Yield, definition, 185